MW01600982

THE INNER LIFE AND THE TAO-TEH-KING

First Edition 1912
Carl H.A Bjerregaard

New Edition 2021
Edited by Tarl Warwick

FOREWORD

The Tao-Teh-King is one of the most enigmatic spiritual (and moral) texts ever created. The actual full translation of the work is technically not even objectively determined due to the nature of the old Chinese language utilized in the oldest discovered variants (several of which post-date this present work!) but the basic premise of the work, providing a basic foundation for the Taoist system, is essentially twofold- the concept of non-action, and the concept "natural-ness." Both of these are discussed at length in this volume, which is an oratory that initially comprised a number of lectures (chapters, in this manuscript itself) which were scholarly in nature and delved into both the academic and historical backdrop of the work and its possibly mythological author- Laotze- as well as the potential quasi-westernized spiritual and mystical significance of the work and its derived spiritual system.

For example, the concept of non-action as beheld by Westerners is here corrected, since simple stagnation, that is, doing literally nothing, per se, is not a proper translation from the initial concept in its initial context. Likewise, the concept of being "natural" or "natural-ness" does not mean stripping oneself of all trappings and barreling off into the jungle to live like a wild animal, but is a sort of semi-vaguely described appreciation or one-ness with existence and with the natural, more "passive" state of things, while maintaining activity within that basic context.

At times the author of this work waxes rather poetic, even including as lengthy final section dedicated to enlightenment philosopher Jean-Jacques Rousseau which has nothing to do, centrally, with the Tao itself. It is fairly clear that Bjerregaard holds the concept of nature in high esteem- indeed, this present work may be tentatively interpreted, at least to some degree, as a typical "backlash against industry" or "blacklash against modernity" style work- not uncommon in the late 19th and early 20th centuries, especially among mystics and occultists as they slowly rediscovered more and more Eastern and tribal lore and dug deeper and deeper into temples, ruins, and libraries, to try and investigate every aspect of the human condition, with each answered question typically spawning several unanswered ones in turn.

The author seems to compare Laotze and Taoism somewhat favorably with Confucius and his system, with the apparent, stated belief that the poverty and issues plaguing China at the time (which were profuse) were the result of philosophical decadence or rather the lack of appreciation for nature, nonviolence, and so forth.

This edition of "The Inner Life and the Tao Teh King" has been carefully edited for format and content. Care has been taken to retain all original intend and meaning.

THE INNER LIFE AND THE TAO TEH KING

PREFACE

These chapters were originally lectures to a small, but select company. They are now revised and published for a larger world. They claim not to be exhaustive, but only an attempt in direction of a mystic interpretation of the Tao-Teh-King, a manner of reading that famous book but little practiced and less understood. The only proper way of reading that book is in the light of mysticism. The book can certainly not be handled like a Confucian document.

I lay no claim to be a Sinologist. I have, however, in many places examined the texts and made translations differing somewhat from others. Elsewhere I have used all the known translations, with which I have usually agreed.

It is more than thirty years since I began in this country to call attention to the Tao-Teh-King. It was then an almost unknown book. Since then, several translations and paraphrases have been published in this country and articles of more or less value have appeared in magazines, but much remains to be done if this treasure is to become known where it ought to be known. I hope my undertaking may be a step in that direction. Without the generosity of the theosophists before whom the original lectures were delivered, the book could not have been published. I owe them my profound thanks.

C. H. A. BJERREGAARD.

THE INNER LIFE AND THE TAO TEH KING

CHAPTER I

The main difficulty in speaking about the Inner Life is the language that must be used. The medieval and renaissance mystics and occultists were obliged for various reasons to use alchemical language and phraseology to express their wisdom of life, because such language was picturesque and easily comprehended by minds of a mechanical and practical turn, minds crude and ignorant of their own psychic powers and processes.

Today we have the same difficulty to overcome as the older mystics. Our audiences are unfamiliar with psychology and so little in the habit of seeing themselves as units, that they really believe themselves to be mere bundles of faculties, forces and states, and are unable to give an account of their mental, moral and spiritual condition. It is therefore necessary to present the Inner Life as if it were something in space and time. It is necessary to speak of traveling on paths, as if such paths were actual roads; and yet, Inner Life and Outer Life, Traveling and Paths, are only terms of psychic conditions. I shall in this chapter speak of passing over bridges as if I literally meant it. I shall be using realistic language, but not talk about realistic bridges. I shall talk psychology. Spiritually understood, there is no Inner Life, there is no Outer Life, there is no Path, no Bridge, No East, No West, no High, no Low- what is there? Well- wait till you have read these chapters and you may know!

I will now do like the genial boy does who wants to know how his machinery is made and put together- he picks it to pieces and examines it. I will likewise pick our deeper life to pieces and try to show what it is and how it works, and, as I proceed, I shall put it together again. A few words about different standpoints and the two; that of the Orient and that of the Occident. For the sake of the deepest understanding of problems which are of the uttermost importance to all thinking people, it is desirable that all theosophic and mystic subjects should be studied from a Western standpoint as well as from an Oriental. Most of you here present are accustomed, I think, to hear these subjects presented in Oriental phrases and in set terminology, all derived from Eastern sources. It has seemed to me desirable that you should hear the same truths set forth in Western terminology. I am sure you can only be the gainers. I propose to set them forth that way. But let me say something to guide you to see the similarities and to prevent confusion. Let me take as an illustration a familiar object, a lens, either concave or convex. The lens remains a lens whatever you do with it, but it reflects the light variously as the light falls upon the concave or the convex. You may call the concave a type of the East, and the convex a type of the West, if you like, or vice versa. The viewpoint and the judgment are personal, indifferent, not real; the reality in the case is the fact that the lens reflects the light. The lens, of course, is the mind.

Because I speak of great truths from the Western point of view and in Western terminology, I differ only from some of you in viewpoint and in personal aspect, but not really; we meet in the middle, in mind; in the Inner Life; in the fact that we both reflect the real, each in our individual way, however. Another illustration. Let us suppose I pass over a bridge: the "bridge of existence," from one end, the Western, and you from the other end, the Eastern. We shall see the Middle of the bridge and the approaches differently, but we shall both be passing the same bridge. And let me add that it would be wise for those of my listeners who have passed over such a bridge from one end only also to pass back over the bridge from the other end. They shall certainly be the wiser for so doing. It is the mystic's way. And let me say further, and, here I hint at a mystery, let me say, that since neither you nor I know absolutely which is the beginning or the end of the bridge, that it is immaterial which is the East or the West end of it. The most important part of the bridge is the Middle; from the Middle of the bridge we may ascend into another plane of existence, and find that that existence is the real one, and that neither of the two approaches have any reality. Nature knows of no Beginning nor End; knows only the Middle; the Inner Life. She spreads out continually from the Center, from the ever-present Now. For that reason, the Middle is called the first or fundamental principle and is the Inner Life. And for that reason, I say, that neither the East end nor the West end have any reality. As for myself, I have long ago come to the conclusion that neither end of the bridge is the real one, and, long ago a wise man talked much about the Middle Path. I, for one, am sure he spoke the truth. And I have found many who also have understood him. What is the Middle? Now I shall not indulge in metaphysics or mysticism, but use a well-known theosophic phrase as my illustration. The theosophic doctrine of "Brotherhood" is a very practical application of the philosophic doctrine Middle; it is the at-one-ing point for all races and creeds; it answers to the One in philosophy. In that doctrine Theosophy proclaims equal rights for all extremes. It is the gospel of "good will among men." It answers, as I said, to the One in philosophy; and to Unity. It is that which Schiller calls the Holy Will and "the idea supreme"; it is the power, that works for righteousness; the "spirit of rest" that ever tries to stay the changeful world. It is the "Love" of St. John; it is "the pure form of thought" of Kant. It is "god incarnate" of Christianity.

All these terms explain what the Middle is; what the Inner Life is. They explain that Middle, which we meet from whatever end we enter the bridge of life, and it is from such a Middle, I said, that we readily swing ourselves to heaven. Unless we come to the perfect realization, that life is one, one glorious whole, and not split up into various antagonistic elements, we shall never come to sound and rational philosophies or religions. Human life is fallen apart and now lies in most unfortunate dualisms of good and evil, of inner and outer, of upper and lower, of heaven and hell. The guilty ones are both saints and sinners; the first in ignorance, the latter in willful misrepresentation. Away! Away! Let us now and henceforth build temples to Unity, to the One, to the Middle, to the Inner Life! Life, Existence, is one, not manifold; one at the core;

only manifold in manifestation. Let us hang on to that. With this doctrine and realization before us, we can without fear examine the characteristics of the East and the West and see how they are merely extremes of a Higher Truth, a Higher Unity. And perhaps you will agree with me that it is desirable that I should speak from a Western point of view.

To simplify matters, let me characterize the two viewpoints. The East is synthetic; the West is analytic; that, of course, makes views different, yet the multitudinousness of the circumference is only the center spread out, so to say. They answer to each other like concave and convex. Do they not? The East is sympathetic and has religion ; the West is intellectual and has culture; that of course separates the two; but as sympathy means heart, and culture means brain, the two make a complete man: One; the Grand Man, Adam Kadmon, the Inner Life. The East discovered the World, the great objective; the West discovered and asserted the Ego, Man. To the East, the individual man is vanity and must be denied. The West declares that the world must be denied; but the discoverer in both cases was Intelligence, Mind: hence they meet. Intelligence, Mind, Heart, is the Inner Life. The essential point is that we always are on the wing, like the eagle. The eagle is only on the earth the few moments that Nature calls. The East does not wish to have any will of its own; it will not assert itself; self-assertion is in the East a sin and an illusion. But in the West a man is despised if he stands for nothing and leaves no monument after him. The East and the West here seem to differ radically. Do they not? Yet these two activities both meet in volition! Will is the name for the core of Man- it is the Inner Life. The essential point is that we have will, because in the will both activity and passivity meet; both the objective and the subjective. The East has discovered the wonderful truths and the laws expressed by the words Karma and reincarnation. In Western philosophical language, and to Philosophy, the same truths are known under the names of Necessity, Determinism, Cause and Effect; hence they are not opposites. The real opposites as discovered by the West and thrashed out so thoroughly, that there is no more life in them, than in the ideas of Sin and Forgiveness. Where the East sees only Necessity and Law, the West sees only Freedom. Different they seem, yet they are but two sides of the same problem: the Oriental is the impersonal method, the Occidental is the personal. Both dissolve in absolute truth and remain as a mystery!

After all has been said that can be said, one Spirit, One Reality and One Truth remains, and the main point is that we reach the One Truth- that is the Inner Life. And so I might continue. There is always a middle Path which leads to the Inner Life, a point of consistency in which there is no creed nor dogma; no East or West. All mystics, all who are in wisdom meet in Samadhi, as they call it in the East; Contemplation or Meditation, as they call it in the West. In Samadhi, or Contemplation, all differences disappear. Samadhi or Contemplation is the Inner Life. The "Inner Life" to the East is, as I said, Samadhi, and to the West Contemplation. More closely defined, the Inner Life can in Eastern terms be described as a fullness of Being, an ecstatic Bliss and a supreme Knowledge; or in the corresponding Western terms, Freedom, Virtue, God, three terms for forms of mind derived from Kant's philosophy. In classical thought they are called the Good, the True, the Beautiful. But these descriptions will not help a rationalistic mind. In the West, people spurn sentiments, exalted perceptions, transcendental moods and subjective states. They are considered vagaries, whims and signs of degeneration. Negative Spirits, those of the order of Mephistopheles, deny the Inner Life. To them it is identical with fancy and romance. Only positive spirits, those of love, know it and live it. Oh! what barbarians!

Those of the Inner Life have the same right to use that exclamation as the Greeks of old had, when they called a foreigner a barbarian. Oh! what barbarians all around! And yet the Oriental description of Samadhi is a marvel of expression to those who know the Inner Life from experience. The peculiarity with the

THE INNER LIFE AND THE TAO TEH KING

Inner Life is this, that it cannot be made intelligible to those who have not experienced some of it. It is experience, not idealistic reason, that tells us that clouds and ice and steam are water. An African under the Equator who has never seen ice cannot understand that water may become as hard as a stone. He has had no such experience. People who live irrationally and in exterior things and who have never experienced anything else, deny the truth the mystics tell. They are like the fishes who did not know water. You know the tale? The fishes asked one another what water was, but none could answer. Then one, wiser than the rest, said he had been told that in the ocean lived a wise fish who knew all, and he proposed that some of them travel to this wise fish and ask what water was. And so they did, and the wise fish answered them:

> "O ye who seek to solve the knot!
> Ye live in God, yet know Him not.
> Ye sit upon the river's brink,
> Yet crave in vain a drop to drink.
> Ye dwell beside a boundless store,
> Yet perish, hungry, at the door."

The Inner Life is a "Wisdom of the other shore" and only comprehensible to those who have crossed over the river or have sailed upon it. Experience, not lecturing, nor hearing a lecture, will make it clear.

> "Measure not with words
> Th' immeasurable, nor sink the string of thought
> Into the fathomless: who asks doth err,
> Who answers errs- say naught!"

"Measure not with words." The Inner life is a "temple of "no-thingness"; no words can enter. In it is understanding, but no creed. The Inner Life is a bloodless altar; its cup is Samadhi, or Contemplation, and its candlestick is insight. The Inner Life becomes an experience only to those who know their God in the form of mercy, never to those who drink of the waters of the lake of the fourfold flood, viz., passion, cleaving to life, false views, ignorance. Nay- it is as Whittier puts it:

> "The riddle of the world is understood
> Only by him who feels that God is good,
> As only he can feel who makes his love
> The ladder of his faith, and climbs above
> On the rounds of his best instincts."

It is the general lack of experience in the higher life that makes it necessary to use such language as I have used; language that seems to deny my assertion that life is one- language that seems to suggest that an impassable gulf is fixed between daily life and the life of the mystic. But it is not so. There is a chasm, certainly, between the two, but it is not impassable; we have evidence enough to believe the testimonies of those who have come to us and told us about that life. Life is one and the chasm is only there for the ignorant, not for the initiate. There are good reasons and plenty of evidence that warrants us in believing that those who deny the Inner Life are not sincere. A comprehensive study of the psychology of all races, creeds, and ages, proves that all people in all ages have found that man possesses certain high and divine qualities and is able to progress through psychic matters into regions of the Self, which seemed to be transcendental. Moreover, it is a fact that all sound minds crave that inner, that immortal life, which alone can give beauty to existence.

It can only be called Satanic, when some moderns dare to assert that the Inner Life, the mystic life, is a product of disease, a fungus growth, a degeneration. It is Satanic-false! It is Devilish-evil. Is it possible that millions of people have lived and fed upon a lie? Is it possible that the sweet-smelling flowers which again and again have refreshed humanity were nothing but poisonous growth! Nay! Nay! Gathering up the various remarks and definitions given, I will further illustrate the Inner Life by returning to my illustration, the bridge and its occult meaning, and thereby I come still nearer to the subject. Coming in from one end of the bridge, the Middle, or the Inner Life, I spoke of, is seen as the "Intelligible World," to use a Platonic term. The "intelligible world" is a term that expresses the idea that the world (Kosmos) is intelligible; can be understood by Thought; is Thought; is over-sensual or ideal; is reasonable. And the world is not "this," the actual, the space and time appearance, but that high phenomenon which appears to the mind and never to the senses. The "intelligible world" is a mental and spiritual influence that corrects our understanding, because it is the plastic power of existence, the power that builds, the power that upholds and that teaches us. It is the archetypal perception of something not in space, yet present everywhere. Something not in time, yet perpetually moving everything else. Something not moved, but the cause of all movement. Something not measurable, but the master of all measure. Something we only perceive when we abstract ourselves from everything the senses are related to; which the desires crave, and which end in death.

But this Something which the traveler thus sees in coming in from the one end of the bridge is not an airy nothing, an astral or unsubstantial something. It is most real; it is the real world. It is, still continuing the Platonic imagery, (1) the original world, viz., the world in which all things originate; (2) it is the typical world, viz., the world of patterns, motives; and (3) the world of all essential thought and consciousness and reason. It is the world of all the ideas of eternal value that lie back of all high and noble thought and action. Plato calls these ideals Universals, sometimes Substances, sometimes Numbers and sometimes Living Powers, Gods. Plato considered them to be indefinite in number and says they are what philosophy speaks of as categories. The highest of all ideas is the idea of the Good. Warning you against the possible error of confounding the "Intelligible World" with the astral plane,

THE INNER LIFE AND THE TAO TEH KING

I now want to impress upon you what this walking in on the bridge means. In Platonic language, it means the opening of the noetic degree of mind, the degree of supreme wisdom which means an insight into the divine mysteries.

And, now, again further illustrating the Inner Life by returning to my illustration, the bridge and its occult meaning. I will explain what is seen in coming in from the other end of the bridge and proceeding towards the Middle. Here the traveler is not met by views, visions or sublime ideas. The traveler enters into an exalted condition; is transfused by sublime purposes, and, gradually, forgetting self, he is coming into a translated and celestial life, a condition of fullness, that excludes all evils, desires and cravings of the sense-man. The traveler is not merely moving towards the Middle, but is drawn towards it, and this drawing is joy and triumph. As the traveler comes near the Middle, he experiences a new energy and a fresh power, a power that comes from hitherto unopened wells of heart and soul. And in that power, the traveler feels a humanity not dreamed of, and, a divinity not even imagined, and a spiritual commerce between the two, which opens all mysteries of goodness, love and perfection. Numerous mystics testify to that. The Sufi mystics speak not only of traveling to God, but also of traveling from God, and by traveling from God, they mean going into the world full of that love, they have received, and, distributing it into the world. Such a traveler from God was St. Francis with his infinite brother-feeling extending to the animals, and such a traveler was Buddha, and, such a traveler was Jesus. Filled with divinity and intelligence larger than their own, they saw into the life of things and made all things holy. The world thus opened is an empire of love. "Love feels no burden, regards no labors, would willingly do more than it is able, pleads not impossibility, because it feels that it can and may do all things," said Thomas a Kempis. Lovers of souls are the builders of this empire. Doers of deeds also build; deeds that touch barren hearts and refresh the sick and the blind. This world holds no altars, no sacrificial fires. No Urim and Thummin are needed to cover the heart; the heart is the Parousia, the Presence, the Fullness.

These, then, are the two aspects of the Middle of the bridge to the Inner Life, seen according to the way you enter the bridge. The mystic is now suddenly beyond intelligence and love; beyond good and evil; beyond East and West; beyond all conceptions and actions or any other mental, moral, or spiritual state of man, and, beyond man himself. In the Beyond, on "the other shore," there lies the Inner Life really, fully; all the other conditions, sublime as they are, are, after all, but approaches. In Platonic language, the Middle is called the first or fundamental principle, the Good. Ages and ages before Plato the Middle was called the Mother-goddess. But in the West they do not say the Good, they say God; and they do not say Mother-God, they say Father-God, and this change in terms robs the Middle, the Inner Life, of its real and sublime character. That change in terms robs the Middle of its life and character and makes it an abstraction. And the West has paid heavily for its mistake. Preachers are now obliged to urge their people "to live the life," "to be doers and not hearers," and they are obliged to arrange Revivals, hoping thereby to quicken the people. All this decadence and decay of religion is a result of the change from reality to abstraction. It must be admitted that in the East, the realistic conception of the Middle or the Inner Life has led to extremes, and crude materialistic notions and worships. The East is as guilty as the West. They are, however, both redeemed by their Mystics. Eastern mystics and Western mystics are the only souls who have come into true and real communion with the Middle, with the Inner Life and into the Beyond.

It is not only the name for the Highest that has caused confusion, sorrow and sin in the religious world. There is another term and image that has been equally troublesome. That term is matter. What is matter? (1) As regards science of today, it must be confessed that it has never seen matter nor weighed it, nor in any way got a real hold of it. Atoms, molecules and ions are not matter, they are force; force is all science knows of. Consequently, science can give only a negative answer. Science does not know matter. In other words, there is no such thing as that commonly called matter. There is substance, however, but that is not matter, as commonly and ignorantly supposed. (2) The ancient people never thought of matter in connection with any physical science. Ever ready with picturesque figures they meant Mother by matter. So it is in Sanskrit, so it is in Greek and all other languages, and, whenever philosophers have entered upon explanations of what that word matter meant. The people who spoke Sanskrit explained it as the Universal Womb, as Space, as Aether, as the Measurer of the Firmament. They talked eloquently of the Divine Mothers where we moderns speak weakly about centers of evolution, centers of force. The Mothers, says Proclus, were *mestetes*, "middles," and "possess mighty power in the universe." Pythagoreans called them "towers of Jupiter." Numerous other terms are known.

Matter then means generation; and note this: to all the ancient people and to all to whom, nowadays, matter means Mother, matter is never to be spurned or overcome. Matter to them was and is the most glorious term they know of for what others call God. This, then, is one signification of "matter," and it is the correct meaning of the word, when used by mystics. But matter has also another significance, and you will see it when I tell you that a Greek, Anaximander, about 600 B. C, introduced the term *arke*, as a term and designation for the first and fundamental principle, and as a substitute for Mother. But arke is a colorless and anemic term that stands for an abstract conception. Really we cannot object to Anaximander and his term; they were both Greek and both idealistic. But now comes the point, now you shall see where trouble arose. Aristotle, about 340 B. C, who understood the term to mean merely a formative and empty principle and not reality, wished to destroy it because it had become a power in Platonism, which he criticized. He therefore placed over against it another term to counterbalance it and to contradict it. That term was Greek for chaos; it is a realistic term, which means "mud," viz., a sort of general mixture of tangible elements. It is this conception of chaos, of mud, that has come down to us, while the conception Mother has been forgotten. It is chaos, mud, and since Aristotle's time materialism, moral baseness, we are bid in mystic life to overcome. We are not bid to deny the Mother. In addition to the Aristotelian conception of imperfection, confusion and low quality, that word Matter has also by Christian philosophy become the bearer of all ideas of moral impurity, defects, sins and baseness. These, too, the mystic candidate must shun. Aristotle and Christianity have certainly conferred a benefit upon us by the invention of a new term and the clear sense they gave that term, but the pity is, that all kinds of fanatics, ascetics, and pseudo-philosophers have completely forced the idea of Mother out of the common understanding and existence, and, that that, which is to be overcome, that which is the outer, and, thus diametrically opposed to inner, is called matter. It ought to be called something else and is so called by mystics.

Can this Inner Life be lived in a workaday world like ours? This is a question constantly asked, and I constantly answer, Yes! most emphatically. It can be lived and is lived. Life is not a snare. I shall in future chapters enter more fully upon this. How to reach the Inner Life! I have already used as illustration: the bridge, and two persons passing over it from opposite ends. I will continue the use of that illustration. It is a good one- that which in mystic life is called the Path. I will now say that one end of the bridge is called Silence, the other Solitude, and that the Middle is called the True Self. Now listen! Let me read you a poem full of suggestion:

"We sat together in the afterglow
And talked of earth's old mystery of pain;
Of wasted toil, of love and anguish vain,
Of little children born to helpless woe.
We talked until life seemed like a hideous show,

THE INNER LIFE AND THE TAO TEH KING

And men but slaves under the cruel reign
Of a blind god, their prayers could not restrain.
-Then we sat silent
     -on the rocks below,

The careless mountain stream foamed at our feet;
Above the dark pine's silhouette hung fair,
One star, in whose calm radiance earth's despair
Seemed childish outcry;—life grew sane and sweet;
For nature's brooding peace was everywhere,
And love eternal through her pulses beat."

Marion Pruyn, in *New England Magazine*, June, 1897.

See the bridge? "We sat silent!"!

The first part of this poem has very likely been the experience of many in this room, and perhaps that line, "Then we sat silent," has also been the experience and has had its natural sequence in peace and quiet, in which "life grew sane and sweet." If that has been your experience, have you reflected upon this, that it was the silence that fell upon you, that brought sanity and sweetness? It was silence that brought redemption; not talk, not bitterness that did it; not criticisms of facts of life misunderstood, not a negative spirit *ivofda*; bitter criticism is the sin of the world today. Sanity and sweetness came when the ravens of restless thought had ceased their cawings; ravens, rooks, crows and jackdaws bring no peace; they mean putrefaction, and so does bitter, senseless talk. Skepticism is not the true beginning of philosophy. The true beginning lies in the recognition of this, "Be still and know that I am God." (Ps. 46, 10), and in learning to commune with our own hearts. I will now say something about Silence and Solitude, and these two words will be the portals, through which, not by which, the Inner Life will appear in some of its majesty and beauty. It will appear that Silence discovers or unveils the Individual Self, and that Solitude discovers or unveils

THE INNER LIFE AND THE TAO TEH KING

Universal Self. What is meant by Silence?

Negatively, the word means "to shut up," to cease talking. Mysticism in its Greek root means to shut up, to close up. Mere silence is of course useless. Mutes are not on the Path, because they are not able to talk. Positively, Silence is the quiescence of a perfectly ordered fullness, viz., after we have become literally silent, the fullness of life asserts itself as never otherwise. Again, in silence, there is a positive realization of the power of presence. A presence, to some, of Beauty; an awakening within of an Ideal, longed for, though forgotten. A Beauty, proud and austere, yet revealing an immortal face; a Beauty that lifts our longings into lovely dreams and the white flames of ecstasy. To others, Silence is like the edge of the day when the dawn slides slowly along the tops of the pines, and they feel a new energy awaken in them, an energy in which they feel, that they hold the worlds in the hollow of their hands. To others, Silence holds the highest Wisdom borne by the rhythmic currents that permeate space. The world calls it inspiration. Others hear the divine thunder: "Be still, and know that I am God," and they go forth as prophets of the Most High, as witnesses for the sovereign of the Past, the Present and the Future. "In silence we become each moment what God already is." Ah, how shall I tell those that have not experienced it what silence is? Those who know it, understand me. My words can be only like the ringing of bells. By Silence we come into the true life, into our right place, and the immortal Life reigns. We discover our individual self. In Silence our normal nature asserts itself and we live; we do not merely think or act, we live, something so utterly foreign, that the modern culture-man does not know what it is, neither does he understand it.

What is it to live? It is to experience an intensity which fully balances the immensity of the objective world. Full of that intensity, that insight, we bear up against any adversity like a thunderstorm, which always goes against the wind. Full of that intensity and this insight, there can be no ascetic dissipation of the eternal fires that lie at the root of the soul. That intensity, that insight, is the synthesis of all the powers we can conceive, and we live neither in fancy, speculation nor in false assertion of self. We are one with existence, as that murmurs in the forest and sighs in the wave and illumines the mountain top and cries on the tongue of the new-born baby or breathes in lovers' amorous talk or shouts in archangel's Halleluyah! This intensity, this insight, is synthetic; it is all inclusive, not exclusive. It will not recognize the theological distinction of saints and sinners to have any eternal value. To it, life is one. It will not lament on account of the ragged edges of sorrow, nor will it merely rejoice in victory. All antagonism, cold as morning chill or deadly as night malaria, is dissolved into the colors of the rainbow of Hope. That intensity is an assertion of Soul and Immortality. It is a realization of Genius, and the Over-man. This was the one end of the bridge- Silence! Now let us pass in from the other end, Solitude. The word Solitude means exactly what its originator meant it to stand for. It means that when "things" have been taken away or removed, there then remains something "alone," and that something is the Ego. Solitude means that the Ego is alone with itself. Do not consider loneliness and lonesomeness as synonymous terms and conceptions. A lonely life is a forlorn, sad and forsaken existence; it is solitary and lacking the soul's craving for a companion. A lonely life is usually the result of conflicts with societary order or a result of sickness. It is abnormal and defective.

Lonesomeness, on the contrary, is most desirable for strong souls. It means seclusion from the rabble and the multitudinousness of daily life. It imparts the idea of terror to some, to those, namely, who are so little self-centered that they must always lean upon somebody. But lonesomeness is not terrible or distressing; on the contrary, the wise seek it as an antidote against dismay and find it to be a tutelary divinity. All who seek the roots of life dig in solitude for them. The "second birth" is in solitude. The "twice-born" enjoy solitude. It would be well for many if they at least could retreat to a "quiet room" like Whittier's:

THE INNER LIFE AND THE TAO TEH KING

"I find it well to come
For deeper rest to this still room;
For here the habit of the soul
Feels less the outer world's control.
And from silence multiplied
By these still forms on every side,
The world that time and sense have known
Falls off, and leaves us God alone."

Yes, Solitude is a state or condition so sublime in character that I may say: Solitude is God's secret meeting place with the soul. Solitude is as Lenau put it, "The Mother of God in man."

The "twice-born" man comes out of Solitude, not out at a whist party or from a ball. In Solitude arise all those images from our past existences which in this present noisy and passionate earth-life have sunk to the bottom. In Solitude there is that which Plato called *anamnesis*, "Reminiscence," a recovery of all past experiences; a fact of the uttermost importance in our psychic life, and, a fact that gives great comfort; we know that we live not in vain even if present conditions are antagonistic. We shall reap the fruits of all our labors, all our hopes, longings and tears. In Solitude arise not only our own endeavors in and towards the greater Life, but also the spectra of all the volitions, good and bad, that filled our surroundings while we lived in the past, as well as the images of cosmic life. Whatever we lost in our studies, the visions of which we do not understand, the beauties we failed to perceive, all, all are again available, are again to Be enjoyed, are again to be studied; and they all come back in a clarified condition and full of an imperial power they never before possessed.

You can readily see the rationale of this. They have been stripped naked of all the incidental and trivial and their burning fire. In utter nakedness they stand before us and call for life. By giving them life they become souls, and, we become prophets, artists, poets, musicians! Oh, the glorious Solitude! Oh, take solitude and let everything else go! Pay the price. Do you remember Goethe's confession?

> "Who never ate his bread with tears,
> Nor through the sorrow-laden hours
> Sat nightly face to face with fears,
> He knows you not, ye heavenly powers."

The "heavenly powers" here spoken of, are those of solitude. But these very powers are the ones that made great men great. The pay was none too heavy! They made Goethe great! These powers of solitude and the ordeal we pass through in solitude brings us face to face with "the Great Alone" and our Genius; nothing else does it. In solitude none of the five senses work. They are merely doors through which the soul passes in and out; in to itself, and out into nature. What I want to emphasize is this- in solitude, we are neither subjective nor objective- we root in neither extreme, we are reflective. We are reflective, I say, we do not reflect or think; nay, the Universal, be it the Good or the Beautiful, finds its true expression through us. In solitude we have, neither ears nor eyes; we are perceptive, however! Do you perceive the difference? We do not have senses, we are the essential of sense. In solitude we are not in manifoldness, we are in unity. These images become the expressions for what I call reconciliation, which sets us free. Here you have in a nutshell the whole psychology of Solitude. See that the emphasis lies upon the withdrawing from externals, from tools, from means, to essentials! This withdrawal must be thoroughly understood, otherwise we shall misjudge and perhaps reject the teachings of the mystics about "overcoming" and "self-conquest."

This subject is the main element in all intelligent life, be it religious, artistic or mystic. No human being attains freedom without passing through this psychic furnace. No human being can ever create any monumental work without initiation in this temple. No human being, who has not worshiped at this shrine and there been baptized in fire and by spirit, can ever understand that myriad named power which we see in Nature, Beauty, Goodness and everywhere else.

Now, in conclusion, examine for yourself and see if I have spoken the truth. If I have spoken the truth, it conforms to (1) the method of nature; (2) to the constitution of the human mind; and (3) to the testimonies of the Scriptures as they have been handed down from age to age.

CHAPTER II

Walt Whitman, our neglected poet, wrote:

"Surely, whoever speaks to me in the right voice
Him or her I shall follow
As the water follows the moon silently
With fluid steps anywhere around the Globe."

And he continues in the same poem ("Voices"):

"I believe all wait for the right voices,
I see brains and lips closed- tympans and temples
unstruck,
Until that comes which has the quality to strike and to
unclose,
Until that comes which has the quality to bring forth
What lies slumbering, forever ready, all in words."

Like Whitman we all wait to hear the right voice. Where is that voice to be heard? The voice that can wake "what lies slumbering," where can it be heard? This sentence, "what lies slumbering," means a great deal; much more than its shortness would suggest. That which lies "slumbering" and which is to be awakened is our most essential nature. It is slumbering, viz., it is unknown to ourselves and to others. It is living in the innocence of a fool's paradise and in untried peace. The voices awaken it to activity and to thought. The awakening is sometimes painful and is followed by many trials, We enter upon the Path at the awakening. It is the awakening of the right voice that makes the difference between one man and another and which gives us any value. That is what happens normally. The "right voice" may also speak to us while we are in confusion or perhaps evil. It is then an awakener in another sense. Of that I shall not speak at present.

THE INNER LIFE AND THE TAO TEH KING

I will show you two pictures. Be not surprised that I call them voices. I have good authority for it. Philo-Judaus, in most of his knowledge a good theosophist, and he had the Hebrew Scriptures as his authority, says that Nature is the language in which God speaks, "but there is this difference, that while the human voice is made to be heard, the voice of God is made to be seen; what God says consists of acts, not of words." (*Works*. English trans, vol. 2, "Art. on Abraham.") Let me show you a picture by the Japanese painter, Okio. It represents a sunrise on the coast of Japan. All you see is a long line of surf tumbling in towards you from out a bank of mist; you see the blood-red disk of the rising sun, and over the narrow strip of breaking rollers three cranes are slowly sailing north. You do not see the shore nor the ocean itself, it lies still sleeping under the mist, you see only the borderland of the great unknown, the breakers, the sun and the cranes. The picture is so simple that it would not appeal to most people. But it contains the whole philosophy of the Tao-Teh-King of which I shall speak in the following chapters.

You have perhaps seen such a scene on an early morning. I have seen it (minus the cranes, to be sure), right outside New York, where the Atlantic washes New Jersey's low, sandy shores. The view is weird, to say the least. It makes a desolate shore look more desolate and strikes you painfully at first. In melancholy you begin to realize that you have before you a picture of life. A vast unknown and a misty immensity envelops you, in which you perceive only the heaving breath of the ocean as of a mighty monster, perhaps dangerous. The breakers speak in unknown tongues and the cranes represent the eternal cry of the human soul for rest. And really, such is life in one of its aspects, the most dreadful one! What a blessing that the majority of people do not even suspect the truth! Only strong souls and initiates are allowed to behold the mystery and to see that we are surrounded by just such uncertainty- Uncertainty! The Inner Life begins in such realizations. It cannot begin in any other way. Yet such a negative beginning is most fruitful. All the entangling meshes of a complex life are hindrances. The Inner Life is, first of all, simplicity; that is, it is unmixed, homogeneous. Hear a legend. In the glorious days of chivalry, there was a knight brave and bold, but stupid as regards learning. He never learned more of the "Ave Maria" than the words "Hail, Mary blessed among women" but these words he repeated always, in time and out of time. When he died it was discovered that lilies sprouted from his grave, and upon opening the grave it was found that the lilies grew upon his tongue! Sancta Simplicitas! Simple enough! Who would follow him? Yet the legend contains eternal truth. A life in simplicity is a free life, a life not in bondage either to desire or the objects of desire, or blurred by intellectual smoke. A life in simplicity has eliminated even the perspectives of the landscape, and stands like Fudji-no-yama with the head above the clouds. A life in simplicity is a strong life, and ignores the clouds that thunder and lighten around its breast, and, it stands firmly on the rock-ribbed cosmos.

It lies so near for anyone that may have been awakened by hearing about such a life, to imitate that which has been seen or heard, or follow some teacher who promises a short cut to the ideals. I would warn such. I would not have anyone copy another who has lived that life. I would have you know it from your own experience. The Inner Life is original. I warn all that "new trees cannot be made of flowers old ones bore," and, that one must not lay withered flowers as offering upon the altar. We live in a new age, and the Inner Life for us must be lived on new lines. It must be, first, natural or true to facts, secondly, it must be human, viz., not ascetic; thirdly, it must conform to all the best results of the lives lived by Mystics and Theosophists in the past. The Inner Life is an original life and mankind today is in as bad a way as it is because there has been copying, imitations. Teachers and leaders have taken their gifts in vain and sold them for money, and smothered their own consciences by the belief that they did mankind good by making it follow them and by making it copy their methods. They conferred no blessing, they hampered the inner life not only in their followers, but in themselves. I need not mention examples, church history is full of them. Prophets turning autocrats, leaders becoming tyrants and heavenly meetings ending in hell, are painted only too frequently in history. If I were offered a high seat in Heaven for organizing a mystic or Inner Life society, I would refuse it. The freedom of a soul is worth more than Heaven. The Inner Life is original. It rests on no authority. The study and exercise of the Inner Life must be as new and as fresh as the morning that breaks in upon that shore in Okio's painting, and shine in its own light as the sun does in the morning; every morning greeting the mists anew and inviting the cranes to rise. And every soul that aspires to initiation must stand there where it sees no shore, but only breakers and the long indefinite line of possibilities. I will have no man or woman cling to another's thought, because "a thought that once has been thought, no man can think once more." The Inner, or the Mystic, Life must be and is original; viz., it is a new beginning; it is fresh from the Original; it is something that never was before, either as light, or as power, or motion; it is a new opening into the sanctuary of the Most High, it raises the curtain to new loves and is the genesis of new born worlds. A true mystic, or spiritually minded person, one who lives the Inner Life, avoids all kinds of "systems," be they philosophical, theological, ethical, or anything else. He seeks what the Tao-Teh-King calls Wu-Wei, and Wu-Wei is taught by the seashore of Okio's painting. The more consistent, the more logical the systems appear, the more they are to be shunned. Their very consistency proves their lack of life and spirit. Any and all systems, be they mystic, theosophic, or handed down by angels or otherwise, are only views obtained from one of the approaches to the bridge of life. The middle lies equally remote from either end, and the middle is the Truth. Of that I spoke at length lately. Life is too rich and too full to be forced into a Procustes' bed of thought, no matter whose thought or will it happens to be. History bears witness to all I say on this subject, and, so does Nature. Go into any garden and you shall see for yourself and hear the old Mother Nature laugh at you and your ideas when you want to force her. Your ideas are not hers. She does not work by "system." She is

THE INNER LIFE AND THE TAO TEH KING

Herself. We ought to analyze into the mysteries of the New Life that today surges upon the shore of existence. The New Age People follow the Stream and they never think of commanding the waves of the ocean to respect the royal feet, as did King Canut of Denmark. What do the waves care about royal feet?

In addition to that which I already have said about Okio's painting, I want to say that the main lesson I would point out in it, is this: In it there is no clamor, no striving of the senses, no lusts, no unreal thoughts. It is Wu-Wei, or the simplicity of life; or as the Tao-Teh-King calls it, relaxation from earthly activity, the simple beauty of life flowing as of itself like a river according to inner law, but not striving in its own will. The painting is a prayer for stillness; that voice which resounds everywhere in Nature, and everywhere with Nature's passionate intensity. And that voice is "the right voice" to all. It speaks always about mystery. Mystery is but another name for absolute truth, for Originality! Now let me show you another picture and ask you to listen to another voice. I have a picture to show quite as powerful as that of Okio, and you shall hear a voice from the abyss as rich as that in the Japanese painting. I shall quote a poet, who ought to be the banner bearer for Theosophists with poetic veins. I mean him who understood so well the occult there is in the landscape:

> "The silence that is in the starry sky,
> The sleep that is in the lonely kills,"

And who realized more powerfully than anybody else that:

> "The meanest flower that blows can bring
> Thoughts that do often lie too deep for tears."

I mean Wordsworth, to whom nature was no puzzling mechanism, but a luminous organism, a personal influx:. Wordsworth, of whom Shelley said he had awakened "a kind of thought in sense"; Wordsworth, to whom a sunrise was the time of spiritual consecration; Wordsworth, who liked to stand;

> "Beneath some rock, listening to notes that are
> The ghostly language of ancient earth;"

Wordsworth, who had communed with "Nature's self, which is the breath of God." I shall read to you a short passage from the first book of the "Excursion." I am very fond of it. It is a voice that speaks

> "...truths that wake
> To perish never-
> Which neither listlessness nor mad endeavor,
> Nor all that is at enmity with joy,
> Can utterly abolish or destroy."

This is the passage:

> "...for the growing youth
> What soul was his, when, from the naked top
> Of some bold headland, beheld the sun
> Rise up, and bathe the world in light? He looked-
> The solid frame of earth
> And ocean's liquid mass, in gladness lay
> Beneath him- Far and wide the clouds were touched
> And in their silent faces could he read
> Unutterable love. Sound needed none,
> Nor any voice of joy; his spirit drank
> The spectacle; Sensation, soul and form,
> All melted into him; they swallowed up
> His animal being; in them did he live,
> And by them did he live; they were his life-
> In such access of mind, in such high hour
> Of visitation from the living God,
> Thought was not; in enjoyment it expired.
> No thanks he breathed; he proffered no request;

THE INNER LIFE AND THE TAO TEH KING

Rapt into still communion that transcends
The imperfect offices of prayer and praise,
His mind was a thanksgiving to the power
That made him; it was blessedness and love!"

This is...

"An Orphic song indeed,
A song divine, of light and passionate thoughts,
To their own music chanted."

As Coleridge wrote the night after he had heard "The Prelude." It is a voice that speaks without sound; a voice that does away with the animal being; a voice that does not need thought for translation; it is immediate; without means it transfigures sensation, soul and form. In rapt communion the soul transcends both prayer and praise, and, becomes blessedness and love; becomes one with glory, one with nature. In "The Prelude" where Wordsworth sings of another magnificent morning, he confesses:

"My heart was full; I made no vows, but vows
Were then made for me; bond unknown to me
Was given, that I should be, else sinning greatly,
A dedicated Spirit."

How mean does not the every-day treadmill seem in the light of such solemn experiences? And how contemptible the waste most people are guilty of; they waste the golden moments in bed and neglect the morning on the mount. Hence they do not expand and know not its beatitudes. A traveler once asked a Hopi Indian, whom he saw praying half an hour as he stood at his door looking over the mesa, what he said. The Indian answered: "Nothing!" He said nothing- but something filled him. What? the Great Spirit filled him with bright presence and a calm sank down into his heart, a calm in which he perceived the eternal, and the horizon of his heart widened. He felt something akin to himself.

THE INNER LIFE AND THE TAO TEH KING

And such is true prayer. He heard "the right voice."

Now, you have heard what Whitman called "the right voice" and these two, Wordsworth and the Indian, who "followed as the water follows the moon silently"; Wordsworth, the man from the sea of the nations, and the Indian, the power of the mountain fastness and the Open. Do you know the soul of either of these? or their experiences? Did you ever go out into the free, the Open, where "the right voices" may be heard? or did you fear and hide in the great city with its confusion of tongues, or, did you, perhaps, lose the key to your own heart? Hear "the right voice":

> "Love thy God, and love Him only,
> And thy breast will ne'er be lonely.
> In that One Great Spirit meet
> All things- mighty, grave and sweet.
> Mortal, love that Holy One,
> Or, dwell forever alone- alone!!

It is not necessary that you or I should retire to the jungle, the hermit's cell, or forsake kith and kin,in order to listen to "the right voice." Nay- the sea, the mountain, and your own heart, speak in the right voice, if we but listen. The sea and the mountain we have always with us. Every woman is a sea; every man is a mountain, and the heart throbs in both. As I said, it is not necessary that we should retire to the jungle, as they do in India and elsewhere. A large city like New York is a jungle, and as full of all the dangers, horrors and sublime opportunities as any mountain fastness. As for myself, I live in it and look upon New York City as a jungle. I can testify that I do not listen to the chattering monkeys; and the wild animals, though they growl and threaten, never hurt me. I let great popular excitements pass by like an electric storm in the forest, and I stay unaffected in my meditations. I have my solitary room and there I find myself undisturbed in my spiritual exercises. Yet, I am no recluse. I do my duty as a citizen and hold men's fate in my hands as much as any ruler of states. I do not wear the mendicant's robe, nor do I carry his bowl, nor do I affect the manners of a pietist. Of what use? Why should you not do likewise? The "right voice" tells you to do likewise! To return to the voices:

> "Of mountain splendor and the mobile sea,
> Which are most Mother Nature's in sooth I cannot tell"
> (After John Chadwick)

...but this I know, female souls seek the mountain and masculine souls seek the sea.

> "Two voices are there; one is of the sea,
> One of the mountains; each a mighty voice."
> (Wordsworth)

The one, that of the sea, surges and sinks back again- a sublime continuance! And thus it has been since time was. The others- the mountains- were plowed up one day in an earthquake and "made the haunts of beauty; the home elect of grace; Nature spreads mornings on them, and sunsets light their face," and that is why masculine souls love the sea and female souls seek the mountains. And by drawing these souls to the mountain and to the sea, Mother Nature speaks in the "right voice" to each; but alas! how often does not the female soul become restless and cry;

> "Away! I will away, far away,
> Over the mountains high:
> Here I am sinking lower each day."
> (Bjornson)

Alas! I have also heard unfaithful masculine souls complain that they never fully understood the mystic song of the sea and that dreams enervated them. They wearied of seeing the sun retire and of sleeping behind his purple skirted robe... And why is this? Ah! unfaithfulness! The masculine is as restless as the feminine. They are both unwilling to listen to Wu-Wei, to "inactive absorption into Tao." They fear to be lost. They will rather trust themselves. They have no faith, though Tao, which is faith, constantly speaks assuringly. Have no fear! The Inner Life does not kill either sense, understanding, feelings or anything human! Only shadows vanish and false activity is as naught. Will you not try to practice thinking without doubting; speaking without duplicity; acting without attachment? Again: I have heard of the wonderful mountains, Fudji-no-yama, of Alborgi, of Kaf and Meru, and other heaven-towering mountains, real and mythical, and I have felt the uplift and I have heard a female voice sing rejoicing:

> "I stand on high,
> Close to the sky,
> Kissed by unsullied lips of light;
> Fanned by soft airs
> That seem like prayers
> Fleeting to God through ether bright."
> (C. G. Ames.)

And I have heard the heart's meditation and triumph:

> "All alone on the hilltop
> Nothing but God and me!
> And things immortal cluster
> Around my bended knee."

Ah, yes! So I have heard the song- but silence and I have also heard the same heart fret and fume, wishing for the absence of desire; crying for a light that did not burn, and asking that the voice would cease to urge- as if the flame which the Mother had started was not a holy flame! What of it, if the heart burned away! It is so the Mother's way. Does she not know?

THE INNER LIFE AND THE TAO TEH KING

Again: Masculine souls have exhausted their strength in lyric songs to the sea, its mighty breasts and the refreshing baths and the wild waves' ecstasy- but they, too, have been ungrateful and with tears repented and said "illusions dwell forever with the wave." Some have later on seen their folly and come lack to the waters of life. Those that did not throw their repentance to the winds and return to the ocean of love will lose their life if they ever come near the shore. Such renegades are never taken back. They have sinned against themselves and must be made over. This is what I have heard on the mountain and on the seashore and I have translated my visions and the voices as best I could. But there is much mystery left. You must understand that there are other seas besides the ocean; and other mountains besides rocky prominence. They all have voices- some to be heard, others to be seen. Perhaps you have read other inscriptions on the mountains, and heard other musical notes scored on the staff of the shore. If so, we understand each other! How shall we teach the others to hear and to see how Okio's picture speaks in low and solemn voice. Wordsworth's in high and triumphant notes. To those who seldom commune with nature, they will appear so remarkable that they will talk about them and write about them in the dailies and magazines. And they will consider them something special they have been lucky enough to see. But to those who live with Nature, these visions and voices are not exceptional; they are common, i. e., they lie open to the perception and enjoyment of all, and always, because Nature is not exclusive, but quite lavish in her goodness. A youthful and poetic mind would be apt to misinterpret

the symbolism and richer glory of these two pictures and miss their real significance. A prosaic and materialistic mind will, of course, remain ignorant of the spiritual values of such experiments. To a lover of Nature, who is one with her, they will be resonant with the deep things of Divinity; and such a lover will feel an interpenetration of all Nature with his or her own being, and he or she will come out of the experience feeling transformed and knowing that something transcendental has visited them. And this is Tao's work. I cannot define it any clearer, but you can experience it and thus know it better. When I now turn from objective nature to the subjective nature within, I also find two voices and they speak loud in the halls of the learned. And these voices are called Idealism and Realism, or Platonism and Aristotelianism. Yon have all heard them, though yon may not have named them as I did. Not having heard them, have yon in their voice- either the one or the other- heard the note of your own mind? It is imperative that yon should hear that note, otherwise the voice is not to yon any right voice, but merely scholastic dust and noise. Which of the voices speaks pre-eminently to the masculine soul and which to the feminine, I leave yon to answer for yourself. Yon have a guide in what I have said about the voices of the sea and the mountain. Those two voices I just now called Idealism and Realism; Platonism and Aristotelianism, were heard at an earlier day in Greece and expressed by Fire-Philosophers on one side and the Eleatics or Philosophers of Being on the other. I mention these because they are two voices which are heard wherever and whenever men try to form their ideas of the surrounding world, and, there is an affinity between the Fire philosophy and some minds in my audience, and, there is an affinity between the philosophy of Being and other minds in my audience. Some of yon can understand the mystery of existence if you consider it under the aspect of eternal change, a coming and a going, a breathing in and a breathing out. And such an understanding is most valuable and most necessary for the formation of character.

Others cannot understand what Not-Being is and how loss, decay and death can be necessary and valuable elements in the cosmos. They demand, according to the voice that speaks in them, permanency and rest. They, too, need to learn all details about their voice in order to build character, different as they are. I need not elaborate or say any more about these two voices. They will readily be seen to correspond to the sea and the mountain voices which I have described in detail. If it is as Aristotle has it, that some men become good by nature, others by training, others by instruction, then I say, that those who are good by nature always and spontaneously hear those voices of the sea and the mountains and the other voices. The others learn in the course of life to listen to them, and both become one with the voices, when they have understood them. Now about the voice within. The "right voice" speaks also in our Inner Man. And that voice is called by many names and described, as is natural, very differently, but we never have any difficulty in knowing what is meant, when we hear the name. This many-named voice, or power, or degree, of the Inner Man, which we aim at getting hold of; that degree which we desire to open and which we wish to develop, is described in various ways, and some of these descriptions I will now give you. First of all I will give my own description. I call it the eternal pattern or plastic power in us and mean by that, that it is the rule and regulation inborn or given to all men. According to it, we know the eternal ways and methods. It always speaks as "the right voice" and we are happy when we listen. I came originally to the understanding of it by pondering upon the meaning of the statement in Genesis, that we are made in "the image of God." I therefore also call it "the image of God." Everyone of you have it in you. It is that ideal you carry in you and which you wish to come up to. That ideal you judge by, when you occasionally admit to yourself and others that you do not come up to the standard. It is there and nobody can plead ignorance as an excuse for disobedience or for not attempting seriously the Higher Life. It may not be wide awake, but it is there and admonishes us, even if we will not admit it. Plato's description of *anamnesis* or reminiscence is in part a very good analysis. You know Plato perhaps. I will not speak of it in detail. But Plato's description is defective in my opinion, in this, that it only recognizes ideals of a former existence, and that is a limitation. I think that this pattern, I mention, is much more than a reminiscence; it precedes anything that can be called so; it is eternal, and, moreover, it not only quickens us, as Plato says, but it commands us; that is, it is or becomes a constitutional part of us, and as such it is or becomes ourselves. It is not a sunset, but a sunrise and a perfect day.

THE INNER LIFE AND THE TAO TEH KING

It is not a longing, it is a realization. It is a compelling voice. It is a voice, which, when we hear it, we follow readily and in joy, because we know we cannot go astray. How could we? Am I not my own voice, aim and purpose? Am I not myself? I am; at least when I am on the Path! I will now give some descriptions from various sources.

Schelling was a German philosopher of modern times and full of theosophical and mystic element. It was he who said, that the Divine sleeps in the stone; rises up in the plant; moves in the animal and opens its eyes in man; Schelling said: "In us there is a secret and mysterious and wonderful power, by means of which we may retire from the mutations of time, and into our inner self, stripped of all that which comes to us from the outward things, and, there under the form of unchangeableness, gaze upon the Eternal. This vision is the innermost and most genuine experience and upon it depends and from it flows all we know or imagine of the supernatural world." Next to Schelling's expression I will place the Greek philosopher, Heraclitus, also full of theosophy and mysticism. And he put it down as his experience: "Though you trod every path, you could not find the limits of the soul, so deep in its essence." Well, is that sense of the Infinite wide awake in you? Has it become Thought in you as it did in Wordsworth? Does it sound as a voice you would follow like the voice Whitman spoke of? Have you perceived it as the sound of your soul, as did the medieval mystics?

Schleiermacher, a preacher, akin to those already mentioned, in speaking of the intuition said: "In it there is contact of the universal life with the individual life. It is the holy wedlock of the universe with the incarnated reason... It is immediate, raised above all error and misunderstanding; you lie directly on the bosom of the Infinite. In that moment you are its soul. Through one part of your nature you feel, as your own, all its powers and its endless life." With this power we see into the nature of things, and, to borrow phraseology from Platonism, it describes the true home of the soul to be the supra-sensible, supra-celestial, world of true Being, where, pure, incorporeal and without passion, the soul leads a holy and eternal life, contemplating the beauty and the excellent harmony of ideas, and, where the soul beholds the indivisible and immutable archetypes of the fleeting phenomena, that flow in multitudinous commingling before the dazzled senses. Ah! For such experiences "the true home" of the soul- "to contemplate the beauty" of eternity- "the archetypes" or the essence of things- is it not worth while? Shall we not now begin, those of us who have not yet realized this "pure incorporeal world," which is "without passions"- those of us who still live in those terrible earthquakes that rend this fragile frame of ours to pieces? Well, friends, "while the eternal ages watch and wait" for some of us to come up higher, let me quote from others who, in "high seriousness," have felt and spoken of that "awful shadow," of the "unseen power, which floats among us" visiting us "as summer winds that creep from flower to flower."

Legends and Folklore are full of picturesque tales and symbolical narratives. Here are a couple of examples:

Boethius (about 470 A. D.) tells us in his book "Consolations of Philosophy," how he, while in prison and in exile, was visited by a woman of reverend countenance, with glowing eyes, penetrating beyond the common power of human eyes, of brilliant complexion, and inexhaustible strength, though full of years. Her stature was difficult to describe; sometimes she appeared to retain it within the common human measure, sometimes she lifted her head so high that it looked into the very heaven and was lost to the gaze of the beholder. This visitor was Wisdom. Who would not like such a visit, even though she should speak reprovingly as she did to Boethius, because she found him busy with classical poetry, neglecting heavenly Wisdom. What business had Boethius (or have we) with anything else than the eternal? Yes, such a visit would be worth a whole life's study as it was to Boethius. The moment he realized who she was, he knew instantly that all his studies had not revealed to him what Man was, and he had to confess it to her. But, humble he was and his confession was rewarded. In free and lightsome song she bid him cast away grief, and, from that moment she was his good genius, teaching him the true philosophy and the mystic union with God. She was his own Soul.

In a Shawnee tale, from our American plains and told by Schoolcraft, I find a parallel to this story. The story is called "The Celestial Sisters" and treats of a celestial sister, a daughter of the stars, who comes down to see "how the game is played by the mortals" and is captured by Waupee, "the White Hawk"; she becomes his bride and thereby his regenerator. She brings him in upon the starry plains, where his second or celestial marriage is celebrated. I cannot here give more of the story. I have elsewhere told it and commented at length upon it. It is a marvelous story and richer than the Greek of Apuleius about Cupid and Psyche.

Of course, Folklore contains many other similar stories. They are all poetic renderings of the same truths which I have spoken of. In numerous Folklore stories do we hear of celestial or mystic visitors that come to free a soul in bondage. In some of them we also hear warnings to the one who receives the visit, and these warnings are to beware of rudeness and curiosity. I will give you an illustration, not Folklore, however, but just as good and to the point. It is a little story once told by a teacher of mine, Professor Rasmus Nielsen, of Copenhagen University. The story is about a student, a lady. We see her at her study table. She has ink on her ringers; surely a proof that she is literary. She is not yet a graduate, but soon she will be. See how she arms herself. Look at this table of studies; seven foreign languages, history, geography, music, singing, drawing, painting, natural history and physics, mythology, perspective and mathematics, fortification and astronomy.

For a moment she rests and takes her attention from an

essay in astronomy on which she is at work. Suddenly it occurs to her that there is something wanting on the study-plan. Says she: "There must be something they call the Inner Life. I can learn so much else, surely I can learn that, too. It would be well to do so; it is always well to know something that others do not know. I wish I could find a teacher in the Inner Life." As suddenly as this soliloquy had sprung up, as suddenly there appeared in the door an elderly sage-looking man, who smiled upon her with compassion. "Well, who are you?" He was, he said, a teacher in the Inner Life and offered to give her lessons. "What are your terms?" He teaches without money or compensation and is always at service. "What?" says she, "without money or compensation," and "always at service?" She is astonished; looks out of the window and- when she turns back, he is gone! Hah! what is that like? He teaches "without money or compensation" and is "always at service" and can't even wait while one looks out of the window. Wonder if the Inner Life is logical? By the way, I forgot to ask about recommendations. The incident was soon forgotten and our student turned to the astronomical essay. What she later found out about the teacher and the Inner Life is not known. But this, my listener might learn, that the Inner Life is immediate, sudden, spontaneous and free of cost. Do not look out of the window; do not hesitate Do not ask for recommendations.

Not individuals only make such grave mistakes. Western humanity has made them again and again. I can supplement my teacher's, the Professor's story by showing you the parallel to his story in history. The history of philosophy furnishes it. Greek Thought degenerated into materialism in Democritus and his successors, and, in Socrates and the Sophists it lost itself entirely in self-conceit. A reaction set in with Plato, and in the Post-Aristotelian thought Greece almost recovered itself. Neoplatonism was full salvation. Neo-Platonism was mystic and theosophic wisdom, that destroyed all self-sufficiency and taught men how to find release from the world and the flesh by an innermost activity of soul and in ecstasy. (Down and up!)

THE INNER LIFE AND THE TAO TEH KING

Men lapsed. Night set in again, and, in the next and following ages the transcendental period established by Plotinos and his school lost entirely its vital force and became mere scholasticism in the Church's theology, and transformed itself into a doctrine of will, such as is manifested in St. Augustine. These two represent a new fall and degeneration once more. The Dark Ages, the Middle Ages, follow and the Inner Life is lost sight of. But redemption comes at last. It breaks forth in the Renaissance and Reformation and comes to its full power in theosophists like Jacob Boehme and all those wonderful men, such as Eckardt, Suso and Tauler, who all live entirely in the depths of the soul. (Again down and up!)

Once again after a time delusions blind the human mind and conceit gets the upper hand. The supremacy of mind and spirit in men like Descartes becomes mere rationalism. English empiricism crops up as an antidote, but on the same low level and, between the two, the human mind is again darkened and comes near its death. A revival begins in Emanuel Kant's reassertion of the spiritual principle, and in the works of the so-called Faith-Philosophers, Lessing, Jacobi and Herder. But the real resurrection takes place when the mystics and theosophs once again come upon the scene. Reinhold asserts "the principle of Consciousness" and lays emphasis upon the fact that, thought always points beyond itself. He therefore demands a higher unity than thought can furnish, and that opens the door for mysticism. Fichte and Schelling both end in Theosophy and become the saviors of many. Finally comes Schiller with his mystic doctrine of art as the redeeming element from all skepticism and materialism of the age. At the same time such Romanticists as Novalis dream and talk only about the innermost essence of things. All this, together with that vigorous protest we call the French Revolution, shake off all trammels; and from now on the individual is free again to pursue its own course. Thus once more did the mystic powers that lie at the root of the human tree revive it and give it new growth. (Down and up again!)

THE INNER LIFE AND THE TAO TEH KING

Has it continued to grow according to the promises of the beginning? Nay, it must be admitted that the negative forces, the selfish powers of the knights, kings and priests and their servants, have succeeded only too well in strangling the new growth. And science, which ought to have been a liberating angel, has only too often and too well furnished the gross and stupid parts of man with indulgences and physical means for enjoyment. Everywhere we again see decay and indifference. Here and there only, and, in isolated cases, have theosophists and mystics arisen with healing on their wings, and upon them depend a revival and restoration as it has depended upon them in the past, as I have just shown you. Will you, all of you, each one individually, come to the rescue? There is no better way to promote one's own welfare than by working for others. All the voices, that are "right voices," all call upon us to do something for the neighbor, and, they all say that we can accomplish nothing of ourselves, nothing in isolation. The future belongs to us if we will work! And, now, in this chapter you have heard two voices in the pictures I have shown. The first voice speaks in two ways, by the melancholy note of the sea and by the joyous triumph of the mountain. The second voice is that of the human heart. All three are voices of Tao, of which you shall hear more in other chapters. All three are One voice, and that voice speaks without sound, and, that One voice is also Tao. Of that you shall also hear more later. To the three spiritual voices answer four mundane voices, and of these I shall speak at the end of this course of chapters. Some of you will understand that I refer to the Triad and the Quaternary. Tao is The Word or "The Silent Speaker," and the little book, "The Voice of the Silence," says, on page 3, that the soul must be "united unto the silent speaker" before she can comprehend "the mystery." This teaching applies to all I have said today. And to hear the voice of the silence that speaks without sound, it is necessary one should learn what it is to fall away from the phenomenal and into the Higher Self, and thus become one with the "Silent Speaker." I have now spoken about voices, such as they come to us in Nature and in the Mind, and my words may possibly have been pleasant to some of you, and my illustrations may have been interesting, but I shall have missed my object entirely if my words have not translated themselves into soundless voices, and if the "Silent Speaker" in you has not united with you. Let me hope

THE INNER LIFE AND THE TAO TEH KING

CHAPTER III

MYSTICISM

Though I have spoken twice about the Inner Life, introductory to my chapters on the Tao-Teh-King, there is still a great deal to be said about it, all of which will be helpful in the study of that book. Upon some points most important in that respect, I shall touch now and hope you will be as happy to hear them as you were with the two other talks. It is especially about the Inner Life in its relationship to Mysticism that I would speak. The two are not identical as some might think. I can define their relationship very readily. If I divide mystics in two large groups and include in the first all pillar-saints, hermit-fakirs of the deserts, Harpokrates and his kind, epileptic miracle-mongers, flagellants, mendicants and other beggars who pretended to sanctity, but really were suspicious characters, not to say criminals, then- these are not Inner Life people. They ought never to have been called mystics. The other group will be composed of saints, yogis, and all those who come under the category of Inner Life people, such as I have deemed the Inner Life in the two foregoing chapters, and, as I shall define it now. In beginning a study of the Tao-Teh-King and Taoism it is well to emphasize that all Inner Life takes its color and terms from its environment. The Inner Life is always Mysticism, but its forms vary according to the soil in which it grows, the atmosphere it breathes and the geographical zones in which it finds its home, and it is always adapted to the historic period in which it appears. You will remember from my last lecture the periods I pointed out and how the mystics came in as the saviors. The reason for the variation of form is this, that the Mystic Life is always more or less of a protest against existing conditions of the actual life in the midst of which it appears. It is only in forms of expression that it varies so much. Its core is always the same, and mystics of all ages and climes understand each other even if they do not speak each others languages. Thus

THE INNER LIFE AND THE TAO TEH KING

in Brahminism Mysticism is ritualistic and must be studied in its symbolical actions. In Buddhism it is nihilistic and must be guessed from its hyper-transcendental forms. In Mohammedanism it is forbidden and hides behind Koranic doctrines or in poetic and naturalistic lyricism such as found among the Sufis.

In Christianity it indulges in extravagant ascetic practices and monastic enthusiasm. In Judaism it has revealed a wonderful philosophy, the Kabbalah, which is a transcription of the divine life as it flows in human arteries and veins and as it reveals itself in the cosmic order of the universe. In our own day Hasidism or Jewish pietism in the form of sentiment and emotional faith is Mysticism of purer water. In China, Mysticism is closely connected with the social-political order of the democratic forms of the empire. Something which the future chapters will show. In connection with the various forms of it which I have just mentioned, many individuals and books come before us and require close attention. In Brahminism the Upanishads claim it. In Buddhism it is the person of the Buddha. In the Kabbalah it is the Zohar and the Sepher Yetzirah we go to. In Hasidism we realize that when we look on material things, we really gaze at the image of the Deity. In China it is the Tao-Teh-King and its author Laotzse, and, in Christianity it is the master-mystic, Jesus, and his disciple Paul. These general remarks are sufficient to show, that the Inner Life is not an abstraction or an airy nothing, but something historical and real, though at the same time it is entirely removed from history and the actual world. In studying Mysticism or forms of the Inner Life under any of these conditions, we repeatedly come in upon the ground occupied by philosophy and religion, because these two together with mysticism are the three mental, moral and spiritual factors in human life, "These three on men all gracious gifts bestow."

But their fields are nevertheless distinct and the three must be kept part in our studies. Philosophy will grasp the Universal in a conception. Religion will devote itself to the service of the

45

THE INNER LIFE AND THE TAO TEH KING

Universal. Mysticism, or the Inner Life, includes both and transcends both because it lives in the Whole, not in any part. It will, as Echardt put it, have Divinity, not merely God. It must also be borne in mind throughout our studies, that Mysticism is The Inner Life, and of the Inner Life I have already spoken. Being the Inner Life, Mysticism is not Occultism, nor anything that comes under that heading in the catalog of the learned societies. To be sure, numerous occult subjects constantly come up and crave our attention for the time being and their relation to The Inner Life must be settled. Occultism, properly understood, is a science of the hidden workings of Nature's powers and Nature's methods. The majority of people do not need occult studies, and such studies would be injurious to most. But all people need the Inner Life, the development of soul powers. Of what use in the bettering of life is a knowledge of manvantaras and pralayas, or, the ebb and flow of divine life, if the student does not live according to such knowledge; if he does not live as Shamsy, who cried out: "From the bosom of Self, I catch continually a scent of the Beloved."

Mysticism or the Inner Life is not the same as Spiritism; in fact it stands sharply over against the delusions that hide under that name. But we meet again and again mystics who have been in some relationship or other to angels and devils, and their records about such intercourses must be carefully sifted. There is Mysticism or Inner Life in Art and in much of our literature, in poetry, for instance. The artist feels it as the plastic power of his art, the writer works by it as his formative energy, to the scientist it is the mystic fire in his test-tube, that subtle cosmic power which he neither can weigh nor measure. Here a warning against bias is needed. An artist or a scientist may be good Inner Life people though they do not speak in the customary language of most mystics. Do not condemn anybody because they do not use the same terminology as you do. I see a most exalted Nature-Mysticism in Michael Angelo's so-called "Aurora," the figure on the monument over Lorenzo di Medici. They did not bury Tyndal in Westminster Abbey, as they ought to have done. When he advocated "imagination" in his famous Belfast address, he spoke from out of the Inner Life. In my opinion, in the Alps he had discovered what the image-making power is. He had seen, what Frederick Robertson called so beautifully, "God's feeling and imagination."

Friends! There is much more Mysticism and many more elements of the Inner Life in the world and in you, than you know. Asceticism is rampant in the history of Mysticism, but a mystic or a theosoph is not necessarily ascetic. Buddha found that the ascetic method was a miserable failure, as regards the attainment of the freedom and knowledge he sought. Jesus may in his youth have lived among Essenes and Therapeutae and applied the ascetic method, we do not know. But this is certain, in the Gospels he is no ascetic, and is blamed by his enemies therefore. Here are two mystics, two who lived the Inner Life, and whose likeness none of us have reached. Neither of them teach asceticism. They teach self-conquests, they preach overcoming; they give examples upon living not swayed or dominated by passions- all of which we must learn, and learn to practice.

They teach especially against making bad Karma; against fatal entanglements, and they advocate the simplicity of the lilies and children. Though Buddha and Jesus denied asceticism both Buddhism and Christianity, however, have upheld asceticism in its worst forms. Such master Mystics and Inner Life men as Buddha and Jesus are not denying the cosmic energy there is in life, both objectively and subjectively. On the contrary they work in harmony with that cosmic energy, and it is for us to learn to do likewise. Most people must, however, overcome much and fight many battles against themselves before they are ready for that simplicity which these two represent or even before they are ready to acknowledge these two as types of the Inner Life. Buddha and Jesus deny the irrational workings of that energy when it appears in our human frame, when it flames like fire broken loose, or like a raging tempest, or as a subtle poison in envy and hatred. Cosmic energy can be a savor of life and a savor of death; it is a savor of life to the strong, to him who is not working for self; it is a savor of death to him who lives only for self, and, to him and all who are ignorant of the nature of cosmic energy.

The mystic is no finished product, he is simply a traveler on the Path, and as such he is learning to "overcome." And what is it we must overcome? To what extent must we all be ascetics? I give as an answer in part the following: The mystic, in Western terms, "seeks union with God" and nothing else. To translate this phrase, "union with God" into the lowest terms, I say, it means "to come into order," "to live rationally." To attain such "order," such "reason," we must overcome all our crotchets, desires and idiosyncrasies, whatever they may be. Not the power which misapplied or run wild becomes crotchets, desires and idiosyncrasies. The power is all right, but our application is wrong. This is the simplest way to indicate what it is to "overcome."

The subject can not be stated in lower terms. Of course, "overcoming" thus far defined is only a beginning. It is followed by numerous other degrees, but of these I need not speak at present. I will, however, touch upon some features of "overcoming" which are of primary importance: of total resignation, of self-denial, carrying the cross. In one word, and in a mystic phrase : we must stand naked in the presence of Self before the real mysteries will reveal themselves. We must be "naked" in order to enter the Path to the Inner Life; free from all those irrational and passionate forms which hinder us. Nakedness means freedom, truth, soul-reality. We must be "naked" because we cannot enter the sacred fire with clothes on; they burn, and thus we will be scorched. Self cannot burn. Do you remember the story from classic mythology about Demeter, who is the Goddess Isis, who placed the little Demophaon, son of Metanaia, in the fire, that he might become immortal? The mother interfered and the boy was burned! Remember also Ishtar of Babylonian legend, who had to drop one garment after another on each of the seven steps in her descent into hell to recover her other half, Ishtubar. At last she stood naked and the doors opened. She returned unscathed. In clothes we burn, but not without them. The same truths come out in the Sufi legend about the soul, which came to the gate of Paradise and asked for admission. Upon inquiry from within: "Who is there?" the soul answered: "It is I," but the door was not opened, and, remained closed for three times thousand years, each time the soul returned with the same request. At last when the soul had learned what the Inner Life is and answered not "It is I," but "It is We," then the door opened at once. When the soul has learned that separateness or clothes are in the way, then it enters into joy; never before.

Did not the cry of Jesus on the cross: "Father, why hast Thou left me?" signify the same? They did! The proof is, that immediately after that cry of nakedness, he exclaimed: "It is accomplished!" (his work.) What can we do in nakedness and not otherwise f In nakedness, we are like Thor. Thor is the spiritual giant, who is not attached to "these" things and who therefore unlike anybody else, can break through Helas Kingdom and make even Hell shiver, shake and tremble. Asa-Thor is the God of rejuvenescence; his beard is as red as his fiery nature; he has the Mjolnir, the belt of strength and the marvelous mail, all symbols of purified or "naked" humanity. Once he rode into Hellheim and brought consternation. Never before had living men entered where the ground was only fear, the walls nothing but pain and the roof made of the stench of death. No wonder Thor's companion Loki advised him to leave. But Thor would not till he had lectured the contemptible shades that stood in rows along the walls and shivered clad only in shadows and pained at sight of so much health; health, they had lost because of fear and the Negative. Only nakedness accomplishes such deeds! No man loaded down with merchandise or in fine clothes comes back out of Hell, or is able to lecture the shades. He is rich, too rich! I Now you see the meaning of nakedness and will understand why anchorites almost always are naked. It is a symbolical help. Enough of pictures!

THE INNER LIFE AND THE TAO TEH KING

After that which I have now said about Mysticism and the Inner Life, it will not be surprising, that I say that Mysticism or the Inner Life is a protest against the actual conditions of its surroundings. The Inner Life is not necessarily so radical as Mysticism, but rather inclined in the same direction. Mysticism is always in its beginning a protest against the traditional and against the actual. It is in conflict with the traditional because it demands originality. It is in conflict with the actual because the actual is usually brutal and of itself in conflict with the Inner Life, a conflict which roots in the usurption of leadership by the actual. The Inner Life cannot and will not recognize the actual for more than a passing show, a necessary face of life. The actual is made by man, not by the Eternal, hence its ephemeral character.

But Mysticism and the Inner Life people have not always been in the right. Let me show a couple of mistakes. Mysticism has in the past condemned the senses. One of the mystics has said: "The senses resemble an ass, and evil desire is the halter"- that is the general idea of the mystics, but the Inner Life as I understand it does not necessarily take that attitude; at any rate not always.

Let me try to say something in favor of a rational view of the senses, the flesh. I may possibly meet with opposition in some of you; may I therefore ask you to listen and follow my explanation till the end and wait with your judgment until I am through with my exposition? Mind is the interpreter and the fashioner of the music that the Divine plays upon us, and I may say without fear of contradiction, that the senses are the mechanics, who mold the divine fire into acts, into deeds. They are the hands of the mind. Can you realize what our world would be if we had no senses? Have you ever thought of it? If mind only existed and no senses, the Word might be spoken, sounds might thrill the vacant spaces and colors might dash from pole to pole or illumine the night, but there would be no human world. The human world is made by the human hand or which is the same, by human deeds and there can be no human deeds without the senses, the flesh! That is a fact! Without the arts man could not utter himself, much less discover himself. He would remain mute and blind. In his desire to speak and to see he evolved them; he demonstrated his desire by the arts. That is the origin of the arts. If there is anything at the bottom of you, you will develop a sense for its manifestation and an art that proves your value! We have the choice: a human world and the senses, the flesh, or, Death as Death will be if we leave out the senses, the flesh. In that case, Death will then be the end of life and not as it really is, an event merely. The denial of the senses, the flesh, means that we declare that all our doings, all our acts, are weavings of smoke, are puppet plays, are perishable time-illusions and not the manifestations of that wonderful existence which Silence reveals. What Divinity is esoterically, we do not know, but to us Divinity becomes something by our acts. In our doings Divinity is unfolded in us. The Greater Life, the Inner Life, cannot admit limited views. In the Greater Life, the five senses (to limit the question to these) are the five fingers of the human hand, and, the human hand is the most marvelous organ (none other excepted) we have. Without a hand, no human society! Think it out and you shall see! Let us learn to honor the senses, the flesh, and, be done with absurd asceticism. The senses are nature's personification in man. "In the senses of the body, Nature mirrors herself to the mind" (Krause), and in "the formation of the human body, Nature authenticates herself as one living whole." (Krause.)

True, the senses drag us frequently over the ragged edges of sorrow! But it is rarely in the open sea that our ship is wrecked. Good sailors run out into the Open when the storm overtakes them, and they avoid the shore. The gale throws the catboat and the timid sailor on the rocks, or on the shoal that he hugs in his fear of the Open. The dangers on the sea are chiefly those of shore and shoal, not in the Open. Keep the rudder true! Run out into the Open! True, the senses are for many fall and destruction. With regard to the senses, the old accusation which Adam raised against Eve holds good. Because fools have used and abused the senses they accuse the senses of undoing them. The accusation is as cowardly and unjust as that of Adam's. True, the senses often leave us empty and forlorn, but it is also true that it is first when the trees are leafless and reach the bare arms up in the cold air towards a bleak sky, that we discover the secret of the forest! Have you seen that? It is so! There is a wonderful symbolism here! When the forest is overloaded with leaves it is intoxicated with life and its mystery simmers away. When a human being is drenched in passionate streams, the senses adjust the exuberance and the pain of the drain reveals their real nature. Never does conscience speak clearer than through the senses and their ravages! The cure of life is more life! Do you see how the senses minister to the redemption of the whole man? I say all this fully conscious of what I say. I glorify the senses, but I will not subscribe to Keat's famous exclamation: "Oh, for a life of sensations rather than thoughts." The senses must always be "spiritualized" and that not merely in Keat's sense. To "spiritualize" to him had only an aesthetic sense and no moral signification. Degeneration is an economic factor in the life of the individual; and, Deity and Nature are not at strife.

I will say, that the Inner Life works with the senses, the flesh, as a gardener does with the soil. He uses the soil to grow his flowers in, and, has no other ground to plant in, and, this is the point, the soil he plants in is organic matter with slight intermixture of inorganic material. Just how the plant appropriates and assimilates the elements we do not know. We see it grow, sometimes very well; but we also see the plants make mistakes and die. Apply this to ourselves. We grow in organic matter, in flesh, which we renew daily, and, if we do not do so, we die. We cannot grow without it any more than a plant can. How we appropriate and assimilate the elements we do know to some small extent, but we certainly do not know how it is that we can flower spiritually and can blossom heavenly on account of this organic life. But we do flower and blossom and some blossoms are very sweet smelling. We know that we make numerous mistakes-probably more than the plants- in our endeavors to appropriate and assimilate food both for the organism, the flesh, for brain and heart, for soul and spirit. Rather than condemn the life of the senses, Inner Life people study them and one result Inner Life people have attained and that is, that they have realized that the senses are poor rulers but excellent servants when trained. It must not be charged against the senses, the flesh, that weeds and poisonous growth spring up and overrun everything. They are not generated by the soil or the senses, but are sowed there. The soil and the senses are simply passive tools to bring them forth, and no more. Yet, the senses have been condemned because of these growths; nobody seems to have seen the irrationality and the absurdity of the charge. The whole absurdity must be laid at the door of the fanatics, and we must in the future acquire more sense. Let me advise my hearers when they next time hear some fanatic in unqualified talk condemn the senses, the flesh, that they ask him what he means. Ask him for instance if his harangues are not of the senses? Ask him where he gets his violence from? Ask him if his God gave him his senses in order to betray him! His answer to these questions will prove what sort of senses he has, and, whether he has any sense. If he does not see the point, you will. In our day we cannot afford to live in the foolishness of the past, nor to be led by maniacs, let us have truth everywhere. Like the gardener we must engage in the study of soils, and find out how to plow our sense-soil; how to loosen it for the roots of the plants, how to water it and drain it, and, keep it free from weeds; how to manure with the right ingredients, and, how to do it in right proportions, how one soil of our sense-nature is suitable for art-cultures and another for wisdom-cultures. Common sense seems to me would advise this. But as it is, in the past when people awakened spiritually, they turned most unnaturally against themselves; they cut away all balancing roots, became top-heavy and were thrown over by the storms. Read any life of any of those people and you shall see it is as I have stated. Now, the New Mysticism has profited by study and will avoid these mistakes. This is what I at present will say about the senses, the flesh. You may now pass judgment upon what I have said and make up your mind what you will do with the subject. The future is yours if you will take it. This I will say, do not misunderstand or misconstrue my words, I have not advocated the free play of desires. I have not recommended license. I have in no way given anybody an excuse for any crime, or liberty to break with common sense morality. I have asked for a more dignified attitude to yourself. I have suggested a revision of old ideas, ideas that have proved unhuman and unnatural. As I said, the Future belongs to you! The Future, even as we now can see it, is vastly different from the Past. To own the Future you must endeavor to find out the tendencies that sway the moment you now live in, and the tendencies, I say, are in the direction of a thorough revision of our ideas about the senses, the flesh.

It is not only our ideas of the senses, that need recasting. Our attitude to Reason is also false, and must be corrected. I think you can see that by a reform of our sense ideas and be deeper understanding of Reason, we shall rise to a higher level than the mystics of the past, and, we shall be much richer in our existence. Browning wrote, "man is not man as yet," but, I say, we may now become man. And how? In the first place by cultivating immediacy of the feelings. By feelings, the mystics and Inner Life people do not understand perceptions as they are defined in psychology. They mean divine gifts, graces, spiritual intuitions, the Holy Ghost and the Image as I defined it in my last lecture. Secondly, "man may become a man" by learning from the Mother! Or to put it in a phrase more familiar to people in the West. We must learn "to live according to Nature."

"To live according to nature" is a terribly hackneyed phrase, and its modern originator, J. J. Rousseau, was far removed from a life according to nature. Nevertheless, that phrase would express the highest philosophy were it but understood rightly and practiced correctly. In the West, the stoics were high and worthy examples of what a "life according to nature" ought to be. They were very near to the truth. If you have no better plans for your conduct, try to live up to Marcus Aurelius "Thoughts" and you can see for yourself. "To live according to nature" is sublime existence, but to live a "natural life" is undesirable, and, it is that life which all Inner Life teachers oppose. At first appearance the difference may not be discovered, but it is there and the difference is radical. I shall come back often to this subject in future chapters and fully explain the difference between the phrases. I think that I shall here and now meet Mathew Arnold's onslaught. In a poem entitled "No Harmony with Nature," he wrote:

> "In harmony with Nature? Restless fool
> Who with such heat dost preach what were to thee,
> When true, the last impossibility
> To be like Nature strong, like Nature cool!"

I will meet this onslaught with the remarks made by Chwang-Tzu, a Chinese commentator on the Tao-Teh-King. Chwang-Tzu wisely said, "You cannot speak of the ocean to a well-frog, the creature of a narrower sphere; you cannot speak of ice to a summer insect, a creature of the season. You cannot speak of Tao to a pedagogue; his scope is too restricted." I think Mathew Arnold, the schoolmaster, has been fully answered by that, and, moreover, a couple thousand years before he was born. The same Arnold went on in the same poem slandering Nature. Like Tennyson, who wrote so many false lines on Nature, he was influenced by some of the misconceptions that inhered in the first presentation of the doctrine of Evolution. Both charged Nature with being "cruel" and exonerated Man, whom they claimed was "sick of blood." A stupid and ignorant boy may be kissed and petted by a fond mother and the rude world blamed for not taking kindly to her darling. Nature does not care for such a boy. So these men, small as they were made by class room and boudoir, found the sympathy and help they called for in clubs and conventional drawing rooms and claimed that Nature was heartless and cruel. None of them ever told us how they had followed the sun across the sky for a day, or seen the moon shine upon Diana in the bath in some secreted lake in the woods. Guess they had no such experience! Nature would never sympathize with them! How could she? They never had watched the opening and closing of a flower; the blowing of the bud, the movements of a star fish or the formation and re-formation of clouds. Such people do not perceive Nature's Inner Life, or man's eternal longings. Nature is Spirit visible and Spirit is Nature invisible. They both maintained that "Nature and man can never be fast friends." Both of these two are like the prisoners in Plato 's cave, who sit chained to the rock and with their backs to the very small opening that leads into the cave and through which comes the only ray of light that ever comes to the eyes of these prisoners. Being unable to turn round, the little they see are faint shadows on the rocks in front of them. As a matter of course, in such people we can find no cosmic emotion, no yearning to feel the pulses of the great heart of the universe. They know neither visible spirit, nor invisible Nature. They are forever strangers to the Mother's voice and have never felt her Presence. I need not say any more; your own acquaintance with Mathew Arnold and Tennyson's poems has told you that they were not Nature lovers. I am sure you will not fear a study of a life "according to nature" because these two did not live according to nature, but in an atmosphere filled with phantasms of human greatness. I trust that my hearers will not misunderstand my words about a "life according to Nature" to mean a recommendation of that which in modern literature and philosophy goes by name of Naturalism. I mean nothing of the kind. Naturalism in this sense means perverted and degenerate human nature. By "life according to Nature," when I use the phrase, I mean Nature- Mysticism, and of that you shall hear more in later talks. Naturalism I condemn in all its ways and forms. It is the cause of the moral decay of today.

Quite often some say, to compliment another: "he is a strong nature," or "he is a strong man," but the phrase is a very doubtful one. Its value depends upon whence this man derives his strength. A strong man may be a "big stick" and as such have his way and will, a way and will that the community may need, because the community develops on selfish and natural lines. But that very man is in all probability a weak man and a man of desires, and a mere baby in the Inner Life. Such a man may possibly be a tool in the hands of cosmic energy, but for all that not create any spiritual force for others or for himself. On the other hand, there are in the world the so-called "silent in the land;" those of whom you never hear till by accident you come across them; those who so "empty" (Kenosis) themselves, that really they do not live, but somebody else lives upon them and in their stead; those whose only motto is "not as I will." These are the strong people, because their silences are eternal work; their "emptiness" prevents strife, and their non-assertions of will establishes Unity, and thereby they become patterns for all the world. The Inner Life loves silence and solitude; but it can also hear the divine voice in the roar of hell, and it can see the divine face in the market place as well as in mountain fastnesses or by the sea. The Inner Life does not love the passing show, but is not offended by vulgarity, nor does it condemn bearers of evil. It exists beyond such things. Babia was asked if she hated evil, to which she answered that inasmuch as she loved God always, she had no time to hate evil.

Mystics ignorant of true methods and without guides have given fight to their desires in various ways, and unfortunately readers of these reported fights have only too often been led to repeat these fights, hence the overflow of ascetic advice in mystic books. Some mystics denying the desires dammed up for them, have found all dams swept away and themselves besides. Other mystics have weakened the desires by diverting their forces, as one does with mountain torrents in order to break their power. None of these understood that the human passions are human parallels to the subterranean fires, which from time to time break forth in earthquakes; nor did they understand that passions are the vortex-powers of devastating tornadoes; powers terrible to us, foreign to us, yet nevertheless engines of the divine workings. Other Mystics have led the waters of passion into irrigating canals and thus added great strength and fruitfulness to their natural gifts.

THE INNER LIFE AND THE TAO TEH KING

Such Mystics were not far from the truth. Other mystics have even given themselves over to desires, calling them heavenly fires and divine messengers. But fools they were, and, soon they ended by burning themselves in these fires. All this relates to one side of our nature, the side we are to fight, to "regulate," to "kill out," the desire life. All Eastern treatises are especially emphatic on this subject. Eastern passions and desires are so much more violent than ours and they need much more radical means for suppression. Now about another side of our nature, equally in our way and needing "overcoming." I mean our intellectual proclivities; and they are especially a Western sin. I do not wish to speak in paradoxes, but I am almost tempted to say that ignorance is the best soil for Mysticism. Mysticism is not literary religion, it is Wisdom-religion. "Learning is the perception of differences. Wisdom is the perception of similarities. As it is, Mysticism can do without learning. "He has scarce thought to any purpose who has not thought beyond words; who has not thought long enough, deep enough, fruitfully enough, to encounter, somewhere, glimmerings of truth untranslatable into words." The Mystic, he of the Inner Life, has thought intensely, that is why he needs no words, no learning. He possesses the Word. And he loves God and the neighbor, and he knows intuitively. Says the Tao-Teh-King: "Dispense with learning and save yourself anxiety." Mystics and Inner Life people could not be caught in Descarte's delusion: Cogito, ergo sum: "I think, consequently I am." "Cogito" to the mystic means "coagito," that is to say, "I act and I think," because "action" or "thought" takes place in him. He is not the actor nor""the thinker."

Mysticism stands sharply over against "desires" and against "intellect," when these usurp the place of wisdom. Intellect is impotent to penetrate beyond the phenomenal world to a vision of a reality transcending sense. Intellect is merely a land surveyor, and is neither the land nor is it the owner of the land. The Ego is both the land and the owner of the land, and it uses intellect merely as timekeeper and as a fence around its "space"or land, just as the Ego uses its other faculties. The intellect is thus a tool, a comparative faculty, and no more. As a comparative faculty, it judges of relations, of forms, forms of mind and forms of the object. But of essence, the intellect knows nothing and can know nothing. Intellect is analytic and can only concern itself with one point at the time. It lacks totally comprehensiveness, the ALL embracing power. It is "conceptual thinking" only, or, which is the same, "we think by means of something else" and not absolutely. Mysticism wants the absolute. And this is the definition of intellect by Mysticism of all ages and lands. Mysticism wants Essence, Being, and not Form merely, hence it has always stood apart from intellect and the limited knowledge it can give, and, relegated it to lower places. By intellectual search we cannot find out the Divine; we may nevertheless have communion or fellowship with it, namely, in heart and feeling. The mystics of all ages, first clear the ground, then they plow and then they sow. Mysticism has always been (1) first a protest, then (2) a positive content. After it has denied the power of intellect to teach us about Essence, or Being, and declared that intellect cannot reveal Essence or Being, it tells us that we, in virtue of our Ego, possess a power that is equal to reach up to the Divine and the Universal, and, which is equal to bring us into union with it. This faculty, which answers to Kant's (so-called) "practical reason" has many names. In the West, the mystics of Germany call it "the spark of the soul," "the ground of the soul," and very characteristically they call it also "synthesis;" and rightly they call the intellect "analysis." The mystics are sympathetic people; they gather together; they do not shatter.

The illusory phenomenon is always in the way. How shall the soul pass from the phenomenon to the noumenon? Human understanding, Echardt reiterates, is useless in this matter. It can perceive things in time and space only. The soul must therefore try to attain what ordinarily will be called absolute ignorance and darkness, but which mystics call "the nothing of nothing" and of which the soul cannot and must not try to form any conception. It is not by an intellectual development, but by sheer passivity, by waiting for the transcendental action of God that the soul can attain the highest knowledge. That ignorance here recommended is not that blindness of mind, that untaught, that un-informed condition which that word ordinarily represents; it is a condition in which the soul separates itself from the phenomenal world; voluntarily renounces all sensuous activity and even ceases to think under the old forms. When the soul attains the nescience, then the soul is re-born; is in the Supreme. Though poor in spirit and having nothing, willing nothing, knowing nothing, the soul is in the highest and approaching union with God. Examined more closely it will be seen that here is no illogical contradictions, nor foolish asceticism. As John of the Cross said: "Spiritual things transcend sense, because they already include it," hence this passivity or negativity is formal only, and not real. The mystic has simply chosen the better part. From now on the soul lives in another world. In the East, where this is so well understood, they say that now the soul is in Sat-Chit-Ananda, in Being-Knowledge-Bliss. Meister Eckardt says that now God takes the place of the active reason. The soul has returned to the state in which it was before entering the phenomenal world; but it has not returned empty handed, nay it has returned plus a recognition of itself as idea in God. Henceforth, to use a term from Spinoza, it sees everything *sub specie eternitatis*. Separated from man, from the external things, from chance, distractions and troubles it sees only reality.

I have nothing to say against mystics or against Inner Life people who reduce intellect to its place and refuse it permission to deal with spiritual things. But I have much against any so-called religious or other person who denies reason. The true mystic and the Inner Life people build their temples with stones and timber furnished by reason or Tao, and, out of nothing else, and they know that temples are adaptations and symbols. Do you know what the word temple means? Well, originally a temple was not a house of prayer for the multitude, nor, a shrine or sanctuary of a god. The "templum" was a certain place "cut off", as the term means, and set apart by augurs, and, it included also that part of the heavens which was visible above this "cut off" place when one stood in the middle of it; of course, it was not a building with a roof, and when it was a building it had no roof. The "templum" was then really a space set apart and nothing else. Intellectually there is nothing tangible in such a space, but to Reason, or the highest sense, there is in it a consecrated form of intercommunion between heaven and the soul. Anywhere, and wherever the human heart stands in the Inner Life, it builds such a "templum." Do not compare this mystery to astrology of the kind of "a penny in the slot," or "around the corner." It has nothing to do with astrology. The space is not a locality in the sense that its earth-place is any more sacred than any other place on earth. Its space is merely pointed out by means of a place and is in no wise tangible. If we had an augur here and asked him to show us the space of his temple he would point to a part or section of the sky and tell us where he saw a certain section of the sky, there would be his temple. If he should take you to the top of a mountain or to the bottom of a valley and say; here is my temple; you would still remain ignorant of what he meant, even if you saw a magnificent building and numerous priests. If you have the Inner Life of a mystic or theosoph you would know the mystery, however. The augurs of old from such a house without roof read the signs of the heavens; the Inner Life people now hear The Word in their temple, not built of stones, but of Reason. They see the law for themselves and see it written in the Kosmos without any augur or other middleman.

You will now understand why the true mystic reveres Reason. It is because Reason builds his temple; not a common meeting place, but his individual space (not place). Reason is Tao, the main subject of the Tao-Teh-King on which I shall talk to you. And you shall hear much about Tao, which means both Life-Truth- Way- Reason. Reason or Tao is not an abstraction, but the constructive and combining power, which out of itself builds up the form or body in which the I^age manifests itself. What the

THE INNER LIFE AND THE TAO TEH KING

Image is, I defined in my last talk. Reason is Form, or
Consciousness. Whatever we may call it, without reason there
would be no manifestation of our real life. We say that we see this
object or that, but we do not. Our eyes do not see it, but through
our eyes we see forms, and Form manifested. When Moses saw
the burning bush, or Jesus the descending dove, or the disciples
saw the three figures at the time of the transfiguration, or when
Arjuna saw the divine forms in nature, they all saw through their
eyes not with them. To explain what I mean by looking through
the eyes, I will borrow a little from Fiona Macleod (William
Sharp). The illustration will be much more effective than words of
mine. The publication was called "The Divine Adventure" and was
first published in the Fortnightly Review and later in book form.
The story is about "Three in One,' that is, Body, Will and Soul
traveling together in a night full of beauty and suddenly coming
upon a secret garden of ilex and tall cypresses, which rose like
dark flowers out of the ground. Flickering moonlight lit up
between the trees, the wild foxes barked in the distance and owls
hooted near by. "Look," said the Body, and there on the mossy
slope under seven great cypresses lay a man asleep on the ground.
In the moonshine his face looked beautiful, and, as if great
sorrows had ached the heart. After a little it appeared that the
sleeper was not alone, but that there were eleven others, lying
about, also asleep. Only one of them was sitting upright as if he
were the watchman of the hour, though slumbering at his post.
Still another, the twelfth one, sat behind the great bole of a tree.
Suddenly the spell was broken; the vision vanished far off among
the hills, foxes barked, and, the owls hooted nearby. All else was
still. This was what the whole man, the "three in one," say-
through the eyes in part, and, in part with the eyes. Individually,
the Body, evidently with the eyes, had seen in the sleepers worn
and poor men, ill-clad and weary, and, instead of the one sitting
behind the tree, a company of evil men with savage faces and
drawn swords. Individually, the Will, evidently also with the eyes,
had seen only a fire drowning in its own ashes, and round about a
mass of leaves blown hither and thither by the wind. Individually,

the Soul, evidently through the eyes, had seen Divine Love asleep; not sleeping as mortals sleep, but resting in a holy, quiet, brooding peace and in communion with Eternal Joy. Around Love were the Eleven Powers and Dominions of the World. And the one that had caused surprise by his appearance was the Lord of Shadows, whom some call Death, others the Unknown God. Behind were demons and demoniacs.

The forest itself was made of human souls awaiting God. Perhaps the story may awaken in you a recollection of similar experiences; if not so romantic, perhaps alike anyhow. I am happy to say that I have had experiences of the kind as just described. I remember William Blake to have said, according to his biographers, that he, of course, saw the Sun set like a big flaming ball, not unlike a guinea. "But," said he, according to report, "through my eyes, I also see hosts of angels pass up and down singing: 'Glory! Glory! God on High!'" Friends! I think it is well, not to be hasty and condemn others who describe a scenery which we may not have seen. One of the party may have seen with the eyes, the other through the eyes. Some see the moon, others the moonlight; which is most bewitching? Who sees best?

Now to return to my argument. I want to point out how many people come to call Idealism Mysticism, and to believe that Idealism constitutes the Inner Life. A sad mistake. It is quite true that we speak correctly at times when we say that Form or Consciousness is all there is. That is, for instance, the refrain of all the Upanishads, and thus summed up it is one of the main teachings of Vedanta. It is true, I say, that it is all there is, but only to us. Only to us! Whether it is all there is to other beings, we do not know; in all probability it is not. That Form or Consciousness must be ours; it could not be that of other beings. Nor can it be said absolutely that Form or Consciousness is all there is, for manifestly Form or Consciousness depends upon Substance. Substance, to be sure, is unknown to us, but that does not change the case; whatever there is, there is and must be Something back of Form or Consciousness. All this has a direct bearing upon what we call knowledge. All we know is, as was said, Form or Consciousness and not Substance. In the West we identify our knowledge of Form with Reality, and that is false. Most of us in the West are therefore idealists and not mystics. True mystics, alone of all, discover the fallacy and reject the claims for Consciousness. They want to go behind it. Idealism is by no means enough for them. Mystics, as well as a great many other people, even professional philosophers, must learn to distinguish between knowledge and reality. The besetting sin in the West is to confound knowledge with reality. The West has a doctrine, commonly held among philosophers, that says that "knowledge is a copy of the real world outside us." In it lies the same error as that the wayfarer so readily falls into, that is, mistaking a fallen branch in the road for a snake. Knowledge is a copy of the outside world for us, but not a real copy, and the difference is enormous.

The mistake is a fallacy which lies at the root of all Western philosophy and it is as pernicious as the phantasms that the desires originate, and, as destructive as those phantasms. Knowledge is of our making. The reality behind the appearance is and remains unknown. When the mystic degree of our mind opens, we discover the fallacy and we care no more for scholastic knowledge or mere Idealism. In the mystic degree the real knowledge appears. That knowledge is no more our knowledge, it is both our knowledge and the universal knowledge. We call it no more knowledge, it is Wisdom. And Wisdom is first of all, "flight from all positive content as from a limitation," next it is pure thought, pure thought from the Inner Life sources. It is not so much a medium necessary in this life, it is rather the sum total of that larger life, which some know now, but which all will reach sometime, when they become free. But while the humdrum of daily life calls for no wisdom, we should nevertheless dissolve this humdrum into its spiritual elements and let these elements permeate our daily existence. It is marvelous how easy life becomes that way. It is wonderful how we renew ourselves.

THE INNER LIFE AND THE TAO TEH KING

Indeed, it is true, as Hermas Pastor a thousand and more years ago said, "that those who regenerate, grow young." The New Mysticism is alive to this and lives that way. Vedanta is merely Idealism and a sublime form of mind, and not enough for the future man, the man of the New Age, the man that lives the Inner Life. Vedanta and Idealism are one of the approaches to the bridge, I spoke of in the first chapter or the voice that we in the West call Platonism, spoken of in the second chapter. Mystics and theosophists of highest order go behind consciousness, or to use the phrase used before, they see through their eyes. And what do they see? They see the World of reason, the Archetypes, or, if I may call it so, they see the heavenly machinery and they experience great happiness. From my own experience with Beauty and art objects, I can say that by a little practice you can look so long upon the symbol before you that the symbol becomes life and reality. At such moments and for sometime after, yon transcend your actual self and know positively that you are beyond yourself. All of this will be of importance in the study of the Tao-Teh-King which is a mystical book, and it will enable you to find the Inner Life by a study of that book.

Thus far, I have dealt with laws of nature. Now I will give you a few historic facts to show what the mystics, the Inner Life people, are good for. Wherever we find Mysticism, we find it in either of two forms; two forms which answer to the two voices and the two approaches to the bridge spoken of in my former chapter.

The one form is active and represented by such mystics as, for instance, those of the Rhine Valley. It is history, that these mystics, during the Black Death (1348-1349) and during the Interdict which lasted more than twenty years, utterly ignored the pope's orders. An interdict means that all bells are silenced, that penance and the eucharist is administered only to the dying; that none but priests, friars and children under two years can get Christian burial and that none can be married. The loss of these religious forms means terrible suffering in Catholic countries. But the mystics buried the dead, married the living and said mass regularly. During the Black Death, which ravaged the Rhine Valley and adjoining parts of France most terribly, the regular clergy could not even for money be induced to bury people, nor to visit the sick or dying, nor to say mass for them. In many places they deserted their parishes. But mystics of the orders of the Dominicans and Franciscans officiated in all cases, and there is no record that any of them died of the Pest. This is active Mysticism. Not a bad kind, is it? The other form of Mysticism is quietistic. (2) In this group I place people who live in their deepest nature:

> ...Beyond occasions and events, And who, through
> God's exceeding grace
> Know release from form, and time and place."
> (Whittier)

I shall describe these people by a story or two attributed to the famous John Tauler and you will please note that this beggar I describe is not held up before you as an example because he is a beggar, but because he is a free man, a man who lives in the Ground of the soul, as the mystics call it. In silence he has discovered the Divine Self in himself and is able to teach the learned, but as yet un-free Dr. Tauler. With this in mind the following queer story will not sound unreasonable and you will understand the quietistic mystic. This is the story. There was once a learned man who longed and prayed full eight years that God would show him some one to teach him the way of truth. And on a time, when he was in great longing, there came unto him a voice from heaven, and said: "Go to the front of the Church, there thou wilt find a man that shall show thee the way to blessedness." So thither he went, and found there a poor man, whose feet were torn, and covered with dust and dirt, and all his clothing scarce worth three cents. He greeted him saying: "God give thee good morrow." To this the poor man answered: "I never had ill morrow!" Again he said: "God prosper thee," to which the other answered "Never had I ought but prosperity"- "Heaven save thee," said the scholar, "How answerest thou me so?" only to receive the reply: "I was never other than saved."

The scholar was perplexed and said: "Explain this to me, for I do not understand." "Willingly," quoth the poor man, "Thou wishest me good morrow. I never had an ill morrow; for am I an hungered, I praise God; am I freezing, doth it hail, snow, rain, is it fair weather or foul, I praise God; and therefore had I never ill morrow. Thou didst say, God prosper thee. I have never been unprosperous, for I know how to live with God; I know that what He doeth is the best, and what God giveth or ordaineth for me, be it pain or pleasure, that I take cheerfully from Him as the best of all, and, so I have never adversity. Thou wishest God to bless me. I was never unblessed, for I desire to be only in the will of God, and I have so given up my will to the will of God, that what God willeth I will."

"But if God were to cast thee into hell," said the scholar, "what wouldst thou do then?"

"Cast me into hell? His goodness holds Him back therefrom. Yet if He did, I should have two arms to embrace Him withal, and even so, I would sooner be in hell and have God, than in heaven and not have Him." Then understood the scholar that true abandonment with utter abasement was the nearest way to God. Again the scholar asked the poor man: "From whence comest thou?" "From God." "Where has thou found God?" "Where I abandoned all creatures! I am a King. My kingdom is my soul. This kingdom is greater than any kingdom on the earth."

"What hath brought thee to this perfection?" "My silence, my heavenward thoughts and my union with God." This is life; this is simplicity. Not only did this beggar have life, he was life. And the report is that Dr. Tauler was so struck with this man and this meeting, that he gave up his preaching and withdrew for seven years to the Oberland. When he returned he became the famous mystic, now so well known in history. What had happened to the beggar which made him so great in life and so profound in knowledge, though he externally was nothing? What did he rest on? He had learned that "it is the ground we do not tread upon which supports us." This ground is Tao, of which more later. If you analyze this story, what will it prove or demonstrate? If we read it "synthetically." The "poor beggar" is certainly not "poor in spirit," nor is his mind covered with "dust and dirt;" and though his clothing may not be worth "three cents," his spiritual superiority is beyond price. He meets the "learned man's" greetings with a parry every time as if they were sword cuts, and he refutes what he considers insinuations and radical misunderstandings of life 's true order and the rationality of existence. When finally asked: "From whence comest Thou?" he gives an answer that comprehends all further and now unnecessary details.

"From God." By that answer he has given an unequivocal reply, such as all mystics would give upon such similar questions. But to the analytic intellect, he has given no answer. Moreover, he further defines himself as a mystic of the heart by the answer he gives to the question: "Where hast thou found God?" His answer was, "Where I abandoned all creatures," and that "the learned man" should be in no further doubt, the mystic continued triumphantly: "I am a king. My kingdom is my soul. This kingdom is greater than any kingdom on the earth." All this is of no value for analysis; the words are not intellectual statements. You can analyze the conceptions "kingdom" and "soul," but you cannot "analyze" this synthetic phrase: "My kingdom is my soul."

This is a specimen of a mystic of the heart, a theopathetic mystic, that is, one who suffers all things. Suffers!- not necessarily in pain! Nay, one who is passive! One who has understood the mystery of obedience to the course of life, no matter what it may be phenomenally. One, whose mind is not bound in Spanish boots of logic, but who has experienced the freedom from illusions which come from living untrammeled by philosophical systems. One, who knows of no "eternal no!" who does not fret at hindrances, who does not try to force locked doors, one who blesses drudgery, one who fears no cross! Lest this word "theopathetic" trouble you, let me recall to your memory that the Greek word *Pate* means a passive state, hence secondarily suffering, misfortune; that you know from your Greek dictionary, and it is well, but you do not know that mystics consider suffering to be a blessing and that suffering is a normal condition to them. Mystics invite suffering as the best monitor against becoming entangled in illusions and sensual or phenomenal states. Nobody better than the mystic has understood the educational value of suffering. This mystic is, as I said, of the class of theopathetic mystics, common in the south of Europe, France, Spain, Italy. He is of the company of Mme. Guyon, Molinos, John of the Cross, Theresa, Catherine of Siena. All of these sang like Mme. Guyon:

> "Love is my teacher
> 'Tis Love alone can tell of Love."-

> "'Tis not the skill of human art
> Which gives me power my God to know;
> The sacred lessons of the heart
> Come not from instruments below."

You notice that this "poor beggar" upon the question: "Where hast thou found God?" did not quote any philosophical system or enter upon any discussion on the "Path to Reality." He is not troubled with epistemological problems. His answer lies on no intellectual plan; he is on the plan of immediacy, the plan of simplicity, and because he has abandoned all intellectual and sensual problems, he stands in the principle of the Whole and answers from out that standpoint. And that he knows his own standpoint and is in full self-conscious possession of himself, is clear from his final answer to the question, "What has brought you to this perfection?" His answer was, "My silence. My heavenward thought and my Union with God." These words could not and have not been transcended by any philosopher or any philosophical system. This mystic knows from out his own soul at once and without intellectual training that which the few philosophers who have attained similar knowledge have only attained through long years of painful thinking. The heart has reasoning powers of its own as much as the brain and the mind have. Before, in a former chapter, when I spoke of the two voices, I at-oned them in the voice of the "Inner Man! Tao." When I spoke of the two approaches to the bridge, I declared the truth to be in the middle. Here are two forms of Mysticism. How are they both the Inner Life? How are they at-oned? Place Nature in the witness box and you shall hear her declare that she is double. Sometimes the beast, sometimes the beauty. Sometimes Life, sometimes Death, and in no case revealing herself fully. She speaks to us incessantly, yet she never betrays her mystery. She is our mother and that explains it. Place Mind in the witness box and inquire about the character of our language, and ideas, our conceptions of beauty, or religious symbols, and Mind declares that an inevitable dualism bisects nature and mind, and, that unity is only attained by a leap out of mind into the transcendental, into Wisdom. Mind will declare that our whole world is a system of nuptials and that only by removing the extremes of active and passive Mysticism do they become one in true Mysticism or Inner Life, Tao, which is the sum total of both. Both of these two forms of Mysticism are found in the Tao-Teh-King and you shall hear more about them by and by.

Now, I will appeal for a life on the inner basis of our existence. Let our motive be love such as sung by Mme. Guyon, Love is my teacher; love alone can tell of love. Let us abandon individual self-assertion and live according to Meister Eckardt, who said (Here is my translation from his Ms. (Fol. 274, 297, 301.) "There is something in the soul, which is above its created nature. It is in itself one and simple; it is above name and knowledge; it is pure No-thing. If you could do away with yourself, you would have all this is in itself. But so long as you look upon yourself as Something, so long you know as little what this is as my mouth knows what color is, or, as my eyes know what taste is. About this, I have often spoken. Sometimes I have called it a Power, sometimes a Light, sometimes a Divine Spark. It is free from any and all names and forms, as Deity is free. It is above all knowledge, above love and above grace. In this power (light, spark), blossoms and nourishes the Divine. This Light (power or spark), rejects all creatures and will have Deity only, Deity simply, and no revelation of Deity. This light (power or spark) is satisfied only by the Simple Ground, the Still Waste, where nothing moves and where nobody lives. It will have only the Silent Solitude in which no distinctions are discernible. This Ground, though immovable and unrecognizable is nevertheless that which moves all and by which all is recognized."

You will have noticed that Eckardt here attempts to state "the thing itself," the eternal reality, the Noumenon and that he all through opposes it to something else, the phenomenon. If anything can or needs be added to this quotation from Eckardt, let me say that this infallible light is in "the light that never was on sea or land," which the poet speaks of. It "lighteth every man that cometh into the world." It is the highest heritage of our nature, the ultimate faculty. It requires no confirmation and admits of no denial. It is direct and immediate in its operation. Our psychologists have no special name for it as yet. They know it in part as intuition, as ecstasy, as the over-soul, but such terms are defective because they smack too much of cognition only. The mystics attribute to this faculty, just described by Eckardt, both sensation, feeling and will and degrees of inner perception not known at all to ordinary psychology. Psychology has not sounded the depths of the soul as mystics have. Psychologists have never succeeded in dealing satisfactorily with Feeling as the fountain of consciousness. The fact is our school psychologies deal in abstractions; but the mystics who know existence as a system of living forces, care not for abstraction or terms; they live in realities.

CHAPTER IV

I shall now begin to talk directly out of the book Tao-Teh-King, the book I have referred to several times in my three introductory chapters on the Inner Life. I have chosen for a text a line from Athanase:

"Our human souls
Cling to the grass and the water brooks."

I am fully aware that this line has no meaning to city people, or to people who are absorbed in city problems. Nor has it any poetry in it for those who have no sense of the Infinite in Nature. Nevertheless, I say that I could not find a more suitable text or motto for today's discourse on "Simplicity," because my discourse will have no interest for city people, for people who prefer the stage to a midsummer-night's revel in the woods, and, who would rather breathe factory smoke than morning dew and the cool breezes of sunrise. Grass is, as I trust you shall see, a type of a simple and sincere life, a life for use, and, water you shall hear Laotzse speak of as a most marvelous element. No wonder then that human souls cling to them. Simplicity, human souls, grass and water brooks are no abstractions. They are real things and not metaphysical entities, nor all poetry. And we need to concern ourselves with the practical, with life and its methods. I shall connect grass and water brooks with Simplicity and the three shall give us an insight into the human soul. To be sure:

"There's not a place on earth's vast round,
In ocean deep, or air,
Where skill and wisdom are not found,"

...or as I said in the last chapter, "There is no place where God's feeling and imagination may not be seen"; but today I will extol grass and water and their union with human souls. I must clear away some difficulties that may arise from misconceptions. While I shall recommend Simplicity, as the Tao-Teh-King defines it, I shall by no means advocate "simple" minds, or minds of "one idea." "Simple" people or simpletons are as a matter of course beyond the pale of our discussion, and, "one idea" people are to say the least a nuisance and usually fanatics. Simplicity as defined in the Tao-Teh-King means balance in the midst of fullness, and is the very foundation both of culture and Inner Life. This brings out the second point, I want to set straight, and emphasize. It is this: Simplicity is a method of Nature's, that lies at the root of all her doings. If I personified Nature, I would say that Simplicity was her one attribute. Again, I shall not advocate "The Simple Life" as it was preached in this country a few years ago. That movement came to naught because it did not rest on fundamentals: It was not Simplicity. It was a counterfeit and no more. It was merely a "knocking off." To knock off on your demands upon life does not produce Simplicity. Retrenchment is not Inner Life. "The Simple Life" and Simplicity are two different affairs. "The Simple Life" is only a compromise and can never produce Simplicity, and Simplicity does not necessarily mean a "Simple Life." Simplicity may be found in the midst of great abundance.

Let me start by asserting, that as far as Nature is concerned, we all start evenly and with the same favors, and say that all the differences among men are created by themselves. In the words of Wordsworth, I will present Nature's case. Listen to what he said in the "Excursion" (9th book).

"Alas! what differs more than man from man!
And whence that difference?
Whence but from himself?
For see the universal Race endowed
With the same upright form! The sun is fixed,
And the infinite magnificence of heaven
Fixed, within reach of every human eye;
The sleepless ocean murmurs for all ears;

THE INNER LIFE AND THE TAO TEH KING

The vernal field infuses fresh delight
Into all hearts. Throughout the world of sense,
Even as an object is sublime or fair,
That object is laid open to the view
Without reserve or veil; and, as a power
Is salutary, or an influence sweet,
Are each and all enabled to perceive
That power, that influence, by impartial law.
Gifts nobler are vouchsafed alike to all;
Reason, and, with that reason, smiles and tears;
Imagination, freedom in the will;
Conscience to guide and check; and death to be
Foretasted, immortality conceived
By all- a blissful immortality,
To them whose holiness on earth shall make
The spirit, capable of heaven, assured.
Strange, then, nor less than monstrous, might be deemed
The failure, if the Almighty, to this point
Liberal and distinguishing, should hide
The excellence of moral qualities
From common understanding; leaving truth
And virtue difficult, abstruse and dark;
Hard to be won, and only by a few;
Strange, should He deal herein with nice respects,
And frustrate all the rest! Believe it not:
The primal duties shine aloft, like stars;
The charities that soothe, and heal, and bless,
Are scattered at the feet of Man, like flowers;
The generous inclination, the just rule,
Kind wishes, and good actions, and pure thoughts,
No mystery is here! Here is no boon
For high, yet not for low; for proudly graced,
Yet not for meek of heart. The smoke ascends
To Heaven as lightly from the cottage hearth
As from the haughtiest palace. He, whose soul
Ponders this true equality, may walk

THE INNER LIFE AND THE TAO TEH KING

The fields of earth with gratitude and hope-
Yet, in that meditation, will he find
Motive to sadder grief, as we have found;
Lamenting ancient virtues overthrown,
And for the injustice grieving, that hath made
So wide a difference between man and man.
...How blest that pair
Of blooming boys, whom we beheld even now,
Blest in their several and their common lot!
A few short hours of each returning day
The thriving prisoners of their village school;
And thence let loose to seek their pleasant homes,
Or range the grassy lawn in vacancy:
To breathe and to be happy, run and shout;
For every genial power of earth and heaven,
Through all the seasons of the changeful year
Obsequiously doth take upon herself
To labor for them; bringing each in turn
The tribute of enjoyment, knowledge, health,
Beauty, or strength! Such privilege is theirs,
Granted alike in the outset of their course
To both- Whatever fate the noon of life
Reserves for either, sure it is that both
Have been permitted to enjoy the dawn-
Both have been fairly dealt with; looking back,
They will allow that justice has in them
Been shown, alike to body and to mind."

Is there not over all this a grand Simplicity? Does not
Nature offer us all the same terms? And this quotation is a
lesson in Simplicity. Nature's method is so simple, that most
people never notice it. And this want of notice is the beginning
of all the future differences between man and man. In this
procedure of Nature, there is a lesson in the Inner Life. I will now
let Laotzse explain how the differences grow up after the
beginning has been made by ignoring Nature's sublime Simplicity.

He and Confucius met once and the following is part of a conversation that took place between them. Confucius is blamed for all the fuss he makes about laws, rules and regulations. It is reported by one of Laotzse's disciples that he spoke as follows to Confucius on the subject of Simplicity: "The chaff from winnowing will blind a man. Mosquitoes will bite a man and keep him awake all night and so it is with all this talk of yours about charity and duty to one's neighbor, it drives me crazy. My lord, strive to keep the world in its original Simplicity- why so much fuss? The wind blows as it listeth, so let virtue establish itself. The swan is white without a daily bath and the raven is black without dying itself. When the pond is dry and the fishes gasping for breath it is of no use to moisten them with a little water or a little sprinkling. Compared to their original and simple condition in the pond and the rivers it is as nothing."

The lesson was severe and throws a strong light upon both teachers' methods. Laotzse would let Nature alone and let everybody remain in original Simplicity, firmly believing that truth would prevail; and, in as much as he spoke at the time when morals were decaying, he meant to tell Confucius that talking about duty and preaching would no more reform the people than a sprinkling would suffice for the fishes which had been taken out of their original element. The only way to reform, he meant to say, was to restore primitive Simplicity. Ignoring Simplicity produces all those fatal complications which now lie like a curse upon us. Confucius' insistence upon laws, ordinances and rescripts had that fatal effect upon China, and, Confucianism no doubt is the cause of China's misery. What will Simplicity do for us! A great deal, surely. Hear what chapter XXII proclaims: "He that humbles himself shall be preserved entire. He that bends himself shall be straightened. He that empties himself shall be filled. He that has worn himself out shall be renewed. He that puts himself low down shall be exalted. For these reasons the Sage clings to Simplicity and is a pattern for the whole world." And as if to repeat what Simplicity can do, the chapter continues with a description of the

THE INNER LIFE AND THE TAO TEH KING

Sage: "He is not self displaying, therefore he shines. He is not self-approving, therefore he is praised. He is not vain, therefore he has merit. He is not self-exalting, therefore he is honored. And in as much as he is not striving, he is not in conflict with others, and no man is his enemy." And the chapter ends in a very remarkable way. It reads, "The ancient maxim: He that humbles himself shall be preserved entire; Oh, it is no vain utterance! Verily he shall be returned home in peace." This closing sentence reads almost as if it meant: "Surely he shall be saved! He shall go to heaven!" as we would say in Western phraseology. Personally, it seems to me, that I have nothing to explain or add to these sublime teachings. Anybody may translate them into his own religious terms and will find them fully answering to all he believes and wishes for, if he wishes for the real root of virtue. Alas! how many do? Somebody, speaking in Western thought, will ask: "What about sin?" Laotzse's remedy against sin is "to feed the root instead of lopping off the branches, " and, surely nobody can suggest a more rational remedy. Killing the sinful is only adding sin to sin. By restoring the errant they may and can change their ways. By "feeding the root," or restoring Simplicity, the world may be saved from desires and false notions and from sin!

Restoring Simplicity means correcting our perceptions of values- but who cares to correct their perceptions of values? Everywhere they answer us that we need not preach. They have freedom and that gives true value to life and the use of life. Is this really true? I think not! The world has a great deal of liberty, but that is not freedom. Liberty has let loose numerous desires and men are being swamped by them and live not in freedom, but in a terrible social quagmire, in bondage to their own lower nature. Many know this, but dare not admit it. Something called "social conscience" once in a while cries out and calls for a halt, but it never advises a return to primitive Simplicity. It raises a gale and a few boats are overturned. Then there is calm again. What can be done? Laotzse tells us. This is what he teaches in the Tao-Teh-King: "By undivided attention to the soul, by restraining the passions and letting gentleness sway it, it is possible to become an infant (to continue as a child). By purifying the mind of phantasms it is possible to remain without a spot." This then is what can be done; restraining the passions and purifying the mind of false thoughts and illusions. The Tao-Teh-King (XVI) continues, "Having emptied yourself of everything, guard your tranquility and remain where you are." Exactly! "Remain where you are," that is, in Simplicity, for Simplicity is restored when self is emptied of "everything" Says the book: "This going back to one's origin is called peace, Returning to the root means rest," and, is a new Beginning. "This going back to the root is called preservation, and, he who is in preservation is enlightened, and, to be enlightened means to be royal, and to be royal means to be celestial, and, to be celestial means to be of Tao."

I said as a commentary upon Laotzse's words "remain where you are," that "Simplicity is restored when self is emptied of everything." That is dark talk unless I elucidate it, and, happily, I think I can do it by calling in the famous Meister Eckardt to help me. Meister Eckardt lived in the fourteenth century; he was a German Mystic and besides this a deep psychologist. He was at one time laboring to assure his listeners that they did not need to fear God's damnation and anger on account of their sins, for said he, when the will in you is changed, everything is changed- Yea! never was! That is to say, in as much as the will is the center or the all of man, then, when the will is no more what it was, all that belonged to that former state is no more either. The sinner being radically turned or changed is subjectively pure and simple again. Objectivity being outside would take its own course, or, in other words, the objective deed and the sin are two different affairs. The sin being subjective, and, not objective, vanishes the moment the will swings round- "Yea! it never was," as Eckardt said, having no root anywhere in the subject, and, the subject being in the everlasting "Now," there can be neither Past nor Future for it, consequently, the sin neither was, nor is, nor will be. Apply this to what I said about the self being emptied of "everything," and, that

that act would restore Simplicity, and you will readily see the truth and the profound signification of the word "Simplicity." By "emptying the self" is to be understood what Eckardt meant by the turning round of the will, and, by the restoration of Simplicity is to be understood the restoration of the eternal "Now." All this is psychology, or the mystery of the working of the soul or self. To put it in theological language, it means that God's anger is gone and forgiveness is absolute by the turn of will. But it does not mean, that karma is wiped out arbitrarily. The objective side of my deed remains for me to atone for, not because God does these things halfhearted or imperfectly, nay, simply because in my growth, I have reached no further than the deeds of the karma. I must labor further with my deeds, otherwise I shall never grow objectively, and, that I must.

What further can be done? Laotzse teaches it in the Tao-Teh-King (XV). It is asked: "May a man not make muddy water clear by keeping it still?" We answer yes, because we believe in the original goodness of man. By keeping still, that is to say, by abstaining from evil, the mud will sink and the water be clear again. The mud is not evil in itself, it is only in its wrong place, when stirred up in the water. No action is either good or evil in itself, but it may be so, when prompted by somebody's wish or when out of order. Again, the teaching is (XXXVII): "Nameless Simplicity" would produce absence of desire, and, "Rest would return, and, thus the world would regenerate itself." Can there be any doubt about it? It is the loss of Simplicity and the sinking into the complexity of things that has wrecked humanity and brought about the frightful moral ruin we see about us. Therefore, if Simplicity could be restored the world would righten itself, as does the ship when the shifted cargo is thrown overboard. We need today single mindedness, candor, and disinterested teachers to give the example of a life in Simplicity. No social nor political revolution is enough. We must go much deeper. When I think of these conditions my mind runs into the scenes in the Apocalypse and I perceive all kinds of horrors coming to produce suitable conditions.

No doubt some will argue that no Simplicity or return of childlikeness can reform the world. And they will say that much more radical means will be needed. Those who argue that way are wrong, and, they are ignorant about the dynamic forces that work in Nature and human life.

Laotzse knew the truth and spoke with insight when he said: (XLIII) "The weakest thing in the world will override the strongest." (XXXVII) "Tao is quiescent, yet leaves nothing undone." (XXXVI) "The soft and the weak overcome the hard and the strong." (XXXV) "Tao is as nothing, yet in its uses it is inexhaustible." (IV) "Tao is without limitation; its depth is the source of whatever is." (XLVIII) "By non-action there is nothing which can not be effected." (LII) "To remain gentle is to be unconquerable." (LIV) "Whoever develops Tao in the world will make Virtue triumph." (LV) "What is not of Tao, soon comes to an end." (LXI) "A woman conquers a man by continual quietness." (LXVII) "Gentleness is always victorious." (LXXIV) "The celestial Tao does not strive, yet overcomes everything." All these quotations fully bear out my contention that Laotzse's teaching about the weak overcoming and mastering the strong, is a teaching that represents Nature's method.

The weakest thing Laotzse knows of is water. Of that he says: (LXXVIII) "Nothing on earth is so weak and yielding as water; yet for breaking down the strong it has no equal." (VIII) "It can get into the most inaccessible places and that without striving. It is therefore like Tao." Taoism has studied water very closely and Taoists constantly quote texts about it. I will give you one, rather lengthy, but to the point. From "History of the Great Light," a famous Taoist text by Huai-Nan-Tsze, Prince of Kuang Ling, I quote as follows about water:

"There is nothing in the world so weak as water; yet its

power is such that it has no bounds; its depth is such that it cannot be fathomed. In length it is without limit; in distance it has no shores, in its flows and ebbs, its increase and decrease, it is measureless. When it rises to the sky, it produces rain and dew; when it falls upon the earth, it gives richness and moisture; there is no creature in the world to whom it does not impart life, and nothing that it does not bring to completion. It holds all things in its wide embrace with perfect impartiality; its graciousness extends even to creeping things and tiny insects, without any expectation of reward. Its wealth is sufficient to supply the wants of the whole world, without fear of exhaustion; its virtue is bestowed upon the people at large, and yet there is no waste. Its flow is ever onward- ceaseless and unlimited; its subtlety such that it cannot be grasped in the hand. Strike it, you hurt it not; stab it, you cause no wound; cut it, you cannot sever it in twain; apply fire to it, it will not burn. Whether it runs deep or shallow, seen or unseen, taking different directions, flowing this way or that, without order or design, it can never be utterly dispersed, its cutting power is such that it will work its way through stone and metal; its strength so great, that the whole world is succored by it, or (literally translated) it is able to support the ships of the whole world on its broad bosom. It floats lazily through the regions of formlessness, foaming and fluttering above the realms of obscurity, that is to say, in the forms of clouds; it worms its way backwards and forwards among valleys and water courses, it seethes and overflows its banks in vast and desert wilds. Whether there be a superfluity of it or a scarcity, the world is supplied according to its requirements for receiving and for imparting moisture to created things, without respect to precedence in time. Wherefore there is nothing either generous or mean about it, for it flows and rushes with echoing reverberations throughout the vast expanse of earth and heaven. It cannot be said to have a left side or a right, filling everything as it does; it winds and meanders backwards and forwards, this way and that, being coexistent in point of time with the entire Universe- for which cause its virtue may be called perfect. And how comes it that water is able thus to bring its virtue to perfection in the world? It is because of its gentleness, weakness, fertilizing properties and lubricity."

And Laotzse himself said: "That which is the weakest thing in all the world is able to overcome the strongest. Issuing from nothingness it returns to nowhere, and from this I know that there is advantages in non-action." This was Taoism, and, you cannot gainsay a single point. Now remember, I was reading this to prove how powerful the weakest may be. Let me now quote a Western man, Ruskin, on water. Indeed, Buskin's enthusiasm (*Modern Painter's*, Section V, "Truth of Water") ought to be ours: "Of all inorganic substances, acting in their own proper nature, and without assistance or combination, water is most wonderful. If we think of it as the source of all the changefulness and beauty which we have seen in the clouds; then as the instrument by which the earth we have contemplated, was modeled into symmetry, and its crags chiseled into grace; then as (in the form of snow) it robes the mountains it has made, with that transcendent light which we could not have conceived if we had not seen; then as it exists in the foam of the torrent, in the iris which spans it, in the morning mist which rises from it, in the deep crystalline pools which mirror its hanging shore, in the broad lake and glancing river, finally, in that which is to all human minds the best emblem of universal, unconquerable power, the wild, various, fantastic, tameless unity of the sea; what shall we compare to this mighty, this universal element, for glory and for beauty? or how shall we follow its eternal cheerfulness of feeling? It is like trying to paint a soul."

I quote this, too, to prove how powerful the weak may be. How marvelous is not Beauty and yet it is intangible. Beauty can take hold of a human heart, when neither truth nor goodness can move it! You have now heard a great deal about the weakness of water and you have verified the truth of all you have heard. Let me now turn the leaf over and show some of the marvels this Weakness performs, and combining the two descriptions as symbolical of Simplicity, it will readily be seen, that Simplicity is a workmaster of miracles and that we never can fail essentially in life if we identify ourselves with it. Water covers seven tenths of the surface of the earth. Not much left, is there? In connection with atmospheric oxygen and nitrogen, it surrounds the earth to a height of two hundred miles, it is estimated. Surely we may well say that we live and breathe in water, yea, we may even say that we are made of water, because three fourths of the weight of all animals and plants is water. Certain it is, that our body could neither be built nor sustained without water. It is water and light that transform the inorganic in the plant to the organic, and thus becomes the source of our energy.

This is directly important for us personally. But water exists not alone for us. Simplicity is not only a human virtue. Water, though seldom chemically pure, is without smell and taste, two of the most animal senses. Being without smell and taste points to its freedom from anything that can be called rottenness; moreover, water is cooling and a solvent for all that which man normally takes into his body and assimilates. Apply this to Simplicity with which Laotze and his followers compare it, and, surely, you can see Simplicity as a "cooling" force, and as a "solvent" of many difficulties. Though water is soft and pleasant, it hides enormous strength. It is composed of oxygen and hydrogen, two of the most powerful gases. Bring these two together under the blowpipe and they unite in a violent explosion. Simplicity contains in itself two equally strong powers; activity and passivity, and, where these two are brought together under the blow-pipe of circumstance, they produce terrific effects. It has been suggested that if the earth ever burns up, as old traditions say it will, then the energy to do it will arise from the Ocean, because the Ocean is simply at present concealing the two fire elements which can and will burn anything. It can then rationally be inferred from this that Simplicity is the same power and the same energy, only on another plane. Do you not think it worth while to pay some attention to this subject of water and Simplicity, as taught in so unique a way in the Tao-Teh-King? Where is the strength equal to Simplicity?

I will wander away a little from the direct subject of my chapter and give you a few problems to think about in connection with water and Simplicity. Perhaps you will have more respect for the Hindus' bathing in the waters of the Ganges, and for the Egyptians of old who held the Nile to be sacred and even thought the rivers were gods. Perhaps you will also reconsider your notions about the frequent illustrations so common among ancient people and in the East to-day. Perhaps you will think of your, own bath in a different way, and, perhaps you will bathe differently now, than you used to. In old Babylonia, proselytes were initiated by baptism and the custom was borrowed by the Levites and transmitted to the church. In Ex. XIX-20, we are told that Jehovah would not come down and give the law before the people had washed their clothes. In John's Gospel (III-5) it is reported that Jesus declared to Nicodemus that nobody could enter the kingdom of God before he was born of water and spirit. All these things and the suggestions they have called forth, I want you to think over in connection with Simplicity. Your meditations upon them can only stir you up to a consideration of all the marvels that we pass by in the ordinary day life, and, call out a desire to change and do better in the future. Anybody penetrating into these mysteries will understand much of the hidden meaning in the voices of the sea, I spoke of in my second chapter, and can neither drink a glass of water nor wander on the seashore without marveling and thinking of mysteries and of veils that do not hide but do reveal. So much about water. Laotzse does not speak of grass, but I will do so in connection with this subject of Simplicity, because grass represents in the organic world the same state of mind and heart as water does in the inorganic. The peculiar character of the grass is its power to adapt itself to the service of men. In its marvelous Simplicity of build it shows humility and cheerfulness. It is satisfied to be trodden on and fed upon. It seems even to cheer up under all kinds of violence and ill usage. Cut it down, and, next day, it multiplies its shoots and sends a rich perfume to you from its withering leaves. It keeps itself green through the winter and greets you in fruitful strength next spring. Have you ever studied that dainty little spear of fluted green, we call grass? It is more marvelous than any church spire, and it teaches the same lesson every spring when it rises up from the soil with song of glorification to the Sun above, and a silent prayer of thanks for preservation to mother earth below. Its Simplicity is so great, so profound, that but few notice it long enough to speak about it, yet, we should know no fair earth if the grass did not fulfill its mission. The earth would be nothing but desolation and we should not be among the living. Nature's primary object with grass seems to be the protection of the soil. If the soil were not protected by an organic covering it would speedily pass away and only the bare rocks remain, because floods would wash it away and the sun would burn it up. Simplicity fills a similar office. The destructive power of man's heterogeneous culture would lay him waste very soon. He keeps himself in check by retirements upon the conservative forces of existence. The grass family feeds us. All our cereals come from the grasses. The grass family comprises over three hundred genera and not less than three thousand five hundred species. In grain the grasses furnish a larger amount of sustenance to animal life than all other tribes of plants together, and, thus they are truly the physical basis of all civilization. Reflect upon this and you will soon see that Simplicity serves the same purpose in the higher life; that is, that the Inner Life so to say, lives upon it. The grass is the commonest of common things, and, therefore the ever-present god. The universality of grass is one of the most poetical of facts in the economy of the world, and, its name is so universal in its signification, that I may almost identify grass with Nature, The word "grass" means to grow, to sprout, and, the word "Nature" means the same; that is, to bear, to bring forth. You have heard much about Simplicity. Does it not all find its realization in grass?

As grass is earth's garment, so is Simplicity the most beautiful garment the soul can find. Both grass and Simplicity are found watching "in all the places that the eye of heaven visits." They love each other like brooks and the watercourses. They follow each other and make gardens for the spiritual man. The grass family has never betrayed its trust; neither has Simplicity. They are back of all man's love and have covered over the sands of sin which human faithlessness has washed down upon so many fair flowers of spirituality. The grasses have spread out the garment and Simplicity has taken the seat thereon. There is still one more family likeness I wish to point out. It is most interesting and convincing. Grasses are endogens and their growth is endogenous; that is, they grow from inside and not by concentric rings as for instance the oak. They increase by the intercalation of new cellular and vascular tissues among those already formed. They are "inside growers" and so are lilies and palms. You will at once see the similarity to Simplicity for that certainly is of inside growth and not of the outside. You can now see why I quoted as my text the poetic sentiment, I started with:

"...Our human souls
Cling to the grass and water brooks."

CHAPTER V

THE SAGE

In the third chapter I spoke of the mystics and toward the end I retold a story from John Tauler about a poor man, whose clothes were not worth three cents, and, who sat like a beggar at the church door, and, how John Tauler was sent to this man for heavenly wisdom. I retold their conversation and you remember how this beggar triumphed over the learned Dr. Tauler because of his Union with God, a union attained as he told him by self-abandonment and absolute love of God. We agreed then that the beggar was a Sage. Now I offer you an Eastern parallel to this tale from the Middle Ages. The difference between that tale and the one which you shall now hear is this, that Laotzse, who gives the information, speaks as a teacher and instructs us in the language of Simplicity about the sage. The Western and the Eastern tales are simply two presentations of the same truth and image. Who and what is the sage? Before I give you passages from the Tao-Teh-King on that subject, it may be well, that I say a few words about the great man in order to distinguish the two. The Sage and the Great Man are two distinct phenomena. Nietzsche was not a sage, nor were Caesar, Leonardo, Michael Angelo, Spinoza, Beethoven, Copernicus. They were men of genius and greatness. Jesus, Buddha, Laotzse were Sages, because they were embodiments of great love and started men on a course of life, more human than that mankind had followed before. The life they started mankind in was mahatmic, that is to say, it was a sublime blending and union of the opposite factors of existence, a union, that does not destroy but raises the opposites above the world by a complete transformation. The others were great brains and furnished mankind with many accessories of life. They promoted culture but not holiness. Jeremy Bentham and John Stuart Mill held Utilitarianism to be the characteristic of the Great Man and Hippolyte Taine considered him an embodiment of the spirit of his time and the will of the people. The world has readily accepted these opinions and judges greatness by these standards. In contradistinction to these, I now shall give you Laotze's definition of the sage, and the difference will appear at once, and, you will see which of the two groups you belong to or want to follow. I will preface my definition of the sage, such a Laotze sees him, by leading your thought beforehand to observe how different Laotze's view is from the view of a sage we get from India, for instance. The views we get from India tend to depress rather than to raise the value and significance of life. They contain no incentives to work or to put forth any efforts against irrationality and wickedness. The Hindu flees the world.

Not so Laotze's sage. The main key to him is activity. He remains in the world as an example; he encourages us to struggle for freedom and never condemns us, though he laments that the world is so bad and so irrational. You see the difference? It is my opinion that we in this country can learn far more from Laotze on how to live, than we can learn from India. If one wants to become a yogi, and wishes to throw away all human value and become a mere wheel in the mechanism of nature, let him go to India. If one wants to be a sage and yet live in the world as a useful member of society, let him study and follow Laotze. The last mentioned object in life, I believe, is American. Who and what is the sage, the holy man? "The sage is occupied only with that which is without self-assertion and he conveys his instructions by silence. He does not refuse the world's ten thousand things, but does not possess them. He works, but claims not the fruit of his action. He has merit, but does not dwell on it and therefore no one robs him of it." (II.) In short, he is in the world, but not of it. If you remember the description of Simplicity, you will see that the sage is Simplicity realized. The sage and Simplicity are two sides of the same truth. They may be compared to the approaches to the bridge and the two voices spoken of in former chapters. The sage is neither self-sufficient nor does he claim the honor for that which Tao accomplishes through him, nor even the fruits thereof. How thoroughly the character of water and grass as shown in the last chapter! "The sage knows no distinctions; he has no 'loves,' but looks upon all men and things as made for holy uses." (V.), that is to say, separateness does not exist for him. Men and women and things are seen *sub specie eternitatis*; only their eternal value counts with him. From a worldly point of view this looks like indifference. It is no indifference. It is wisdom; for consider: there are men and women enough all around us. They are common enough; they are everywhere and as plentiful as workers in a beehive or anthill. The mere fact of shape and organic structure is nothing remarkable. Nature uses the same sex-model throughout all her kingdoms; everywhere she moves by means of dual forms. But where is the one among either of these sexes who is more, something more than merely a human form? The one who is a species rather than a specimen? The one to whom we can apply the eternal measure? The woman who will and can be recognized because she is Woman and not a special and separate individual? The man, who is not a semblance, but a reality? Where are the ones who cause us to exclaim, "Ah, I have seen a soul! I have felt the Presence!"

Such exclamations are proper when we see a man or a woman who uses the body with absolute and joyous freedom; and whose mind rests in majestic peace and who is master of both. Such an one is mahatmic, or a sage, a great spirit. We have mahatmic spirits of various degrees among us. They are the ones, whom the sage considers; the others are children, and some are merely possibilities. In the world it is heresy to say anything against the world and its things. The world wants all of us to be as worldly as it is itself, and to look only for self-interest and provide "bread and play" for the mob. In common justice to the sage we must, however, say that he has as much right to live in his own way as the world has to live its way. The world does not consider him a valuable asset, why should it complain because he sits apart? Let him alone, he does not hurt the world. The Tao-Teh-King thinks well of the sage and declares (VII) also that "the wise man is indifferent to himself and thus becomes the greatest among men. Because he does not seek his own he accomplishes his own." As little as the wise man seeks his own, so little does he proclaim himself as the "greatest among men." By acting that way he gives the world no cause for irritation or hatred. Why he succeeds by "indifference," I have elsewhere explained. It is because this sort of indifference is Simplicity. In confirmation of my explanations, I will here again quote the Tao-Teh-King on the subject. The reasons for the sage's success and his superiority is this, that (XXII) he adapts himself to Tao, therefore he is "preserved to the end" and becomes a model even for the unwilling. He "bends himself" therefore he becomes straight, and he is "filled because he empties himself." Though unknown and unrecognized he toils incessantly for the good. Though that toil wears him away, he is constantly renewed. On this point of toiling and wearing away, yet not dying, the world least of all can understand him. The reason why he does not die lies, of course, in the fact that he draws life from the deepest wells of existence, and those wells are only open in the sage. The deep wells never dry up; they are not filled by surface water; they flow with perennial streams which come from the innermost earth. It was that kind of wells Isaac was told to dig up when sent to dig up "the old wells." To the sage, work is not toil; it is recreation, growth and laudation of Tao. Work is the key to all spirituality. Because the world does not know the difference between toil and work it condemns the sage as an idler and a useless member of society. It is further said (XXVI) that the sage never loses his gravity and daily walks with dignity. He never forgets himself even if glorious palaces should belong to him. This is readily understood when it is realized that he is a quietist. His Quietism is "concealed enlightenment" to the world; nevertheless in it he becomes the good savior, a savior to whom nobody and nothing is "outcast." In the mysterious balance of things, he outweighs all misery and degradation by being "the enlightened one" and one who is free. In his intensity, the sage balances the world's immensity. Being one he outnumbers the many. Because he rests in the endless, he commands the finite. He was always in the world, but the world did not know it. In connection with the gravity of the sage stands the fact that he (XXIX) "abandons pleasure, extravagance and indulgence."

That he should be far from pomp and levity is a matter of course. But the sage is no pietist or hypocrite. On the contrary, he is a devotee of beauty, beauty both in the human and in nature. Being rooted in Simplicity he can appreciate beauty as nobody else. Simplicity being the kernel of all beauty, he and beauty are one. Beauty to him, is, of course, not show nor stimulated desire, it is the supreme form, that otherness which only from time to time strikes common people and professionals; that power, which lit upon Chaos and Heaven and Earth came forth, and, became cosmic order.

Again it is said about the Wise Man (XLVII) that "he does not travel, yet he has knowledge; that he does not see things, yet he defines them." How would an emperor or even a police inspector get along if he did not get daily and hourly reports from everywhere? How would any manager of affairs who did not see for himself and learn by reports, how would he "define" things or affairs. He could not do it. He depends upon a complicated state machinery and reports. Not so the sage. It appears that there is a universal exchange bureau in the spirit to which he has immediate access, access at any time and anywhere. The sage lives in the spirit, hence things appear to him not fragmentary, but essentially and as they really are, both in their primary forms and in any and all of their derived forms. His world is the sum total of all the factors of the universe; factors which are both positive and negative; factors of both birth and death; factors which are the forms of existence. His world has been described in all that which Laotzse says about Tao; in all that which Plato dreamed about Ideas, and Jacob Bohme revealed about the Nature-powers called "mothers."

The sage does not strive. He knows that Tao is One and he

follows Teh, or virtue, which is neither more nor less than following Tao, for Teh is Tao realized. As little as anything can be taken from Tao or added to Tao, so little can anything be taken from Teh or added to Teh. Teh, virtue, is a constant. Why then should the sage either strive or care for names or distinctions; they can only be human inventions, and cannot affect either Tao or Teh. The sage wastes no energy in striving, he applies himself to Tao, and, Tao gives him the true perception or understanding of the nature of things and their value. He also applies himself to Teh, or Virtue, which instructs him how to use things and by right use of things he attains power. Said a Taoist: "The man of virtue, Teh, remains indifferent to his environment. His integrity is thereby undisturbed and his knowledge transcends the senses. As a result of that his heart expands to enfold those who take refuge in it. Such is the man of complete virtue."

It is said of one who does not strive: "He will bury gold in the hills and cast his pearls in the sea and not strive for wealth or for fame. He will not rejoice in old age or grieve over early death, nor will he pride himself of success or feel sorrows in failure. He will not feel rich because he ascends the throne, nor glory because lie may rule the world. His real glory is to know the One, Tao, and that all things are but phases of the One." It is interesting to compare this sublime indifference to the stoicism of Marcus Aurelius. The Roman looks upon such things with contempt. The Taoist treats them as unimportant. Both stand aloof and separate from them. The sage has "the gift that abides," the anointed eye, which sees the light that never fails. God still speaks to man. The mountains especially call to the sage and they show him the hidden life. In ever ascending scale he rises upon the spiritual sense of all scriptures, and praying in the spirit he goes out into the wilderness. Everywhere he is in the midst of "the salvation of God"; nowhere is the divine face hidden; "the little things," as well as the first born, the "sons of God," guide him. Thus and therefore, it will be seen, that though he does not travel as the curious and the idle do, nor examine as the learned do, he nevertheless knows everything.

It may now sound surprising and contradictory to hear that the Tao-Teh-King also says (XLIX) that the sage's heart is not set upon anything, that he has no fixed opinions, or opinions which he calls his own; but a little consideration will show that that is necessarily so. How could he who lives in the universal, stay in the particular? He would not even claim the universal as his own. Only small souls beat the drums and the smaller they are, the larger the drum. Professionals especially are zealous about their so-called discoveries and panaceas. Contrary to all such, the wise man, says the book (XLIX), "accommodates himself to the minds of others." That is to say, he does not force his hearers or pupils to exalt him or to speak in the forms of his thought or copy him. He accommodates himself to them. If his hearer is an artist, he speaks in art phraseology; if his pupil is a philosopher, he falls in with him and uses abstract terms; to a woman he speaks in life terms and with love, and, to the child he uses pictorial illustrations. To all he is sympathetic, and, they confide in him. The sage "universalizes his heart" (XLIX) and thus becomes a savior.

And how does he thus become a savior? He does it by such behavior as I already have described; a behavior, the key of which is Simplicity. Salvation is not brought to anybody by forcing them into another's mode of thinking or living. Salvation comes to whosoever needs it, by letting him reform himself, by letting him overcome himself, and thereby allowing the Higher Self to reassert itself in him. People would be righteous if let alone. It is pressure from outside and the preaching of false notions that cause people to do wrong. Remove desires by putting no false value upon things, and nobody will desire them. It is the law that makes sin, said St. Paul. Leaving out for the present any discussion about the metaphysics of "the law of contrariety," so called, this can be said, that by making distinctions we create crime and antagonize Tao and Teh. Rightly says Laotzse, that by setting value on rare things of sense we disturb the peace of the mind. (III.) Who can deny it? Predilections are the cause of sin and crime and our alienation from Tao and Teh. If nobody made distinctions, no breaking of rules would take place. The human heart is not radically wrong. The core is right and sound. Our book says (LXII) that "Tao is the guardian of all things," and "does not even forsake those who are not good." Yea, the book even says (LI) that "Teh (or virtue) nourishes all things, increases them, protects them and watches over them."

In the face of such declarations, who dares throw stones? who dares malign the people? Let the hypocrites go and hide! Do not stand in the way of a soul! Every flower will seek the sun if let alone; none turns away. The sage is the good savior! and the sage never advertises himself, and the sage is always poor; he carries his jewels in his bosom (LXX). He never speaks up in the congregation. Those who do not know, do the talking. All this about the sage, I have read in the Tao-Teh-King. Go and read for yourself. You may find much more. You have thus far, in this chapter and in the last, heard much in praise of Simplicity and about its natural types, water and grass. You have also heard who and what the sage is, and how he uses Simplicity. All of this has conveyed ideas of Reality to you. It must have appeared that Simplicity is something fundamental; something structural, something cosmic. Let me now finally translate the word Simplicity into moral concepts and thus come a little nearer to our human existence. Simplicity then is first of all sincerity. Sincerity in the Latin is *sine ceray* "without a flaw." Certainly Simplicity is completeness and uprightness. It is a vase that rings true when struck. Simplicity is whole-hearted and simple-hearted, or, in other words, it is synonymous with singleness. Plato applied the word Simplicity, (aplous) to God, "who is," he said, "perfectly simple and true both in word and deed." Plato uses the word Simplicity again in the Republic about the just man.

He means, and we ought to mean by the word Simplicity, that a just man is perfectly at one with himself in motive, aim and end in his relations to the Divine and to his fellowmen. In an old work, "The Testament of the Twelve Patriachs," a work of Hebrew origin and character, Issachar, the fifth son of Jacob and Leah, is represented as Simplicity, and, he represents himself to his children as one who has walked all his life in Simplicity. He lays emphasis upon his being a husbandman and recommends his children to find contentment in husbandry and to shun mercantile pursuits because these lead to transgressions.

That of being a husbandman is a point I would emphasize as a necessity for the full realization of Simplicity. City life, with its complexity, is ruinous. The old adage is true: "God made the country and the devil made the city." By being a husbandman, I do not exactly mean being a farmer, though Issachar was it. I mean that country life, life in the open, and not city life is the true life. If we cannot flee the city, we can nevertheless in many ways place ourselves in direct relation to the country. Let us do that! An outlook to Nature will make a path to Simplicity! And now in conclusion : What can be done for the restoration of Simplicity! We talk and boast of culture and civilization, and what is it? Nothing but sham! I say "nothing," and do so perfectly conscious of what I am saying, and do not think I am exaggerating. The proof is to be found in all the misery around us, a misery that never ends. I am not blind to the marvelous industrial and commercial progress of the world. I profit by it in many ways, and so do you, but eternally, what is it? It is not as stable as clouds, and, those who promote the so-called culture, make gains that last no longer than mosquitoes in the fall. The only lasting thing they gain is terrible strength of will. That lasts, and, will send them back like blind moles to burrow in the earth. By and by the Powerful and the sages will change places. To die poor now but wise is great gain. Cannot something effectually be done to introduce Simplicity? Can we not call to arms all those who have realized the Overman in themselves, as they say? Why not send them to vitalize that Overman? Let them introduce Simplicity! Who will be first to preach and practice it?

THE INNER LIFE AND THE TAO TEH KING

I now come to that special purpose I had in mind, and to which I referred before. My purpose is to connect Simplicity, the sage and the Tao-Teh-King, and that not merely as logically related, but standing in a life relation to each other as Mother, Father and Child. Before I proceed to do so, let me explain my method in these papers. In these chapters I am endeavoring to translate all scholastic and intellectual terms and expressions into living conceptions, into the forms that answer to our personal existence. In all of us there lie images, words, sounds, symbols, and so forth, of various kinds, they are the epitomes of ourselves, and by means of these images we, in the most direct manner, get hold of ourselves and are taught. I am trying to get hold of such images in you, in order to explain my subject. It is easy enough to spiritualize any idea or conception, and to raise it very high, but the result is that it becomes so utterly attenuated that it loses all practical value. As soon as an idea is so thoroughly denaturalized that it has become a mere nothing, it has also ceased to awaken anybody who lives in flesh and blood. I say, it is easy enough to wander off into high-flown language and poetic imagery, but it is very difficult to move the other way; and yet that is most needed, because people need a foothold, and they get it not by a talk above their heads, but by bringing the truth and the spirit to them in tangible forms, in forms that correspond to their own lives and their own experiences. Indeed, it is an old truth that "invisible things are discerned from the foundation of the world through the things which are made." And why is that the truth? Why is it self-evident? It is so, as John of the Cross says, because "spiritual things include them." By right use of visible and tangible things we may lay hold upon the invisible and intangible, because they are included in it as the higher in the lower. As I said, people need a foothold from whence they themselves can begin to work up on the Path.

You remember I have laid much emphasis upon originality and have condemned all kinds of copying and ascribed much of humanity's misery to lack of originality and to copying. If a lecturer or a preacher can come down, not to platitudes or childish talk, but to the living images that lie in every human mind, he can reach that mind and do it good. By infusing those images with power, by purifying them, by electrifying them, by explaining them to the mind that possesses them, that mind is infused with vigor and awakened to itself. Being awakened, it will live for itself and be on the Path, and, that it should be awakened and caused to live for itself is the object of all preaching. A preaching that does not aim at that nor accomplish it is no more than babbling or beating the drum. If you will go back over the preceding chapters and reexamine them, you will see that I am struggling to do this very thing I am talking about. Instead of screwing the subjects up higher, I have attempted to take the scholastic machinery to pieces and I have substituted living powers for all mechanical and inorganic details. I have made all abstractions into living personalities; I have painted dramatic scenes and appealed to your feelings and love-nature rather than attempted to instruct. I have used veils that reveal, and, thus I have gained the same effects as Greek sculptors gained, when they wetted the drapery they put upon their models: they revealed, yet they never offended propriety. I have, if I may say so, rather "lowered" idealistic expressions; I have done that by clothing them in flesh and blood, and, I know I have attained some satisfactory results. An experiment with that which I have called Western and modern phraseology will prove more of a success than might have been expected.

It is most singular, that this method which I have called Western and modern is the very method of the ancients. In the East, today as of old, all preaching and teaching is by personal intercourse, and, experience in European universities has shown that it is the only real way by which to impart spiritual seed. Abstract and mechanical subjects may well be taught from a platform, but spiritual life never. The reason for this is plain. Consciousness is more than a physical fact. In the Universal, the individual person is a species, but in the physical world an individual is almost meaningless. One crystal is like another; but one soul is not like another. All those high-flown, abstract and difficult terms and phrases and conceptions in which so many teachers, both mystic and others, have buried that life which these terms and phrases originally stood for, all these terms and phrases are not of the spirit of the Orient. The West and part of Asia under western influence made them, partly in Greece, and partly elsewhere, during the development in the East of what is called Western progress, Western culture and civilization. In its attempt to gain a reasonable understanding of living forces and acts, the West and part of Asia invented all these terms and phrases and they unfortunately forgot the original aim and end, and forgot that these terms and phrases were only to be symbols and no more, and they forgot life altogether. They hugged and kissed petrifactions and do so now. By forcing posterity to learn by the brain and not by the heart, we have now come to our present desperate conditions. We have the shell, but the nut is not in it. I am trying to retranslate terms and phrases into life. Like so many others, I have lived in the blind man's paradise and been satisfied with painted canvases and with words. But time came when I could no longer square the murmur of the forest with the pages of a book; nor comprehend why I should not worship a beautiful body, but raise my eyes with devotion to a manufactured and unsubstantial puppet god. Time came when I could no more find peace in thoughts formulated by others and not by myself; at that time I began to use my own innate images as symbols for my thought. Time came, also, when my will refused to be tied conventionally; at that time I dared to be myself, and I entered the Path.

Having found it necessary for myself to give the life-element its absolute freedom and experiencing it as the first step in the approach to the Path, I now apply the experience and present to you what I call the "inside" of those terms and phrases which philosophy and ethics abound in. I translate them into lifeforms, which I have experienced, and some of them must strike you as they have struck me. And I know they are of eternal value. I am confident that if you start with life-images, your own reason and the image in you will clothe these life-images with their celestial garments and you will discover yourself to be on the Path. It is my experience that nobody can enter the Path by any other method. And upon examination you will find that it is the true psychological process. It is Nature's way when she is allowed freedom with us. Now, then, applying this principle of translating philosophical and ethical terms into terms of the living, I say that Simplicity is but another term for mother and that the sage is but another term for father and that the book, the Tao-Teh-King, is but another term for child. I mean to say that the love-power in us will feel Simplicity as the Mother-power. And that the wisdom-power in us will recognize the Sage as the Father-power, and, when I shall have spoken about the book, you readily will acknowledge that the book must be the child-power. Indeed, this translation seems to me so simple that I feel it ought to have been unnecessary to mention it. These conceptions, mother-father-child, are living-forces in us, and lie nearer to us than the abstract terms Simplicity, sage and book. We can grasp them by our inherent vitality and the image, and thus at-one ourselves with them, and having done that we can hereafter raise them to any potential power we wish. In the conceptions mother-father-child we get living footholds and cannot lose ourselves in fancies or miss the real in existence. They will readily transform themselves into the Path for us. But I must proceed. From this talk about Simplicity in the last chapter and about the sage in this, I come naturally to the subject of the ancient people who were so far ahead of us, and to the books they have left behind them. I will therefore say something about the recovery of the ancient wisdom and speak especially in praise of the Tao-Teh-King as one of the marvels of ancient wisdom. I was laughed at the other day when I recommended a certain learned man to read the Tao-Teh-King and advised him to learn something from people of another race and of prehistoric character. I urged the digging up of old wells, and as he was a minister, I referred to Isaac who dug up the "old wells" and found them flowing with fresh water. With scorn he refused to have anything to do with the ancients, barbarians, he called them. He wanted, he said, only the newest new; only the mental products of this, his own age. For, said he, "there is and can be no connection between myself and those ancient ones." I never argue with a man that stands in his own light. What would be the use? I left him, only asking him if there were any connection between him and his ancestors of yore? Did you make yourself? How about your nationality and race characteristics? What vital connection is there or can there be between you and the theology you learned at the seminary? Of course, the answers to these questions would refute his conceit, but I did not force the answers. To refuse to read such an old book as the one I referred to, or to learn of the ancients is as rational as not to recognize the spring of the day. Surely the day spring is older than any book. People cannot deny it. Why not deny it? But they do not. On that point Nature forces them to learn her lesson, it is so her ministry; on other points, they are left free to act and unworthy as most of their free-will acts are. They arrogantly refuse to listen. This is another of the many faults I have pointed out from time to time in our modern life and another source of many of our troubles.

An age cannot stand apart from the age that precedes it, as little as an individual can stand apart from its parents and other ancestry. To learn what to-day means, we must return to yesterday's task and its lessons, be they finished or not. Nature's method points the lesson. The spring of the day or morning; the noon, and the dusk and the night resemble Spring, Summer, Autumn and Winter. Nature has arranged it so, by making the diurnal revolution of the earth upon its own axis correspond to the annual revolution of the earth around the sun. And Nature makes all her children move in that fashion, and by so doing she both repeats herself and teaches new lessons; she constantly renews and constantly returns again to the same point, but on each stage she teaches something new and forces a new development. We are constantly in the midst of her, yet never see the beginning nor end, but we are constantly taught nevertheless. Anyone refusing to reconsider the old teachings is a disobedient child and must necessarily be crushed sooner or later, because the wheel of Nature's rotation cannot be stopped. Modern culture is near being crushed because it does not follow Nature's method. It has cut itself off from Nature and attempts to rest upon self alone. Though I was laughed at, as I told you, I nevertheless recommend a return to the old wells, and I recommend that we dig them up again. From experience I know that modern culture does not contain the essential life.

From experience of a long life, I also know that there is a stream of clear water flowing through much of the ancient learning and that he who drinks of it never shall thirst again. One of the old wells that gushes forth such pure water is called the Tao-Teh-King. It is with this well, as with so many of the old wells, they must be dug up. The digger is the Inner Life and the sensible people of to-day who long for the Inner Life. Let me talk a little about wells and caves and on their symbolism, or, how they are to be revered, because they are veils that reveal; and not veils that cover up. I wish to speak of wells and caves because of the water that flows from them. In Nature they play a part that resembles the work of the heart in our organism. As life flows from the heart and returns to it, so water flows from the caves and returns to them by way of the clouds. In my last lecture, I described at length the importance of water, such as Laotzse and his disciples saw it, and I added what Science had to contribute ; it is therefore quite natural that I now should say something about its source or sources. And whatever I shall say adds to the instruction given about Simplicity and the sage if you will make the application. In the first place, wells or caves do not originate the water, to speak properly. They are the vessels that gather it and send it forth in different directions. In the Alps yon may climb a mountain, the St. Gotthardt, and from that one mountain see three rivers flow out in various directions. The Rhine is the conflux of these three rivers. The three rivers start in icy caves. The three rivers united in one as the Rhine have been the leaders of much of the most important

THE INNER LIFE AND THE TAO TEH KING

European history from the time of the Romans. Why, we do not know. The fact is there. From three repositories on St. Gotthardt these rivers are sent forth. The mountain gathers the water and stores it up in glaciers and from these it fills the wells, and the wells give birth to the stream. The mountain, the glaciers, the caves and the streams are ever the same, yet they are never old, but remain ever young and fresh. Ancient Druids and priests of Nerthus heard \he eternal passion of song that reverberated from each drop of water that fell in the cave. That same song is heard today, though not understood. In that song Mother Nature assures the devotee that though her children forsake her, she will forever and ever keep sending streams, young and fresh, into the world. Though people think only of using the streams for selfish purposes, for saw-mills, sailing and shipping, she will nevertheless continue to submit and ask no rewards. St. Gotthardt, of course, means "God's Heart," and the song is one of assurance that Love never shall cease to flow from God's heart. Look upon caves and wells and springs in that way and you shall see that such symbolism is even richer than other meanings often attributed to them.

The Tao-Teh-King is such a mountain like St. Gotthardt, and from it springs three rivers: Tao and Teh and the King. Tao and Teh are living forces and King is the book containing them. No matter how much foolishness commentators fill it with, the original stream is as pure to-day as ever. And now I will tell you the story of its origin and you can interpret it yourself. The legend is, that Laotzse, disgusted with the corruption of the court, left his home in the territory of Chow, and in order to travel West as he wished to, had to go through a mountain pass on the border. A friend of his was the warden of that pass. While staying with this warden, Laotzse wrote his book. The point I wish to call attention to is that it was written in a mountain pass, it was born in a pass. There is a connection between a cave, a mountain pass and the three rivers, called Tao and Teh and the King. Think it over and you will readily see it and yon will discover that mystery, and that mystery will be a key to the understanding of the book. The book is, as you readily can infer, I mean to say, more than a book and its meaning is not understood except by those who have heard the voices of the sea and of the mountain, voices I spoke of in my second lecture. Many can read the book and many have read it without any mystery. But I can assure you that only those get its full meaning who can listen to its sentences as they would listen and interpret the flow of water from out of a cave. I know I am mystifying some of you, but I dare not express myself any clearer. Moreover, your own discovery will be of far more value to you than anything I could say in plain language.

I have said all this about caves and wells, because I argue for the digging up of that old well, I call the Tao-Teh-King, hoping that when I have got so far as to have led your thoughts to it as a well of old, I may be able to take the next step and put some life into that cave or well, and henceforth call it a Heart, a living source rather than a cave or an inorganic hollow. If I can get that conception of Heart accepted, I will be understood when I say that Tao-Teh-King flows with living water, which will quench all thirst and none shall thirst again after having tasted its waters. And I have used the language I have chosen because this so-called book is no book in the ordinary sense of a book. It is a living being. It is an avatar, a revelation and can only be fully comprehended if treated as coming from the heavenly cave, whence are born anew Heaven and Earth every moment. It was a great misfortune for Peter Schlemilch that he cast no shadow, but it is for the Tao-Teh-King a proof of its celestial origin that it casts no shadow. It is light itself and does not stand in derived light. I am not exaggerating. Your own experience will prove the truth of what I say; but no intellectual research will do it. No flippant criticism ever won fair love, nor will the book reveal itself where conceit reigns. The silver thread that runs through it is spun out of love's heart. As the spider spins its web out of its own organism and lives in it, so is this stream of life, called Tao-Teh-King, flowing as a living soul into the real student.

THE INNER LIFE AND THE TAO TEH KING

Birds gather twigs and leaves for their nests ; all material from the outside. The learned collect fragments from here or there, and putting these fragments together with bits of fancy steeped in midnight oil, they call the product philosophy. But bees and spiders do differently, and so do the sages. The honey the bee brings home has been rejuvenated by the bee and transformed from inorganic stuff. The web of the spider is its own body. The sage is not a collector. He is a spontaneous producer. As the book is of such a peculiar nature, it will not surprise you that I should say something about how to read in it- I say "in it," I do not say "read it." You never can do the latter. The first characteristic of the book is that it can be read like any other moral treatise and will yield splendid results. Its teachings treated as merely human sense must by all be considered as high and noble as any ethics taught anywhere. Moreover, from a purely literary point of view, there is not a single sensual blot in it on any page. It never falls below propriety, no matter what straight-jacked school may hold up the standard of what is proper and right. In other words, the book naturally and literally is a model catechism in public and private morals. Reading it as such requires no special attitude or devotion. But reading in it is different from reading it, and I confess I find it difficult to say just what I mean. But here are some leading thoughts. You have perhaps seen old devout people reading their Bible with folded hands before them and reading with prayer for enlightenment. If you have not seen or heard it in reality, perhaps you have seen paintings in which this was shown. To say the least, that custom of the folded hands and of prayer is very beautiful. Some also cross themselves, and that represents to them an act of faith. In India no Brahmin reads a text without intoning the Om, and no Mohammedan begins or ends a prayer without reciting his creed- "La-ilaha-il-lal-laho," and so forth: "There is no Diety but God," and so forth. Everywhere, where people have any degree of the Inner Life, and even where only ancient ceremonies remain, they utter themselves in words of praise, thanks or adoration. If they do that spontaneously, their ejaculations will stir them profoundly; all externals will vanish or recede, thus permitting the soul to unfold and the spirit to become free. In that unfoldment and that freedom there is absorption into the Divine, and the outcome is either high ecstasy or an illumination. It is told of an old woman, who was ordered by her father confessor to say seven pater nosters, that when she next time came before him and was asked if she had done as directed, she answered No! she had come no further than "Our Father" of the first prayer, and why? Because the intonation of that appellative had thrown her into ecstasy and absorbed all the rest of the prayer.

If you can learn to say Tao with that fire, you will understand what I meant by calling the Tao-Teh-King an avatar. But if you cannot say Tao, say or act as your heart and imagination prompts you. Do or say something! Again. All sentences and sometimes single words, no matter what the language may be, are merely hieroglyphics that represent an image that passed before the mind of the writer. It is that image we must get hold of when we read. If we do not get hold of it, we do not get from our reading that which we ought to get. To get that image, we must let the sentence read present itself before our inner eye. We do that best by meditation, not by prying into its meaning, possible or impossible. The sentence contains the Image, even if the sentence is poor linguistics. Sit still and meditate, that is my advice!

The power of single words is forcefully illustrated by a story told by Dr. Kober about Jacob Bohme. The two were walking in the fields, when the Doctor happened to use the Platonic word "idea." No sooner had he pronounced it than Jacob Bohme, in ecstasy, exclaimed, "Ah! I see the heavenly Virgin!" Bohme had never heard the word before. The explanation was perfectly rational and is easily explained, because "Idea" to Plato means a God. Bohme caught the Inner Life of the word. I myself possess several such words. One of those words I got from the Tao-Teh-King, and I have prepared a chapter on it, which you will find as you continue to read; that word can throw me into an ecstatic condition, and I have found a couple of images that will unlock many mysteries of the Inner Life as well as the outer. There is nothing marvelous about this, and I do not consider myself better gifted than any of you. Some of you probably possess similar words and images, but have perhaps not brought them consciously into use. I have come into possession of these words and images by devotion and by perpetual meditation on them.

Will you not do something of this kind? You need no teacher. The teacher, the sage, is within. All you need is Simplicity, Truth of life and the Mother.

CHAPTER VI

LAOTZSE

I will now give an account of Laotzse and his book. I will first tell the little that is known about him, personally, and then I will examine the character of the historic period in which he lived, and it shall be seen what a remarkable man he was. Finally I will give a summary of his book. He was of a good family, possibly of royal descent, and born 604 B. C. in Ku, a hamlet in Tsu in Honan. Very little is known about him, but we know that he was librarian or custodian of the archives of Cho, a city in south-western China. He was called by many names, such as "the old philosopher," because, according to tradition he was white haired like an old man, when he was born. Tradition also tells that he was 80 years old when born, having been all that time is his mother's womb. He is also called "the ancient prince," "the old child," which means "he who even as an old man remains child-like;" he was also called "the greatly eminent ancient master." After his death, the title of *Tan* was conferred upon him. Tan means "master" and is the same as the title "Christ" given Jesus, and "Buddha" given to Sakya-Muni. As we now say "Jesus, the Christ," so Taoists say Lao-Tan: Lao, the master. Much has been fabled about his connection with Babylonian and Chaldean history, but no historic authority exists for any of those speculations.

I want here in the name of justice to all of the ancient prophets and teachers to protest against the modern scholars' theory of borrowing. It has become the custom among scholars to search for plagiarism everywhere among the ancients, denying the old wisdom-teachers any originality. In this country among the half studied it is common to hear that all teachings are derived from India. It is about as intelligent as to say that our civilization is derived from the Hottentots or from some African negro. The natural question, therefore, is; where did all this wisdom which it is claimed was stolen from somebody else- where did it originate? Who originated it? Our wiseacres never ask themselves this question! The truth about the ancient wisdom, as about wisdom today, is this; the human mind and heart are everywhere and always were capable of originating it for themselves without teaching or impulse from another. All ancient wisdom has originated spontaneously, and that is the explanation of its origin.

If you, my reader, would live truly and not lose yourself in all kinds of distractions, you could equal or transcend Laotzse, Buddha, and all the great teachers, and you could do that without any teacher. All you need to do is "to be as you are," like those most ancient Chinese the Tao-Teh-King speaks of, said: "We are what we are," and who did not know who ruled them nor cared. Yes, that is all that is needed! That Laotzse was a genuine theosophic mystic and not a copyist appears from his book, the Tao-Teh-King. In the 20th chapter he makes the following confession, the only known personal statement we have: "The multitude of men are happy, so happy, as though they were celebrating a great feast. They behave as though it were springtime and they were ascending a high tower. I alone remain quiet, alas! like one who expects nothing of the future. I am like a baby who cannot yet smile. Forlorn I am; oh so forlorn! It appears that I have no place where I may find a home. The multitude of men all have plenty and I alone am empty. Alas! I must be foolish? Ignorant I am; oh so ignorant! Common people are bright, so bright. I alone am dull. Common people are smart; oh, so smart. I alone am confused; oh so confused! Desolate I am, alas! Like the sea. Adrift, alas! one who has no place where to stay. The multitude of men all possess usefulness. I alone am awkward, and a rustic, too. I alone differ from others; but I reverence the Mother."

This is the description of a man on the Path and also his groans, but there is no bitterness in them. It is the lamentation of a man who has moments when he is very unhappy because he feels the world's indifference to its own welfare and feels his solitary position and longs for a company he cannot find. As a sage, he is homeless and feels it when others rejoice around him. By the way, this condition of homelessness, this being a man without a country and a home, is one that comes with various degrees of force to all who are on the Path; you may hear them moan, but you never hear a cry of bitterness or anger, or regret. Do not consider such lamentations to be signs of weakness. It cannot be avoided; it must be endured and the rewards are sure. The time will come when we no more crave for sympathy. You have read about this in "The Voice of the Silence." Cheer up fellow sufferer. Paul was a fool for Christ's sake. Laotzse was a fool for the sake of Tao! And his lamentations are exclamations in moments of loneliness, moments that even the wisest and the most self-centered people have. At the same time, as they are cries of suffering they are also witnesses to his greatness. No mean man, no mere hypocrite would or could so frankly characterize himself that way. Laotzse's Theosophy centers around the two words Tao and Teh and his book is called Tao-Teh-King, which means, the Book about Tao and Teh. What these two words mean, I shall, in this and in subsequent chapters explain, and you shall find, I trust, an incentive in them to dive deeper into the mysteries which they reveal. Personally, Laotzse is the center of his book and also the beginning of a radically new development of the human mind and heart. It is not easy nor necessary now at the beginning of the study to define fully what the mental and moral state of China was just before Laotzse. You will see that easier when you shall have become familiar with the book itself. I will therefore omit such definition and description for the present. But it is possible to indicate what the historic appearance of Laotzse means by comparing him and his appearance to some contemporary and later movements in history. I will try to do that.

Laotzse was born 604 B. C, or at the time when Rome was just built and in early childhood, and not yet of any universal value or significance. Nearly two hundred years later than Laotzse, Greece began in her way to talk about the same problems which Laotzse already so long before had fully stated, and moreover introduced into life, in a most vigorous way and by great disciples. By comparing him and his work with Greece and Rome in point of time you see how the new cycle, which he and they represent, begins with him as a sunrise and ends with them as a sunset. And here are some other facts to prove the same point. As Laotzse is chief among Turanian people, so is, at this time, Babylonia chief among the Semitic people, and typified by Nebuchadnezzar. At this time he had subjugated Judea, destroyed Jerusalem and awed Egypt. Nineveh was razed to the ground the year before Laotzse was born and three years later Daniel was ennobled for his interpretation of dreams. Ezekiel saw allegorical visions. In India, a little later, Sakya-Muni, the Buddha, began to preach the true doctrine of freedom and right knowledge. In other words, on a limited space on the face of the earth, reaching a few degrees north and south and stretching from the western part of China towards the Mediterranean sea, a peculiar awakening and revelation took place. The space may be inscribed in a geometrical figure of a parallelogram of a few degrees north to south and a few more east to west. (See Diagram.) One might imagine a great temple erected upon that parallelogram with its entrance in the east, represented by Laotzse, and its altar in the west, represented by the New Age, which is upon us. Its southern wall would be represented by Buddha and the Gita and the northern by Jesus. Such a design and idea is not so fanciful as some might think. It is a fact that Laotzse, the Gita, Buddha and Jesus, and let me add to them the New Age: these four represent the essentials of the Great Cycle we live in. Their ideas, their historical sequence and the power they have exerted, all confirm the conception. Historically, it is easy to verify what I say, namely, that there is not a single wisdom idea to be found among us which was not born then; nor is there a single religious idea, that we today characterize as of eternal value, which was not born within that parallelogram I have drawn. We of today are simply the inheritors! And what have we done with our patrimony! Have we invested it to get its full power in current value? I think not! I believe there is much in the teachings and life of those four, Laotzse, the Gita, Buddha and Jesus, that we have not yet discovered. I hope the New Age will discover it.

The parallelogram, I have drawn, and the ideas I connect with it, point to the ideas mentioned in a former chapter on templum. I believe the templum of our cycle stands in the heavens above that earthly space. Do you understand me? I think it worth while for you to study these suggestions; they are not only occult, but they are historical, too, and everyone of you is historically affected by these sages and the movements that sprang from them. Everywhere else outside that parallelogram on the face of the earth, where man lived, he existed upon remnants of other civilizations, if civilizations they can be called civilizations radically defective, when compared to the new forms that came in. Such historic facts must not be overlooked or thought of as of no or little value. On the contrary, they are of the greatest value. Someone will now ask about the value and significance of India and all its marvelous religions, thinking perhaps that I misjudge India's position. They will want to know how these are related to Laotzse, to Greece, and to the mighty Semitic force of the days I speak about. I can answer those questions easily. India and all its religions and customs lie on an anterior plane of development. India, or Brahminism, was not human as the human is represented by Laotzse; it is and was god, man is and was of no significance; the gods are and were all and everything. But with the other peoples, man is born as Man and his significance in the world economy is established. That is the difference. Brahminism knows of no sage who is active in the world and desirous of raising the world. Buddha and the Gita are the ones who first see and establish the basis for freedom. Brahminism knows of no such struggle as that which took place among the Semites, the object of which was the establishment of a Kingdom of God, the One, among men. Brahminism was priest-craft, and fought for its own glory and the glory of its gods. Brahminism knows of no such mental boldness and revolutionary ideas as those which lie in the Socratic dictum: "Man is the measure of all things."

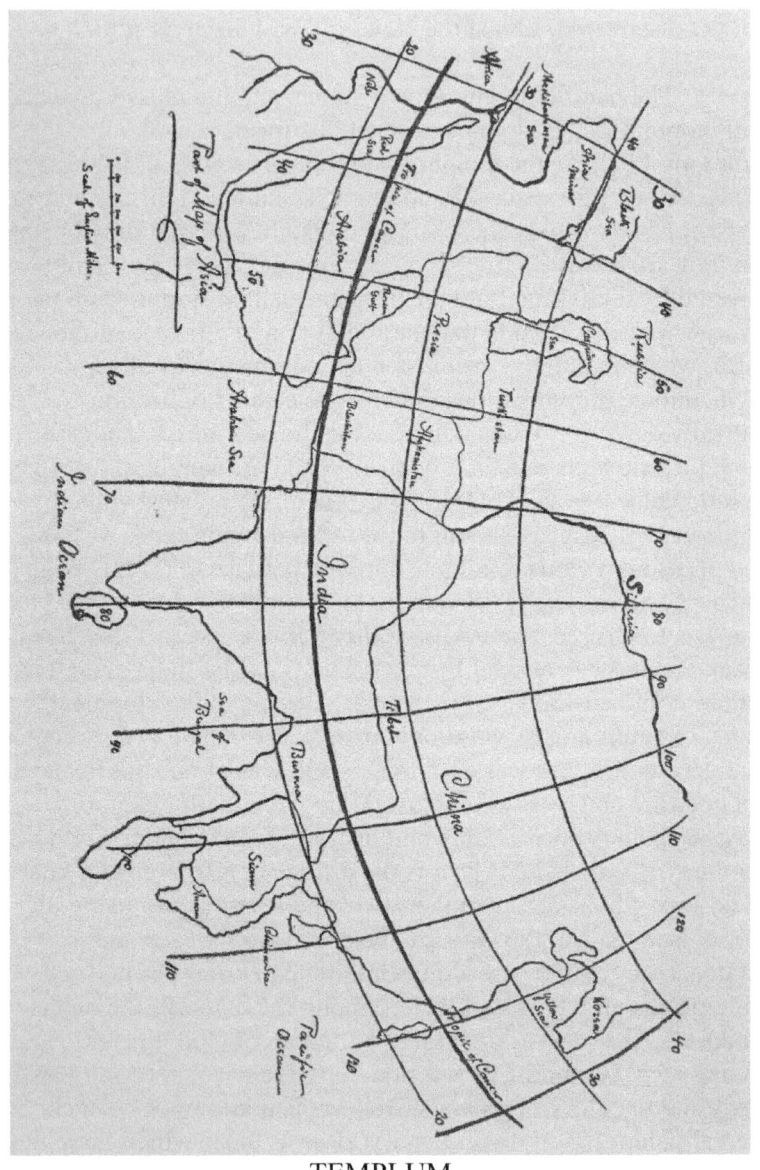

TEMPLUM

THE INNER LIFE AND THE TAO TEH KING

It is easy then to see the radical difference between Laotzse, the Semites and Buddha on one side and Brahminism on the other; and, it must be acknowledged that the progressive ideas are with the former. As for the Bhagavad-Gita, it is not a brahminical product in the sense, I have given Brahminism. Its ideas belong to the very period I am defining and for which I claim so much. An historic and a comparative study will show that.

As for other factors, which I have not counted in, I may anticipate questions about Zoroaster and the Fire worshipers, which plainly lie within the territory I mention. My answer is simply this : I point to the fact that they have vanished. Excellent and wonderful teachers they were, but the eternal, the upbuilding element, was not in their doctrine. Zoroastrian doctrine was mainly an ethical philosophical doctrine of the perpetual fight of good and evil, a dualism that contains no redemption, like that offered by Laotzse, Buddha, the Gita and Jesus. As for the Hebrews, they are the progenitors of Jesus, the last prophet and Master-Mystic. For the rest, their glory lies with all the other Semites, by whatever name they be mentioned, all of which were the standard bearers of belief in the One. At the time of Laotzse they were sadly degenerate, but had already established the work they had to do. I do not think there are any other interrogations that I need anticipate and answer. You are now acquainted with something about the character of the time in which Laotzse appears and you can see the momentous importance of his appearance. It was, as I called it, a revelation, a beginning of a new historic cycle, and, I repeat what I said before, we are still in it. I shall now make some comparisons between Laotzse, the Gita, Buddha and Jesus and their systems of religion, not as they exist in the world today, but the religions such as these masters taught it and instructed their disciples in it. Laotzse's system is summarized best as a system or doctrine of Wisdom and Virtue. That definition will be and is accepted by all students of the book, the Tao-Teh-King. Buddha's one object was to emancipate mankind from sin, sorrow and death, and to teach the doctrine of right knowledge and right living.

Jesus boldly bid his disciples: "Follow me and love one another." He was the first and so far the only founder of a religion whose doctrine was personal. Another comparison. Laotzse was not missionary in any sense, but rather the formulator and teacher for others, who became propagandists. The Gita is clearly a Krishna-Logos doctrine and the law of Union of self with Self by the fulfilling of one's duty. The Gita is full of intense activity, even war. It is a gospel for struggling man. It is a character builder, not a book for home-reading. Buddha was missionary in so far as he preached the doctrine; but he was not an organizer. His followers organized the brotherhoods, not he. Jesus was both a preacher and an organizer of brotherhoods and made His own person the center. Now, if I leave out of consideration the personalities of the three sages, Laotzse, Buddha and Jesus and also the historic systems that have sprung from them, and have regard to the character of their teachings only, then the result is, that there is a gradual development from the universal in Laotzse to the Individual and Personal in Jesus. And such development means psychologically that we begin by learning and end by becoming realizations of that which we originally learned. And that too is the sum total of the Gita. If I now take the final step and seek a comparison between these four and the fifth degree- I mentioned before and called the New Age- what then is the result? It is this, that these four are found to be preparatory to a final transcending condition in which we may be lifted in to a higher wisdom, and an interior union: into God-Wisdom or Theo-Sophia. They are our saviors from the lower to the higher. Summarizing what I have said, the result is a clear view of the essential steps upon the Path, (1) Instruction in Being, "Wisdom and Virtue"; this degree is represented by Laotzse; (2) a vigorous attempt upon the attainment of freedom; this degree is represented by Buddha; (3) a personal realization of freedom; this degree is represented by the Gita and Jesus; (4) an identification of the traveler with the Path and his transcending into God-Wisdom or Theosophy; this degree is represented by the New Age.

I have claimed for Laotzse what a follower of Confucius will deny. I have claimed first place for him in China because he is the one who carries over into the New Age that begins with him, the contents, the inner value, the kernel of all the wisdom the previous ages had acquired, and, he is also the one who communicates to the New Age of China that begins with him, the virtue, or, the right principles of conduct, which the previous ages had discovered. Confucius did no more than formulate ancient ceremonies, the most external of all forms of life. Moreover, this ceremonialism has been the bane of China. In view of these facts, I have a right to claim that Laotzse is the regenerator and the true transition from the prehistoric times to the historic in China. There may have been Taoism before Laotzse, that is to say, similar ideas may have existed, and, no doubt they did, but that does not warrant anyone in saying, that Laotzse stole them. Such ideas as those of Tao and Teh always exist, they are part of the constitution of the universe. They have been discovered time and again, but each time revealed in a different way suitable to the age that discovered them. Laotzse discovered them for his age and the subsequent times and interpreted them for the Chinese, and, for us in a new and fresh form. You may discover them and interpret them anew. Thousands of years hence somebody else will again discover them and interpret them.

All these discoverers are benefactors, and original, not plagiarists. In a similar way, the eternal ideas of Buddha's preaching, those of the Gita and those of Jesus existed, before they appeared in that form which Buddha, Vyassa or Jesus gave them. These prophets and teachers discovered them for their ages and for us. They are couched in forms that still harmonize with the constitution of our minds. A word or two about Taoism after Laotzse. Taoism as a system and in relation to Laotzse, is much like Christianity in its relation to Jesus; in both cases is the founder ignored, his teachings shamefully perverted and a priestly system substituted for the founder's benevolent and sublime ideas. Taoism has temples and a pope. It is full of spiritism, superstitions and pretenses. It is a mixture of alchemy, polytheism and yoga practices. It is degeneration and disgrace. But there are Taoists outside these forms, just as there are a few friends of Jesus outside the Churches. There are many translations extant of the Tao-Teh-King. They differ widely both as to sense and value. The cause of all the different renderings of various passages is easily seen. The translators pursuing their scholastic methods and applying the grammatical rules of Indo-European languages could never hit upon the right symbolical meaning of the Chinese characters, which are symbols of ideas and not verbal representations of words. Unless the Chinese characters are interpreted, both as to sound and to ideographic form, they never can be rightly understood. I will give you a couple of illustrations. A Japanese, now studying at Columbia University, has told me that false intonation caused a missionary to say to his pupils: "Go to hell," when he wanted to say: "Go home." Another missionary attempted to teach his pupils the Lord's Prayer and made a fatal mistake in the very beginning of that prayer. He wanted to say "Our Father," but he did say "Fat pig." In the texts I shall use, I have avoided the scholastic and distorted translations, where the ideographic interpretation was the obvious one. Hence I claim that I have been able to detect many a mystic sense, and, been able to harmonize many expressions, thereby gaining an insight into the Tao-Teh-King hitherto unknown. I have been engaged with the Tao-Teh-King since 1877, or for 32 years, and my interest in the book is ever increasing. I place it very high among the treasures that have come to us from the East.

The book is not only full of mystic lore, but also thoroughly practical. In fact, it is a hand book in the "Conduct of Life." It is a life book, not dry philosophy or metaphysics remote from the problems of life. If a man had no other guide for his spiritual conduct, he would not be the loser, on the contrary, his struggles for light on the Path would be easy, because the book is simplicity itself.

In regard to the many disputes about translation of certain terms and all the fuss those translators have made, I will quote a recent translator and commentator (C. Spurgeon Medhust) who makes the following note appropriately to chapter 2: "A lotus pond will serve as an illustration of the difference between the holy sages and the younger members of the race. Covered with broad green leaves and brilliant blooms, it irresistibly attracts child-souls. They wade into the water, sink in the slime, and desperately struggle for the fragile petals; but the sages, their elder brethren, remain quietly on the bank, always alert to aid any who requires assistance, content to admire, content to enjoy without desiring to possess, yet actually owning the flowers more truly than the struggling crowd in the slimy pond. We are feeblest when we are grasping." The child-souls are the noisy and ignorant translators who "know all about it," yet never even know the A B C of the Inner Life. Let me for a moment drop the thread of my subject and ask you to notice these words of the quotation just read: "The sage i.e., content to enjoy, without desiring to possess." What sorrow we do bring upon ourselves when we rudely rush in, into "the garden of the gods" to pluck flowers, which we vainly think we own, because we have torn them off. In how many ways is that done? Hereafter try to enjoy beauty without possessing it!

I shall now attempt to give you a summary of the doctrines of the book, but I shall leave the word Tao untranslated for the present, because the word means so much and I shall devote several chapters to it. But that some image may stand now before your mind, I will say that the word means both Nature, Logos, the Word and Reason, and also the Way, the Truth and the Life; it may also be translated both Deity and God. Keep these meanings in mind and you may profit by the following, which is a general summary of the Tao-Teh-King, leaving the word Tao untranslated. Tao existed as a perfect, but incomprehensible Being, before heaven and earth were; is immaterial and immeasurable, invisible and inaudible; is mysterious, yet manifest, without shape or form; is supersensuous and hidden from our eyes; is incapable of being named or denned; and the book says, "One needs not to peep through his window to see Tao, Tao is not there. The farther one goes away from himself the less he knows." Tao is in ourselves first of all. This then is Tao as unmanifested. But Tao is also manifested. Hear: "Tao is the external foundation of all things; is the universal progenitor of all beings and only capable of being named by means of the works. But he who would gain a knowledge of Tao's nature and attributes must first set himself free from all earthly desires. Unless he can do that, he shall not be able to penetrate the material veil which interposes between him and Tao. Tao is only revealed to those who are free from desires. He who regulates his actions by Tao will become one with Tao. Tao is the source from which all things come into existence- and to which all things return- and Tao is the means through whom this takes place. Tao being eternal and absolutely free, has no wants or desires, is eternally at rest but never idle, does not grow old, is omnipresent, immutable and self-determined, loves all things and does not act as a ruler. Because Tao creates, preserves, nourishes and protects all things, Tao is glorified for this beneficence and held in high honor." You notice that all this is about Being and Not-Being; the profoundest subject we can discuss.

Tao is both the beyond and also the present. Again, Tao is the foundation of the highest morality. Tao alone bestows and makes perfect, gives peace and is the universal refuge, the good man's treasure, the bad man's deliverer and the pardoner of guilt. Here again, is Tao in a new aspect; in the aspect of the moral power in the world, or as the judge and savior. Is not all this glorious? Do you wonder that my interest in the book is ever increasing. Surely you will wish to hear more about this book and its messages on Teh or Virtue. Teh, or conduct, or virtue, is the exemplification of Tao, the realization of Tao, Tao brought into life. I will now supplement this description, which is put together from accurately translated sentences from the Tao-Teh-King, by another general description of Tao drawn from Laotzse's famous disciple Kwang-zse. It is in the form of an instruction given by a teacher. It is a most practical instruction and Tao is defined in relation to immortality and the endless life. I shall say something about it after having read the instructions.

"Come and I will tell you about the perfect Tao. Its essence is surrounded with the deepest obscurity; its highest reach is in darkness and silence. There is nothing to be seen, nothing to be heard. When it holds the spirit in its arms in stillness, then the bodily form will of itself become correct. You must be still, you must be pure, not subjecting your body to toil, not agitating your vital forces, then you may live long. When your eyes see nothing, your ears hear nothing, and your mind knows nothing, your spirit will keep your body, and the body will live long. Watch over that which is within you, shut up the avenues that connect you with that which is external, much knowledge is pernicious. I will proceed with you to the summit of the 'Great Light' where we come to the bright and expanding (element); I will enter with you the gate of the dark and depressing element. There heaven and earth have their controllers, there the Yin and Yang have their repositories. Watch over and keep your body, and all things will of themselves give it vigor. I maintain the (original) unity (of these elements). In this way I have cultivated myself for 1,200 years and my bodily form knows no decay." (The translation is Legge's in "Sacred Books of the East.")

Evidently Tao is here transcribed as immortality and the endless life, but you must not forget that this is not from the Tao-Teh-King, but a product of Taozseism or the schools that founded their teachings upon the Tao-Teh-King. However, the Taozeists deducted this teaching of longevity from the master's book, hence it may well be considered to be in it. Now, I will attempt to explain some points of this "instruction," which may have been clear to the Chinese pupil of that day, but certainly is not to us of today. In the first place, the teacher takes the pupil to "the deepest obscurity," to "darkness and silence." That means he takes the disciple beyond himself, beyond the world of time and space, and, that "beyond" is always described for obvious reasons in negative terms, such as the "deepest obscurity," "darkness and silence." And literally, of course, there is nothing to be seen nor heard, because the state is beyond the senses, such senses as those which make seeing and hearing. Coming into that high state, "the spirit lies in the arms of stillness;" a poetic expression for the fact, that the spirit now is there where there is stillness, because no motion or change of any kind takes place nor can take place, simply because it is the immovable world, the primal world, the world that is perfect rest in itself, but from which all motion proceeds. In former chapters I have defined this world and its conditions in detail.

After stating this, the teacher admonishes the pupil to be still and pure, that is an important injunction. He who is still is the powerful one, and he only because, in stillness the inherent power is not fretted away; we are self-controlled and that is power. The pupil is also admonished to be pure, that is, he is to be sincere or simple. The meaning of simplicity I developed in the fourth and fifth chapters of this course. If the pupil is pure, or, which is the same, single minded, he is, as a matter of course, in stillness. Stillness is not possible without purity, and, on the other hand, stillness produces purity. No man is strong unless he is pure, and no one can be pure without being strong. The two qualities condition one another. Next, the teacher says to his disciple under those conditions just described, "your spirit will keep your body" and "the body will live long." In other words, the teacher has shown the pupil how to manage to live long. Is that an object in itself- to live long? Nay, certainly not! The only justifiable reason for living long is to be of use to ourselves and to others. For no other reason should we wish to live long. What do I mean by being of use to ourselves? I mean, that we should wish to live long in order to recover all the results we have attained in former lives; results which now lie more or less dormant in most people. Unless those results are recovered by an awakening, our present incarnation goes for naught or may even be a hindrance to us. By being of use to ourselves I mean then: (1) That we awaken. (2) That we recover our buried treasures of spiritual life. (3) That we proceed further on the Path. As a matter of course, we cannot proceed unless we have something to travel on, and that which we travel on is our past. The teacher speaks of this last point, when he says to the disciple: "I will proceed with you to the summit of the 'Great Light.'" And, finally, the teacher repeats his injunction, "Watch over and keep your body, and all things will of themselves give it vigor." I need not now stop to speak on this final admonition. In the third chapter, I spoke extensively on a rational treatment of the senses, "the flesh," so called. All that which I then said openly or more or less veiled relates to this subject now brought up.

We will now return to the subject in hand and will let Laotzse himself speak. The master himself has said something equally as startling and, of course, something that is utterly incomprehensible to people who are ignorant of the occult powers which Tao gives. Laotzse in the 50th chapter writes: "I have heard it said that a man who is good at taking care of his life may travel over the country without meeting a rhinoceros or a tiger, and may enter an armed host without fearing their steel. The rhinoceros finds in him no place to insert his horn; the tiger finds no place to fix his claw, the weapon finds no place to receive its blade. And why is this? It is because he is beyond the reach of death." I have no time to tell you all the silly things that have been said by the ignorant about this. You yourself will understand that the pure and good are always protected, and, that one becomes immortal when all desires are killed. Normally the sage escapes the wild animal because he is in truth and they are not; their ferocity and thirst for blood is not truth. And because the sage is good, or partakes of God, the evil cannot touch him, evil has no real power. It is as Kwang-zse said: "The sage is a spiritual being. If the ocean were boiling he would not feel hot. If all the rivers were frozen hard, he would not feel cold." The mystery is further explained by Su Cheh who says: "Nature knows neither life nor death. Its going forth we call life, and its coming in we call death." The sage belongs neither to those who pursue the path of life, nor to those who pursue the path of death, he is beyond life and death and therefore invulnerable; cannot be touched by death. All this was about Tao. I shall not say anything about Teh. I have already summarized Teh in two former chapters in which I described it as "Simplicity" and the "Sage." I shall, however, come back to it as we proceed. I will tell you in the words of Goethe what to do with this book:

> "Once through the forest
> Alone I went;
> To seek for nothing
> My thoughts were bent.
>
> I saw i' the shadow
> A flower stand there;
> As stars it glisten'd,
> As eyes 'twas fair.
>
> I sought to pluck it-
> It gently said:
> 'Shall I be gather'd
> Only to fade?"
>
> "With all its roots
> I dug it with care,
> And took it home
> To my garden fair.
>
> In silent corner
> Soon it was set;
> There grows it ever,
> There blooms it yet."

THE INNER LIFE AND THE TAO TEH KING

This is what you shall do. Take it home and plant it again, it will then flower forever. To pluck it off as an ornament about which you may prate and pride yourself is only killing it. Only too many treat the books, the ancients left us, that way. They are to them merely like flowers in the buttonhole. In the second chapter I spoke of a young student who wished to add one more item to her study and chose the Inner Life to be that study, and, while she was looking out of the window, her teacher vanished. I want you to take warning from that story, too. Merely to study the Tao-Teh-King as one of several other studies will not be any more either than a flower in the buttonhole that soon fades. Nay, you must transplant this book into your own home, into your heart, root and all, and, to do that you must go out into the Open to learn how nature works. This book is not merely a book as thousand others. It looks like a book. We call it a book from its appearance just as we call flowers flowers, because we have become accustomed to do so. We have lost their language and can no more speak to them or hold conversations with them about the warmth they feel at their roots, or answer the whisperings of their leaves to the winds of morning and evening, when mother earth changes her garments from light to dark, or, when she says her morning prayers to the Sun. And that is why we call them flowers and think we have said all that can be said to characterize them. Our fairyland is lost.

Most people have lost what they never really possessed and yet their better self followed them always and called. To avoid this catastrophe I advise a study and a life according to this book out of doors, that is, under the guidance of nature.

The book is a series of nature notes; it is nature mysticism. It is a song that comes from nature's heart and not from any university. It is nature, or spirit made visible. You may also turn the sentence round, and say that the book is spirit showing us invisible nature. Both sentences are true and the study may be begun either by starting in spirit and ending in nature or starting in nature and ending in spirit. If you understand the last chapter on

"Simplicity and the Sage," you will do as I have done and still do. I study this so called book in the Open. It is only in the open that we see spirit and nature to be One. Some future day, when you and I shall see a new heaven and a new earth, we will be playing the sentences of this book on instruments, and its accords will bring us in harmony with the root of existence. I am not saying this merely to utter some extravagant thought. I have had some experience with Chinese thought that warrants my expressions. I shall speak more of this in future chapters. Take the book home!

CHAPTER VII

LONGEVITY

In the last chapter, I quoted a learned Taoist on Tao as Longevity, and I tried to explain the master's instructions to the pupil- all, except one sentence, which I left for this chapter. That sentence was: "When it (Tao) holds the Spirit in its arms in Stillness, then the bodily form will of itself become correct." I will now try to elucidate what "Stillness" is. What I call my "elucidation" will appear to you as a roundabout talk and not as a direct elucidation. It cannot be anything else because the subject is transcendental. I think, however, it will be an elucidation and I hope so. In the six preceding chapters I have again and again quoted mystic authors about the necessity of overcoming desires, lusts, passions, or whatever all those wild and blind forces of Nature be called, which are in the way of our development in the spiritual life and which only too often destroy us. It is now high time that I speak of other disturbing elements, elements far more dangerous than Nature's wild play with us. These other disturbing elements, I shall now speak of, have their very roots in our Ego, in our own will. Lusts and passions are merely parts of our make up and are not fundamental; they are mere forms of our objective existence; they are only external to us; they are residents of the flesh, and merely visitors on the soul's domain.

I shall now lay special stress upon the conflict in aim and end there is between mind and inclinations, between our spiritual will and our physical will, the two wills of St. Paul, with which most of you are familiar. In short, I shall lay stress upon a fact well known to those who are on the Path, or the Narrow Way, so called, namely this, that volitionally we are in conflict with ourselves; or theologically speaking we are in sin. I shall also try to point out how this conflict arises and can be brought to an end, or, how we, to use theological language, can be saved. This subject is of

uttermost importance, whatever creed one may hold. It is a
fundamental question for us all. Let me tell you now, right here at
the outset, that this inner conflict I shall speak of and will illustrate
in various ways, this inner conflict was unknown to all those
peoples who lie outside that parallelogram I described in the last
chapter. The conflict arises or comes into history at the moment
the new cycle is ushered in, and it governs the whole period of this
our cycle. By and by in other chapters you shall hear Laotzse
describe the "paradisaical" conditions, if I may so call them, that
prevailed in what he calls "the ancient days," or in the previous
cycle, an absolute proof that these conflicts we now know, and
which mankind has known since his day, did not exist before his
time.

The vedic writings do not know this conflict as we know
it. Perhaps there is a glimmer of it with Zoroaster. But Buddha was
fully aware of the conflict and preached it. The Gita also knows
about it. Jesus preached it, and some of the Christians have talked
themselves deaf, dumb and blind about it, yet they never
understood it fully. It was only very late that the Greeks
discovered the problem. Homer knew what "folly" was, but not
what "sin" was. Aeschylos and Sophocles knew something about
"penalties," so called, or, the karma that follows upon
disobedience to our Higher Self, but could not formulate the
principle. Not even Plato came to the bottom of the problem. In
spite of all the talk for nearly two thousand years in Christendom
about sin and salvation, I do not think it has yet been understood
how it is that we sin, nor how we may be saved. That a devil is the
cause of our sin is folklore and no more. Children may believe it,
but not mature minds. I shall not pretend to know the final
solution, but I have lived with the problem before me since a time
when many of you were not yet born, or, at any rate, were too
young to have discovered it. And I have had some experiences that
may be of use to others. Those experiences, in the form of tales
and poems, I shall present to you, in part, in this chapter, and in
part in the next. Now, then, to the subject.

THE INNER LIFE AND THE TAO TEH KING

That which I now say will answer to the experience of most people- in some degree. The strongest and most individual people know more about it than the weak and those that pass through life like sleepwalkers. Those that know nothing of these things are either children, saints or beasts. There was a time when yon began to assert yourself, began to have your own will, as you called it; and there was a time when you said or thought that you knew the truth of life better than your parents, friends, or teachers. In those states you involuntarily (or voluntarily) broke in such a way with your antecedents and your betters, that the break perhaps never has healed. An antagonism entered into your existence, which has left a permanent disturbance, a disturbance which must be distressing to a normal mind. Such splits, breaks or diremptions may in some be so deep that a permanent pain remains ever afterwards, and they may be deadly. You will naturally ask many questions relating to and about these breaks, such as about their origin, their psychological nature. I will try to meet some of these questions. The others must wait till their turn comes. At present I limit myself to a most characteristic feature of that cycle which begins with the time of Laotzse and his immediate disciples, and I say that the characteristic feature is this, that the principles of form, law, order, truth, are revealed or laid bare, and are discovered and realized by man. Of course, there was form, law, order, truth in Nature before this time, but the human mind was not so constituted reflectively that it could grasp or formulate these principles. I take it for granted that these terms, form, law, order, truth, are understood. If I am mistaken, let me state how I use them. I say they are various aspects of the same idea, and that they express the manner of appearance of substance, or, that Something which underlies the phenomenon. Take an illustration. Here is a silver trumpet. In its case, the silver is substance and the appearance of the silver in this case is the form (not the shape) of the instrument we call trumpet. It is not important as regards the form, or the trumpet itself, whether the substance be silver, gold, copper or brass. Trumpets are made of any of these metals, but it is most essential that the form in which the metal is cast or hammered, is after a certain fashion and for a certain use, because the fashion and use determine whether it is a trumpet or another instrument.

In other words, the form becomes the essential and the substance is not the essential. Again, this form, called a trumpet, must be in a certain shape in order to be a trumpet and not a clarinet, for instance. But that is another matter; I only say this to call attention to the difference between form and shape. Take another illustration. You and I are all in the form of man and that is our determining quality. We are made of substances physically not different from the substances in animals. Hence you see, as regards ourselves, as it was with the trumpet, the form is the essential. That we differ among ourselves as to shape is another matter. From this it will appear that form is the manner of appearance. And I want to add that we in philosophy often ignore substance, and only value form, and that confusion therefore often arises. That is my use of form. I might also use the words law, order, truth, for the same purpose, only in varying aspects of the same subject. With this note, I return to my subject, and when I now say, as I shall say, that the principles of form, law, order, truth, first appear in the cycle that begins in the time of Laotzse, you will understand that mankind at that period for the first time discovered what form, law, order, truth are cosmically and psychologically, and in contradistinction to substance and positive laws laid down for the conduct of life; two conceptions which did not give us that power, which you shall hear me say follows, the discovery of the principles mentioned.

Now, then, to my exposition. These principles arose in man's mind about five hundred years (or a little more) before Christ, and were fully established as ruling powers about five hundred years after Christ. It took mankind about a thousand years to add that intelligent element to its mentality. I said these principles arose. They did not arise as a growth simply, their appearance is so sudden and unconnected with the foregone state, that their appearance looks more like a gift, a divine gift. I usually call them a gift. For proof, you need only look into the literature that is left and to examine the extant monuments from the previous cycle. It would indeed be most instructive and interesting if I now pointed out to you the nature of those literatures and monuments, but I cannot enter upon such archaeological details. My present object is not archaeological or historical, but moral and practical. Both among Semites and Aryans you hear of law books, but they are not of the nature I speak of; they are not of cosmic character, nor psychological. They are formulas for the conduct of life, sociological edicts, but not thought-forms, as I will call them for the present, not revelations of what we call philosophy and art, but ought to call Theosophy or God-wisdom, because these thought-forms are revelations of the constitution of the cosmos. I call them thought-forms for the present, as a most suitable term, but you must understand that these thought-forms stretch in variety from Laotzse's Tao to St. Paul's "gifts of the spirit" denned and described in Corinthians, Chap. 12. The term is therefore very elastic and contains much more than merely "thinking."

These thought-forms are declarations, that, besides will, there is in Nature and in Man another power just as mighty as will, and because this other power is intelligent, seeing, and not dumb or blind, so much more superior to will. These thought-forms given to or revealed to man gave man from that moment a tremendous influence in cosmic affairs. In virtue of this peculiar light, man, who before was un-free, now could say "I" to himself as never before and was able to throw the force of this will against the course of events and thus mold them to suit himself. Before this event man was neither conscious of himself nor conscious of what he could do with himself or for himself. After that revelation man could and can now say as Pascal has formed the expression and done it so well: "Man is but a reed, weakest in Nature, but a reed which thinks. Were the universe to crush him, man would still be more noble than that which has slain him, because he knows that he dies. The universe knows nothing of this."

THE INNER LIFE AND THE TAO TEH KING

I feel tempted to add "and this knowledge and thought crushes the universe. The universe is as naught against that thought, that knowledge." Do you grasp the mightiness of man, his thought and his knowledge when in conscious possession of that wonderful power? Pascal's words are a formulation of the difference between the universe and man and it is indicated what his tremendous power is: Thought. Like everything else, this power can be misused. When misused, those breaks I talked about arise. Before I now proceed to illustrate the breaks by stories, tales, I will show the law by which the persons of my stories should have acted, and, if they had done so, there would have been no break.

That law, formulated at this same historic period, is found in the Gita in the instructions given to Arjuna. Arjuna is perfectly conscious of his own power to have his own will, and he wishes to have it, at the same time that duty demands that he shall obey and destroy the usurper of the oppressed land, though to do so involves the killing of both friends and relatives. Krishna teaches him that he must drop all fears and personal interests and carry out the duty imposed upon him as warrior and prince and realize that it is Ishvara, who is both lord and law, who is the doer and not Arjuna. Arjuna must realize that he must fight without passion or desire, without anger and hatred and without fears. This is the Gita. It is the formulation of the law for men of active and combative tempers. The formulation lacks totally any and all expressions that could place it parallel to the Sermon on the Mount. And that is its weakest point. The little book "The Voice of the Silence" supplies most of the defects. The same law put in forms applicable to us, to you and to me, will be something like this. Life is not ours; we are not its originators nor responsible for events or the outcome of events. Under no circumstances must we judge according to our own inclinations what ought to be done, but simply do or not do, awaiting the course of developments, which will show us what and how to do. And to this I may add that developments will come quickly in moments of doubt; they will not let us wait long. I may also say that they will come in the way best suitable for us. Now you know how hard it is for us to believe this and wait. How impetuous we are, and why? Because we have that tremendous power I spoke of before, and wish to use it, wish to satisfy our own vanity, to prove how mighty we are, all because of ignorance till instructed.

I will now tell you some stories to illustrate how we act and how the law works. First, I will give you a prose rendering of Schiller's profound poem, *Das verschleierte Bild zu Sais*. A young Greek, burning with thirst for knowledge, came to Sais in Egypt to study with the priesthood and explore the secrets of the land of Romitu. It happened one day that the hierophant brought him to a lonely temple where the youth beheld a veiled statue, of which the high priest said: "That is Truth." The impulsive student at once demanded to know why he was not brought here before:

> "When I am striving after Truth alone,
> Seek'st thou to hide that very Truth from me?"
> "The Godhead's self alone can answer thee"
> Replied the hierophant, "Let no rash mortal
> Disturb this veil," said he, "till raised by me..."

The boy from Hellas could not understand so singular a command. There was Truth, only covered with a thin gauze, and he not allowed to raise it! Inquisitively he asked his wise guide:

> "And thou
> Hast never ventur'd, then, to raise the veil?"
> "I? Truly not! I never even felt
> The least desire." "Is 't possible? If I
> Were sever 'd from the Truth by nothing else
> Than this thin gauze"- "And a divine decree,"
> His guide broke in. "Far heavier than thou think'st
> Is this thin gauze, my son. Light to thy hand
> It may be but most weighty to thy conscience."

THE INNER LIFE AND THE TAO TEH KING

An insatiable desire consumed the youth. At night he could not sleep. In the day he sought his way to the isolated temple; he found no rest anywhere. One night he lost control of himself and found his way into the temple. Suddenly he stood in the sanctuary facing the veiled statue. The goddess stood before him more mysteriously than ever. In the dim moonlight, which fell from an opening above, he gradually approached the statue, till with a sudden bound he reached it with the cry:

> "Whatever is hid behind, I'll raise the veil."
> And then he shouted: "Yes! I will behold it!"
> "Behold it!"
> Repeated in mocking tone the distant echo.

He spoke, and true to his word he lifted the veil. What did he see? Probably nothing but the statue of Isis. He was found unconscious next morning at the foot of the statue. To the priests he only said:

> "Woe to that man who wins the Truth by guilt,
> For Truth so gain'd will ne'er reward its owner."

This young Greek, evidently a man of high order, was perfectly right in his search for wisdom and in going for it to Egypt, but he had not up to the time of his transgression discovered that the main lesson in all temple methods and for him was not learning, but obedience. He was an embodiment of self-assertion. Learning brings conflict and unrest, because it keeps us on this plane of life. Obedience to our Higher Self brings that stillness about which Qvang-zse spoke, and of which you read in the last chapter, a stillness in which Tao holds our "spirit in its arms," a stillness which gives our form its perfectness. Learning is all very well for its purposes, but I have already in another chapter told you how little mystics care for it, and told you that learning is not of the heart or will, but only of the brain, and therefore not the method that produces heart culture, or, which is the same, the

Inner Life. Only heart can teach heart; only will can control will. Intellect and learning are strangers here and do not know the right knock. Spiritual life moves on a curve of love, not on a straight line of logic, and the magic chain that binds men to men and to Divinity, is forged by love and spirit. If this young man had learned obedience and lived in obedience to his Higher Self he would have been brought into that stillness, in which our grosser self burns up, in which no physical instincts are aroused, and no sense of cupidity stirred, and nothing sways our selfishness; a stillness that is pure white flame and spiritual tranquility, a stillness which Laotzse (XVI) says "returns us to the root" or origin of existence; a stillness in which Isis would have raised the veil according to promise and thereby also lifted his longings into an eternal transmutation and bliss. By practice of silence and solitude, stillness would have come. That which to us in our moral and spiritual life is silence and solitude is, in the cosmic life, called stillness. In other words, silence and solitude are subjective conditions, stillness is objective. What a difference between this young Greek and that beggar I have told you about in a former chapter and whom Tauler met. This young Greek is an awful illustration upon "taking" before time has come; upon "having one's own will," upon self assertion, and thereby coming into that dreadful conflict I spoke of and said that it was much more serious than any conflict with lust. You heard from his own mouth how little he knew of non-action (Wu-Wei) or Inner Life, and you heard the awful confession of the dying man. What application dare I make as regards yourself? I dare not make any, but I may ask if not in some such way some of you may have brought yourself into a suffering that now tortures you?

But the break may be only intellectual, as it is with many. People simply break with the ideas of childhood, instead of outgrowing them and substitute for those ideas some crude and ill understood scientific notions; notions that contain no life marrow to fill their bones and hence leave them weak. These people are ever afterwards incapable of anything definite and become a burden to themselves and others, but they are not sinners; they are only in confusion, and that is bad enough. Some one will now say that if we let this great, wonderful and also dangerous power alone, we would be better off and they will hypnotize themselves into that belief. That, too, is false and I will demonstrate it by another story. The story is called "The Love of Indra" and is found in the Ramayana. I give it in a slightly abridged form as translated by Mrs. Frederika Richardson in her "The Iliad of the East." This is the story:

"There were some young maidens standing just on the threshold of life; for childhood is the vestibule merely; it is hung with pretty pictures. Just at this point paused our young maidens, half awed by the tumult, half fascinated by all the movement and the light. It chanced that at this moment the gaze of Indra fell on them, and beholding them, so beautiful and so pure, he loved them. Flashing earthward, in a form of fire, he kissed them on the lips, and left them with blanched cheeks, and eyes aflame. They knew a god had been with them, and thrilled them by his touch, and yet had winged his way back to his High Home ere they had tasted aught of passion, save its first sudden pain. So, with a fever on them, and a vague desire in their innocent breasts, seeking Whom they knew not, What they could not say, they wandered forth; and Love, who breathes only in the upper air, led them to a Hilly Country, where the large stars seemed smiling near. And there, still far beyond them, but looking down with deeply passionate eyes, they saw the great God, Indra; and he held out his large arms, wooing them to the fire of his embrace. The hearts of the young maidens failed them. Fain had each been to turn her back; but her soul within of a sudden found its wings, and bore her, in a rush of superhuman ecstasy, to the arms of the enamored God. Thus, ignorant of the bitter cost to mortals, who press up, with quivering lips and heaving breasts, to meet the desire of the Sons of Heaven, did they receive the 'sorrowful great gift,' the Love of Indra. Our little maidens, having no previous knowledge of all an immortal's love involved, fretted against the crown Indra had laid on them; because, although it wrapped them in a light, it scorched and tore their smooth young brows, and mingled with its beams of gold the lifeblood of the wearers. 'We are faint,' they said, 'and weary! The bloom has faded from our cheeks, and all the youth of our hearts is dying! Our eyes are tired with beauty! Tired- and light is but a splendid pain. Our hearts are spent with passion, this eternal rapture will destroy us. Oh, that we could rest! Rest, rest, from the fever of our lives, ere it exhaust our power, and we die!' So, one day that this longing for rest overcame them, they strayed from the mountain of Meru, where the Gods quaff sparkling nectar, and hearken to the song that dies not."

"With their hands to their ears the faithless brides of Indra fled from the witching strains, and sought the sheltered valleys, where life is calm, and men and women pass slowly through the stages of time; marking progress merely by the succession of season, and dying, at length, because they have dwelt too long, not lived too much. And in their wanderings they came upon the country of the Uttarakurus. Oh, that was a pleasant land, and surely just the spot where our weary fugitives might find the peace they longed for. There were no extremes of heat nor cold, no excess of light nor depth of gloom; all was equable and tempered calm, like the inhabitants themselves, whose dispositions were inaccessible to all violent emotions, which overstrain a delicate frame. There was no need for any exertion either; for in a wood, hung from the boughs of the trees all that the heart could desire; jewels, and raiment, and luxurious couches, and delicious viands of every description; one had only to walk thither and gather them. The flowers in this country were of gold, so were the mountains; the rivulets were so choked up with gold that they slept between their banks, and did not attempt to sing. The women who dwelt there were all youthful and lovely; the men were all courteous, and learned in saying pleasant things; old age, or disease, or poverty, or suffering, or grief, were not known here, it is probable that all such things were soaked away out of the land by the black and terrible river, that swept with its sinister floods the borders of the

Land of Gold, and rolled, muttering ever words of menace and despair- that were not understood by the smiling Uttarakurus. Amid this luxurious people the pale wanderers paused; and, struck by their strange beauty and their wanness, born of an ardor unknown to any here, the inhabitants flocked around them, saying, 'Stay with us and share our lives.' Then, at first, a pang of unsatisfied longing held back the souls where Indra had set his love. But, little by little, each sought to reason herself out of the memory of those rapturous moments spent up among the mountains. 'Help me to live it down!' cried out each weary heart; and the appealing hands went forth, seeking for some stay. They met the smooth palms of the bland Uttarakurus. 'Let us lead you along the path of pleasure,' they said to the brides of Indra. But the beloved of the Sun god found no delight in the golden country, nor in the wood, nor in the company of the smiling Uttarakurus. 'Better to have died in a god's embrace,' they moaned, 'than to crawl through the long days in this hateful city.' But they had made their choice; and Mahendra, god of the Firmament, has no welcome for renegades! In the heart of the Golden Land his curse found them out. 'Have ye forgotten,' he cried to them, 'how, in the lone Hill Country, ye lay awhile on my breast, fainting almost with rapture, while the large stars were smiling near, and the night hung, still, around? Have ye forgotten how, pale and beautiful, ye stepped through the groves of Nandana; and how light robed ye in splendor; and the stars I had laid in your bosoms glowed there, and flamed with a glory that shamed the pale orbs of heaven? Why have ye thrown by your crowns, whose gems flashed through the ages, witnesses to the past and the future that ye were chosen as the spouses of Indra? What though your slight heads were bowed, and your fragile strength near broken; was not my arm around you? Who would not totter and fail, to be upheld by the amorous Indra? What though your spirits growth were too swift for your delicate frames? As guerdon for your shortened lives, my love had made ye immortal. But ye have loved ease better than glory. O, foolish ones; ease can never be yours. Ye have tasted an Immortal's love. And your glory ye have abandoned. Dwell, then, as Exiles and Strangers in this town ye have preferred to the mountains; and, since ye have dreaded the tempest, endure the torments of the calm.'"

"And so, in the city of the Uttarakurus, dwell these pale women with the lustrous eyes, who were once the beloved of Indra; and they hold no friendly intercourse nor have sympathy with any; each morning gives fresh birth to the wild desire, that gnaws their hearts, each night finds them in a dead despair; for the pitiless curse of Mahendra drives them down to their unhonored graves!"

Here again it is self-assertion, not non-action (Wu-Wei) that creates the trouble. These girls had no faith and yet they were in the presence of the Great Love. Having been chosen by Indra, they were supposed to be giant spirits and able to live in that sphere of light and life, which is Indra's domain. Had they been common girls, their faithlessness would not have been surprising nor their punishment so severe. They should have allowed themselves to be burned up. Indra's stinging reproach accuses them rightly of disobedience to their call. Nature's method with common people is essentially different from Indra's. Those educated by nature run their full course before they discover her method with them. For such, the rule is that not till emotions have had their full course will they rise in intellectual light. They are like firebrands which, burning without flame, are merely smoking annoyances and not lights. The very moment an emotion rises to white light condition, it becomes the savior of its offer.

Laotzse says apropos (XL) "Stillness overcomes heat." Surely before long these girls would have discovered what Laotzse also says: (XXVI) "Stillness lies back of all motion." Even we, without being called by Mahenda, may climb a mountain and discover that stillness is there and not in the valley. How much more those girls, so favored! Take the story literally or symbolically; either way it is full of lessons on my subject of the inner conflicts of the Ego. Everywhere it is action, actions, and again actions of our own, namely, on the plane of this life, that cause our diremptions, that split our personality in two, that breaks off our harmony with our Higher Self. If we let the Higher Self in us act, this will not happen. If we let our Higher Self act, we shall be in stillness and Tao will take our "spirit in its arms." Do not misunderstand this point on non-action, Wu-Wei. The meaning is not the idea involved in the washerwoman's hope. Have you heard of her:

> "Who always was tired,
> Who lived in a house where no help was hired.
> And whose last words on earth were:
> Where no sweeping ain't done, nor churning nor sewing,
> And everything there will be just to my wishes,
> For there they don't eat, and there's no washing of dishes;
> And though anthems are constantly ringing,
> I, having no voice, will get rid of the singing.
> Don't mourn for me now, and don't mourn for me ever,
> For I'm going to do nothing for ever and ever."

This is not what Inner-Life people understand by "Non action" or "Stillness." They mean by Non-action, Wu-Wei, the withdrawing from all this world's interests and activities, all of which lie on a plane of life they do not want to have anything to do with, because their longings are not satisfied with such interests or activties. Their hearts pant for the Living God, as does the deer for the water brook. The Inner-Life people seek stillness or such a condition beyond the senses, where no noise or sound heard by the senses is possible, a stillness which is the kernel and core of the cosmos. In my first illustration I had a man and his intellect in the center. In this second story which you have just heard I had woman and her emotions in the center. They both fell because they said No! to obedience or the law of their life. The man's law of life is intellectual, and in due course of time his life swings around to its opposite: emotion, and the two complete him. The woman's law of life is emotion, and in due course of time her life swings around to its opposite, intellect; and the two complete her. This is the normal evolution. But when the breaks, the splits, the diremptions occur, an abnormal condition sets in and as my stories told, the results are frightful. Would we be better off if we did not make use of that tremendous power of ours! Perhaps we would not suffer then? That also would be a mistake and I will show it by a story of my own, modeled on a few elements I have borrowed from the Hungarian. I have named my story "The Copyist." It runs as follows:

Our friend is a copyist in a government office. Like everybody else, he wanted to go to a certain masquerade, but unlike everybody else that went, he had nothing wherewith to buy a costume. He had an idea. He sold himself to a Jew to carry advertisements through the halls and ball rooms. And so, fitted out in a gorgeous dress, full of announcements, he partook in the revel- after a fashion. Soon he found himself the target for all the wit, good humor and ill will of the assembly. Poor devil, he stood it for a while; but soon, too soon for him, he found out what it is to sell oneself for mercenary purposes, even though one might see the masquerade of life. Behind every masque, it appeared to him, a pair of eyes followed him. The advertisements sewed into his costume seemed to burn like hot coals, and excited his highly overwrought nerve-system and completely prostrated him; his throat seemed to be on fire; his eyes grew inflamed and unsteady. He began to feel as though he were about to be attacked with brain fever.

At last he managed to find his way out from the hilarious crowd, and got into a distant cabinet, to an alcove turned into a kind of flower-grove by greenery and sweet-smelling flowers. The light was reflected by transparent needles, like stalactites, hanging from the ceiling, and it fell brightly upon a basin filled with fish of brilliant colors. The soft murmuring of a little fountain readily put him into a state of trance, and he dreamed. A large leaf fanned gently his fever-hot forehead, but only gloomy thoughts would rise in his sick brain. Ah, yonder they amused themselves and were almost lost in the whirl of passionate enjoyment. But here was he, not only hungry and exhausted both mentally and physically- not so much, however, from the past few moments of excitement- nay, back of this hour lay years and years of unmanly indulgences, and recollections now arose in his mind, none of which could infuse any self-respect into his weak heart, or bring fresh thoughts to his withered soul. Poor fellow, only once, this one time, had he tried to gain admission to what appeared as the ideal brightness of life, in which so many seemed to live and enjoy themselves, and here was he, an outcast. Dimly he saw it; he had gained admission as an uncalled one, and by dishonorable means! Everyone could see it, every piece of his costume bore the advertisements of the Jew, Abraham Trailles, No. 32 Fools lane. What was there to do but to return to the meanness and low life where he belonged and for a few years more drag himself along to an unhonored grave.

Suddenly he felt himself touched upon the shoulder. Half sleeping, half beside himself, he looked up, and beheld: on the large leaf over his head he saw a beautiful woman, sweet as a sylph, slender and tiny, but gracefully strong, and in a dress of pure, fine linen. He noticed particularly a large fan in her hand. A pink masque covered the upper part of her face and left uncovered a mouth of exquisite forms and lines. She seemed a fay indeed. He gazed upon her with admiration and attraction, and asked gently: "Who art thou, sweet maiden?" "Dost thou not know me?" she replied, and removed the masque. It seemed to him he had seen that brow before; those eyes and their dreamy looks. Had he not often unconsciously thrown his mind into the mystic realms of the ideal world and there beheld this ideal of woman: His own personal self. Now she was near him, so near that he might clasp her in his arms. "Dost thou know me now? I played with thee when thou wast little and sung songs for thee. Surely thou canst not have forgotten it. But where didst thou go to? Thou keptest thyself in the house while I picked flowers in the meadows and gathered green leaves in the forest or watched the cuckoo, or listened to the songsters in the trees. Where wast thou while I sat by the brook and the lark hung in the air overhead, ringing out its peals of joy over life? Where wast thou in the time of thy yout?" "Eight hours of the day I spent in the schoolroom and under the whip of the schoolmaster."

"Dost thou remember the day when they sent thee out into the wide, wide world? Dost thou remember that I followed thee and spoke to thee of trusting in me, and I would keep thee and preserve thee? But thou didst forget me when thou earnest to the gay capital. Thou didst lose thyself among the many people and their vanities! I sought thee at thy revels and in thy garret, but thou didst not know me. When thou lookedst upon the beautiful women, I stood before thee, but thou didst prefer flesh and blood to soul. Never, never didst thou come to me!"

"What didst thou do when thou wast young and gay no more, when thou wast poor and miserable, when thou hadst become a ruin to thyself?"

"I worked; I worked; I tried to save myself. Ten hours a day I copied in the office, and at home I copied- I copied always!"

"And now. What dost thou do now?"

"I copy still!"

"And, in the future, what wilst thou do?"

Our friend, the copyist, was fairly startled by that question, and humiliated, too, for he had nothing to answer but to say- "To copy, still!" He burst into tears; he cried the hot tears of remorse. But suddenly, as if in a fit of over-natural energy, he opened his arms and tremblingly exclaimed, "I will love thee, I will embrace thee, I will own thee." Then it happened that the maiden's fan

141

opened wide and covered her face; and lo! he beheld smiling landscapes, youth in its native richness and with its prophecy of love, and the thousand forms of life's beauty and charm, all in harmonious forms and living colors. The vision revivified him, and forgetting himself and his degraded position, like another Faust, he rushed out to embrace this sweet genius, that held the pictures in her hand, the lady who so charmed him. A gentle stroke brought him to his senses. "Stop, my dear Mr. Copyist! To love me! To embrace me! To own me! I fear thou art too old! We have grown apart! Thou are no more young and strong; thy hair has turned gray and thin; thine eyes are no more lustrous and thy soul is withered, thy spirit darkened! Thou art no more fit for love. Know this, that I, thy soul, thy youth, thy personal being, thy Self is no reality, for thou hast not given me life; I am, and must remain to thee a dream, a phantom. Thou hast lost me, though thou never didst possess me!" She disappeared.

Like a madman he rushed into the ballroom to catch her. He set everything in confusion and drove every one aside and frightened all. He was mad. Next day an old doctor stood leaning over a dying man in the hospital of the poorhouse. The dying man was unknown to all around him. Just before he died he was heard to say, "I lost what I never possessed!"

Commentary is hardly necessary. The story explains itself. A copy of that man can be seen all around us. Business life grinds a man into the dust of indifference, and, as if to make his misery so much greater, life gives the flickering taper a whiff of fresh air in the last moment, and the darkness seems so much greater. This copyist is a warning example on not to bury one's gifts in business, that may overwhelm, or in the soil, where they may rust. We have our gifts for use- but not for abuse. It must not be overlooked or ignored that all of these three persons mentioned are people of higher orders. They are of that class which life or nature invites to the university method called heavenliness. They are not of those for whom a common school method of earthliness is enough, because they are not yet ready to quit earth. Nature has two methods by which she educates us. The one, the common school method of earthliness, is applied first and to all, and consists mainly in learning to overcome lusts of all kinds, and in awakening the soul. When the pupil has attained some practice in overcoming lusts and begins to see beyond his own notions, the other is offered, not applied. There is a vast difference here. The first method is applied because it contains a great deal of compulsion. In all our earlier stages of awakening we are not voluntarily active; we learn only because we must. You hear that frequently from people. They tell you that life has made them do so, and forced them to believe so and so. Such expressions clearly show that their progress has not been one conducted by inner love and high aspiration, but has been a result of necessity.

The other method, the one I have called the university method of heavenliness, is offered to those who desire it, not to those who yet see no need of it. Only those desire this method who discover for themselves that there is such a method and who not only can see that the present world is vanity, but whose inner need craves for the Higher, no matter whatever the cost. I look upon the three persons I have used as illustrations as three persons who had come near enough to call for the higher method. Hence it was offered, but- they failed! Now, to come back to what I said in the beginning of the chapter, about the breaks, the splits, the diremption you may have experienced. Like these three persons, you rose in moments beyond yourself both in light and love and you demanded higher light and profounder love. When they were not forthcoming, you stretched out your hand to take "the Kingdom of God" by force like that young Greek, or you gave up and ran away from the greater love offered, like those girls of Indra, or you wasted your resources in false loves and dissipations like the copyist and as only too many do, who believe themselves geniuses before they are out of the mind's swaddling clothes. The hope these three had for stillness or for a world that cannot be moved was not based upon obedience to their Higher Self, but was simply momentary fancy. Hence the failure and suffering, when the higher method of heavenliness was offered them.

Beware! Ask not of Spirit to be trained! Learn first the principles of obedience to higher Self; first then will the revelation of those principles of form, law, order and truth be a blessing.

Beware, when the test comes! Do not act before the right moment, when Isis raises the veil! Do not fear the great love! Do not ignore the repeated calls! Beware, when the critical moment comes!

In spite of all dangers, we must develop that thought-form or those principles I called form, law, order, truth. We must develop them; if we do not, we never come to conscious possession of ourselves, or of those principles which are offered so freely to us in this cycle, and not coming to conscious possession of ourselves or of those principles is a calamity I cannot find word for. It means the loss of the thousands of years of this our cycle- a loss which perhaps to those ignorant of the nature of the loss means little, but which to those who have even a slight idea of the value of such time is an irreparable loss- who knows if there ever be another opportunity? Who knows? Without swinging out into the immensity of space and the thousands of years, think only of the poor copyist and his fate. How can he repair his loss of that which he really never possessed?

There is no psychological ground in him on which he can work and where is it to come from in the future? We cannot imagine his salvation, his restoration, on any rational basis. I am now where I leave the subject of this chapter for the present. I shall continue it in next chapter and hope to finish it. But I have yet something to say to you. Does it not appear to you that those of us who have some idea of these important subjects ought to go out into the world and preach to our follow men "to make up" before it is too late? Who will serve in this ministry? We will enroll you this day!

Ought we not to get out as missionaries to tell our fellowmen what treasures the Inner Life offers and offers for nothing, if we but will let go all kinds of entanglements with "this" world, a world with which we really have nothing to do. Our home is not here! It is yonder! Ought we not also tell our fellow men that in as much as they live in this cycle, they have the benefit of all its characteristics, even that mighty power of thought-forms I have spoken of, but that they bring curses upon themselves by misuse of that power? And should we not show them that they are in a bad way and that the world at large lies in suffering, because that great power has been misused? Ought we not preach obedience?

There is no need of an ordination or commission from somebody else. The witness of the Higher Self within is both call and ordination. We are all in a Universal Ministry, as many as have understood the motions of the Higher Self.

CHAPTER VIII

NATURE WORSHIP

I take up the thread where I left it in the last chapter and will now speak about Stillness as Nature's essential life. I maintain that had those three persons- the Greek- the maidens- the copyist- remained self-contained, they would have discovered how nature's stillness embraced them and they would not have fallen so deep as they did. I shall now, as I have done in all the foregone chapters, point to Nature as our mother, our monitor, our educator and trainer in the Inner Life. To prevent misunderstandings, I repeat what I have said several times before; nature is spirit visible, or which is the same, the only form under which we can see spirit in activity is in nature (and in man, of course, but for the present I leave man out and consider nature, the greater of the two).

Ever since the time of the Gnostics we meet in the ancient writings with testimonies about Sophia, Heavenly Wisdom, that came in personal form to those who lived the Inner Life, and even in our own day there are people living who have received visits of Sophia. She is Deity revealed in nature, and, is described variously in all holy books, but always as man's best friend and companion and his example. I say, therefore, Nature is Sophia and Sophia is Nature. I may well appropriate as my own the following lines:

> "There are Three Testaments which show
> What God both is and does;
> And he who well the first would know
> The second must peruse;
> Nor will he in the second speed,
> Unless the third he rightly read."

The three testaments, or which are the same witnesses in

the world, are God, Man, Nature. He who would know God, must know man; but to know man, one must read nature carefully. I think these lines justify the eminent place I give nature for the present and in these chapters on the Inner Life in connection with the Tao-Teh-King. Of the thousands of examples that could be given, I will mention only one upon her teachings, one to show how she can and does teach us to worship, and, worship I call the highest expression for our spiritual life. I call it the highest expression, because worship gives movement, unity, and system to our life and actions. You must understand I am talking about "worthscipe," the old Saxon form. That word means value, appreciation. Nature is teaching us to value life, to rejoice in God's gifts. She has not prepared for our use any liturgy of canned flatteries or strings of petitions, nor does she lay down the law for the Deity what to do for us. Such unworthy acts are not hers. She is neither browbeating Deity nor shaking us with fears. She gives us an example and pattern for life and happiness, and rejoices in the value, the worth of life. And that is worship, acts worthy the Deity and for our upbuilding.

Do not tell me when I shall have read Whittier's poem, entitled "Nature 's Worship," that the poet has simply personified some of nature's actions and read into them something very characteristic. Do not say that, for you have against you the great multitude of scholars who know about these things, and you reveal your own poverty as regards Inner-Life experiences. Man learned his method of worship from nature; it did not spring from out his own mind. As regards worship (worthship), as in all other fields, order or method came first and existed before man found a name for it. Our definitions come long after we have discovered the facts in nature. At this day we know of numerous facts and ways of nature, but we have no name for them. Our thought-form system is but of recent date as I told you in the last chapter. Man's heart craved for expressions, and as he felt the power of such actions, attitudes and motions of nature which Whittier describes, he imitated them, and he does likewise to this day, when he comes down to the bottom of his heart, and until he does it, he never attains full God-wisdom nor the practice thereof, call it religion or anything else. Such acts follow and are identical with the second birth. Did not the real great prophets live in the open? Yes, all of them! Those that came from monastic cells, were not of the first class. Wonderful as Tauler was, I have this against him, that he pulled the cap down over his eyes, that the flowers should not disturb his meditations. Buddha took the text for his first sermon from a fire in the woods across the river where he was sitting. As for Jesus, you know how his parables abound in nature-life; how he preached from a boat, loved mountains and always traveled in the Open. And Laotzse either starts with a nature-symbol or ends with one. You shall hear enough about that as I proceed with my chapters. I repeat it, the great masters live and have always lived in the Open, and that is why they and we have a common ground to meet on. I say we and mean those who associate with the spirit abroad. Examine into this and you will see it for yourself.

By nature the superficial observer understands all the tangible manifoldness that impinges upon his senses, and that manifoldness only. But that manifoldness is only the fringe of that many-colored carpet which the great mother has spread out for us to walk upon. She herself is nature in a different sense, namely, she is the weaver of that carpet and those fringes. She is both object and subject, both doer and the deed. And she is as personal as you and I; and that is why we can have company with her. When we call her mother we are not merely indulging in personalities, we are speaking as does heart to heart. That many cannot understand this, condemns them and proves most conclusively that they are not on the path. Nature has woven symbols of the most varied designs into this carpet, but they all lead us to the solitary roads, where she is ready to meet us. These solitary roads may look like green meadows or barren mountain tops, like woodlands or deserts, like the open ocean or the still lake. Whatever they look like or whatever we call them, she has provided them for our sake that we may meet her in seclusion and solitude and have a heart to heart talk. It is not true that she is indifferent to the individual, caring only for the race. Nature never falls into those terrible disturbances which we human creatures fall into because we will not learn the principle of non-action. Nature is beyond such a conflict, to say the least. Will you please notice, how intensely active nature is in the illustration I shall give, and yet how quiet, how still, how sublimely "non-active" she is. Nature is always double, not to say multiple, in all her doings. Outwardly she seems to be bent upon beating her own record for multiple productions, but her real doings lie behind the array of facts which is the all so many of us only see. Nature in these "real doings," which are volitional, always points beyond herself and therefore she is our example. I shall read to you Whittier's only too little known and less understood poem: "The Worship of Nature." Please notice that she acts like a human person.

> "The harp at Nature's advent strung
> Has never ceased to play;
> The songs the stars of morning sung
> Have never died away.
>
> And prayer is made, and prayer is given,
> By all things near and far;
> The Ocean looketh up to heaven,
> And mirrors every star.
>
> Its waves are kneeling on the strand,
> As kneels the human knee,
> Their white locks bowing to the sand,
> The priesthood of the sea!
>
> They pour their glittering treasure forth,
> Their gifts of pearl they bring,
> And all the listening hills of earth
> Take up the song they sing.

THE INNER LIFE AND THE TAO TEH KING

The green earth sends her incense up
From many a mountain shrine;
From folded leaf and dewy cup
She pours her sacred wine.

The mists above the morning rills
Rise white as wings of prayer;
The altar-curtains of the hills
Are sunset's purple air.

The winds with hymns of praise are loud,
Or low with sobs of pain,
The thunder-organ of the cloud-
The dropping tears of rain.

With drooping head and branches crossed
The twilight forest grieves,
Or speaks with tongues of Pentecost
From all its sunlit leaves.

The blue sky is the temple's arch,
Its transept earth and air,
The music of its starry march
The chorus of a prayer.

So Nature keeps the reverent frame
With which her years began,
And all her signs and voices shame
The prayerless heart of Man."

This ought to shame most people; it shows how nature is stillness, or in that essential condition so highly praised by all mystics and so intensely sought for. This shows how nature is in the condition of the sage, such as you have heard Laotzse define him, as the one who "acts non-action" the one whose work is always on the plane above this and yet whose effects are visible on this plane. Nature is the one who is not hasty with the hand, like that young Greek, and not afraid of losing the bodily life, like those girl loves of Indra, and, not indifferently wasting the measures of time and at last finding that that was lost which was never really possessed. Nature is in no such conflict. Neither is the sage. Nay, the sage is he who lives in simplicity, such as you have heard me describe it from the Tao-Teh-King, and, simplicity and stillness are synonymous terms:

> "The harp at Nature's advent strung
> Has never ceased to play.
> The songs the stars of morning sung
> Have never died away."

Indeed, nature sings, and "there is always a song, my dear, somewhere" as the Hoosier poet told us. But he did not tell us what the song was about and failed to interpret her notes. Another has done it. I have heard it from another poet, Chr. Fr. K. Molbeck, a poet far away and in the Vikings-land, whence some would least of all expect to hear a translation of nature's call. That poet interprets the song to be a call to us to be still. Here it is in prose, as best I can translate it:

"Oh, man, thou who like the wild wind rushes over earth and ne 'er throws the lead to the bottom of thy breast; thou, who would fathom life, but forget its source: seek for once thyself and God- but still! End this wild rush, this restless sighing! Put the ear to thine own breast, where thy soul is in prison!"

"Dam-up and seal the flood of thy lusts; seek then thyself in the depths of thy bosom- but still!"

"Stop this hurry and haste from one door of life to another. In this noise, how can thou expect God's voice to hear, or thine own; neither of them come like thunder storms; they visit the heart like gentle winds- and still!"

151

THE INNER LIFE AND THE TAO TEH KING

"Ye generation of men, full of evil and hatred, rushing through the world with tongue cursing and murmuring, what is thy goal? What seekest thou in the tumult? Behold the flower grows towards heaven- and still!"

"Hear, everywhere in field and meadow, a prayer for stillness is lifted up. Even midday's golden mouth bids stillness in the woods. The stars along the coasts of heaven, playing silver harps, bid thee be still!"

"Be still" is the refrain "of the song that is always, my dear, somewhere." Be still! is nature's call, because stillness is her innermost, her mystery! Stillness is Nature's Truth and Beauty! Nature never says a word about Truth, but with infinite patience and in stillness she forces us to hear it. She has time to wait. Nature never sings her own praise; but to all, she is goodness, especially to those who will quietly sit down at her table and take her bounties. She does it in stillness. Beauty is her wayside sacrament administered in every flower, and, she goes about spreading beauty everywhere and does it in stillness and without ostentation. Beauty is her hallmark and you find it even in the dust on the flower by the highroad. In spite of man's heedless conduct the dust falls harmoniously. In her workshop she is ever building, but in stillness she plans. On the stage of life, we see the players come and go, but never herself; she stands still in one of the wings. She makes us talk, but she herself has no speech or language; she is stillness. In short: "Forward," is the mad cry of the world! "Homeward" is the gentle sigh of the heart and Nature! "Homeward" is the meaning and the aim and end of the "be still," Nature's imploring call. These two words "homeward" and "be still" connect with each other. Home is stillness and stillness is home. The two express themselves in worship and there is no- nor can there be- worship where there is no home in God, or stillness of God. Nature is anxious for us to come to worship or to worth-ship, which is the real word or meaning. To worth-ship means to consider valuable. We ought to do as she does and as Whittier expresses it, strike the harp and each with our own tongue sing praises like the "stars of morning;" we ought to make prayers or lift up our hearts and look up into heaven, we ought to kneel or prostrate ourselves like the sands on the shore, and, thus we shall be baptized with water drawn from the eternal wells; we ought to offer glad faces and happy thoughts, and, they shall shine like glittering treasures equal to the song that comes from the hills; such glad faces, happy thoughts and songs are incense, that comes back to the worshiper laden with "sacred wine", and where they are offered there is the Lord's table, indeed. The thunder cloud plays the organ and "dropping tears or rain" wash away any grief or sobs of pain. That is the kind of worship nature knows of and has practiced always and long before she saw man's face, and it is that kind of worship she is anxious to have us learn, and she tells us we cannot learn it except we be "still." In stillness alone Tao "takes us in the arms."

Can you imagine what it means to be taken into the arms of Tao under such conditions? Would it not be glorious? Would it not be heaven? And yet they await us! They can be had for the asking! And they cost nothing! Why tarry? Behold the fowls of the air! Consider the lilies of the field! Remember the sage whom Laotzse so graphically described! They all know about stillness and are ready to testify and to teach! Why will people not be taught these simple lessons? I will tell you. You have perhaps witnessed the scene that is enacted every time the wild geese come down from the North on account of the intense cold. When the tame geese in the farmer's yard hear the honk! honk! up in the air, they spread their short wings and run from one end of the yard to the other and make a tremendous noise- and that is all. They do not rise upon the wing and fly away! They have forgotten to fly! And so it is with people. They have forgotten to fly! They may well hear the speakers' call and the song of the spirit and their blood may throb quicker and they wish loudly- but they have forgotten to fly, and come no further than the door of the meeting place.

THE INNER LIFE AND THE TAO TEH KING

When outside and on the street they forget to rise to
heaven following the honk! honk! Let us pray for stillness! When
the heart throbs violently and restlessly! When fortune's wheel
whirls fastest, let us pray for stillness that we may measure our
soul and our longings. When bitterness and loss assail us, let us
pray for stillness that we cast our anchor safely! People are
earthbound and fear to rise high up like the eagle and see the sun.
As soon as they unawares have forgotten the earth for a moment
and felt the breezes of freedom, they hasten to come down again
for fear of falling. They are really "souls in prison" and oh! the
pity of it; they prefer the narrow streets to the Open, because they
do not know that they are in prison. They have been born there.
Their parents were prisoners before them.

If that young Greek, and those girl loves of Indra, and that
poor copyist, had sought nature in the open, not in a temple
service; on the mountain top and not in the land of the
Utterakurus; near running brooks and in green fields and not in a
counting room, then they would have learned what stillness is,
and, they would have realized stillness in silence and solitude and
been saved, because "Tao would have taken their spirit in the
arms." Whittier's next stanza was:

> "And prayer is made, and prayer is given,
> By all things near and far;
> The Ocean looketh up to the heaven,
> And mirrors every star."

Yes, indeed "prayer is made;" the mute appeal in the dogs
and horses eye is a prayer, that is both a petition and a groan for
relief. Who is so dumb and stupid that they never could imagine
the golden bridge which the moon throws across the ocean is
"prayer given" or prayer answered? When the poet next sings
about ocean's waves kneeling upon the strand like a priesthood of
the sea and how they bring their gifts of pearl, he happily
personifies what can be seen in cathedrals abroad, in

THE INNER LIFE AND THE TAO TEH KING

Mohammedan mosques and often in the seclusion of a cell, when a human soul feels the need of crawling upon the knees, and thus finds relief for an inner burden. Of course those of you who have never felt the need of such an art, cannot comprehend the poet's imagery. Whittier must have had that experience; else he could never have penned the next two lines:

> "And all the listening hills of earth
> Take up the song they sing."

These lines mean not merely that echo answers back the song of the sea. They express a literal fact. If you ever shall have an opportunity to stand on the ocean strand with miles of desolation around you, you will learn to understand how sea and land embrace and kiss. Nowhere else and never at any other time. At such a time you will learn what Nature-Mysticism is and you will learn how to pray. I know of one place where you can hear such a solemn duet sung by the ocean and the shore. Where the North Sea howls upon the coast of Jutland (Denmark) on those places where the Vikings of old landed when they came down from Iceland and the other isles; that is the place. Only a devoted and worshipful soul like Whittier could ever discover that the earth offers incense and that the incense burner is the "folded leaf and dewy cup," or compare the early morning mist, that of summer morning at 4 o'clock, to the wings of prayer, or see "sunset's purple air" as altar curtains, and so forth throughout the poem.

Only persons who have spent nights and days, mornings and evenings in the mountains, or in great forests or deserts, or on the shores of the ocean, can catch the note of stillness in the transcendence of these things, but I think all ought to be able to see that in all this there is a condition of blessing, that there is no conflict, no inner rupture, no loss of peace, no sin; but on the other hand sublime teachings for us on how to do, and what the Inner Life is. Let me tell you about something I want you to do in summer on an early morning. Get up early enough to have time to rub the sleep out of your eyes, and get out to meet the sun, but you must be on the hill on the edge of the woods before the sun gets there! If you do, you will be able to attend a morning service such as the small birds conduct it, and you shall never forget your experience and perhaps discover what religion really is. At dawn, the birds in certain localities all seem to be touched by the solemnity of the hour. No man knows why or how. It seems to me mother nature is the bandmaster and director of the music. Though each bird sings his own song, the myriad voices blend in one concordant whole. All the birds seem to be actuated by unity of purpose with the feeling of some larger consciousness. Beginning with the desultory calls of woodpeckers, the song sparrows, robins and catbirds all start in, and in some way the thrushes give the symphony a devotional character. The thrushes are always solemn; a tone of invocation predominates. The Veery or Wilson thrush is truly called the high-priest of the mystic lore of the forest. When the twilight is no more, the warblers take up the strain and express contentment of mind and heart. With them ends the morning service, and the bobolinks, these little light hearted rascals begin to bubble over with gong. Their merry jingles come up from the meadows, bubbling, rippling and lyric altogether. All this is not poetic fancy of mine. Lovers of nature and life in the open will verify my words and experience.

Whence this accord? Nature, the great mother, falls in with all these voices and leads the song, and therefore there is in it a personal address I Go into solitude and you shall hear it. There is reconciliation in it. There is religion in it. Nature will teach you what prayer is and how to sing such as lips never sing, but such as the heart does it, when it offers its own warm blood as the sacrifice and lays itself upon the altar as an offering. Some day I trust you may realize that Nature is Tao and Teh, and that Whittier in this poem has helped to show what stillness is, in which "Tao takes our spirit in the arms." If you are at all familiar with any of these attitudes just described, you must sometime or other have realized the solemnity and reverence shown everywhere where nature worships, and she worships everywhere. Come out again! Come out on an early morning to hear the prelude to the day's symphony as it is sung in the woods. I have heard it many times, and I assure you, you shall spend a happy day, if you do. All the mud that sticks to your shoes will fall off, you will not bring it home again. As regards stillness, the subject of this chapter, you shall understand that it does not merely mean cessation of sound or noise, as with us men, but that stillness to nature means jubilation and an intensity of purpose of which men know nothing. To us such words as simplicity and stillness are merely negative conceptions. To nature they are positive and realities, the very condition the sage wishes to bring men to. I now come to the balance left of that sentence in which "stillness" has played so prominent a part. The balance of the sentence relates to Tao taking us in the arms. This idea of being taken into the arms of Tao I now shall try to illustrate.

You are all familiar with a number of ceremonial actions, actions which you yourself use as expressions of your feeling, though in all probability you are not consciously aware of their import, or why you do them. Among such ceremonies implying spiritual actions the most common are those of "shaking hands," and, other actions of the hand, such as embracing friends and relatives; kissing, taking off the hat. Such actions represent the sympathetic system in our constitution, and they express our feelings towards the neighbor. This sympathetic system in our constitution seems to be gradually sinking into the sea of our personal life. All the actions I have referred to, and numerous others of like nature, no more play the part in our life they used to. In the cycle anteceding the one in which we now live, they were exceedingly important and were the terms in which men's feelings expressed themselves, and they were invaluable. They have survived in some weak form or other here and there even in our own cycle, and, they still are the essential characteristics of those people who are the remnants of earlier prehistoric races, such as among the people we call wild and uncivilized. These sympathetic feelings are now sinking into the sea or gradually receding in our personality, giving place for other systems and other terms; such as for instance, that system called thought-form which came in a cycle characteristic at the time Laotze wrote his book. I shall not speak any further about the loss of the sympathetic system, that must wait till another time. Now, I must speak of the thought-form system that arose at the beginning of our cycle.

This new system, which I for convenience have called thought-form, is not unfamiliar to you. I will show you. I will suppose you to be a lover and suddenly to have been struck profoundly by another person and realized what "sameness" is, or, in other words, "love," for love is essentially a feeling of sameness, of identity with the beloved. In this feeling of sameness, this familiarity you and the beloved have met and determined not to be separated again and both found the essential peace which only such a union gives. No more seems necessary. Up to this point it was the sympathetic system that acted. But now the other system steps in. It is a psychological fact that neither of the two rest in those feelings, in those inner assurances. Both begin very soon to inquire into each other's life and ideas, not mention making inquiries about wealth, or fame, or history. These things do not concern my subject. They begin to inquire, because the thought-form system in them clamors to "see" the beloved, to understand the beloved, to get a picture according to mind, it demands a form rather than an emotion as an expression and will not rest without it. Examine yourself and you shall see the correctness of what I say. All lovers do that, except Jack and Jill; they remain in the sympathetic system.

Every intelligent mind is restless before its object, till it, in a "corresponding" way, has masticated and swallowed and assimilated it. First, after that, does it possess the object as an object of consciousness, and this possessing the object in consciousness is the demand of every intelligent mind, the very characteristic of intelligence and the demand of the thought-form system. To use Qvang-tze's phrase we "take the object in our arms." You readily see the close correspondence between the sympathetic system's action of taking a friend or relative or the beloved "in the arms" and the same action under the form of understanding by the thought-form system: Both systems act in a similar direction and on parallel lines, but their methods are very different.

This action of the two systems on our relative plane of life illustrates what Tao does on the universal plane of life. And as we human beings on our plane come into union, so Tao on the universal plane brings us into union with itself. Tao "takes us in the arms" when we have come into stillness or, which is the same, when sameness or identity has become a fact. You can now see the meaning of that sentence of Qvang-tze and you can readily understand that we are perfect when that happens. I am now done with that sentence I started out with.

CHAPTER IX

TAO

Look at the diagram (No. 1), it is the motto for this chapter. It is a picture of Tao. I shall use the word Tao very little in this chapter, yet, not only the frame of it is of Tao but its content is about Tao; yea, I dare almost say it is Tao. The diagram will explain itself as I proceed with my expositions; I say expositions, because I shall really give two ; the first one is a short one, consisting of four paragraphs, and, the second somewhat longer going over the same ground as these four paragraphs though very differently. The first exposition runs as follows:

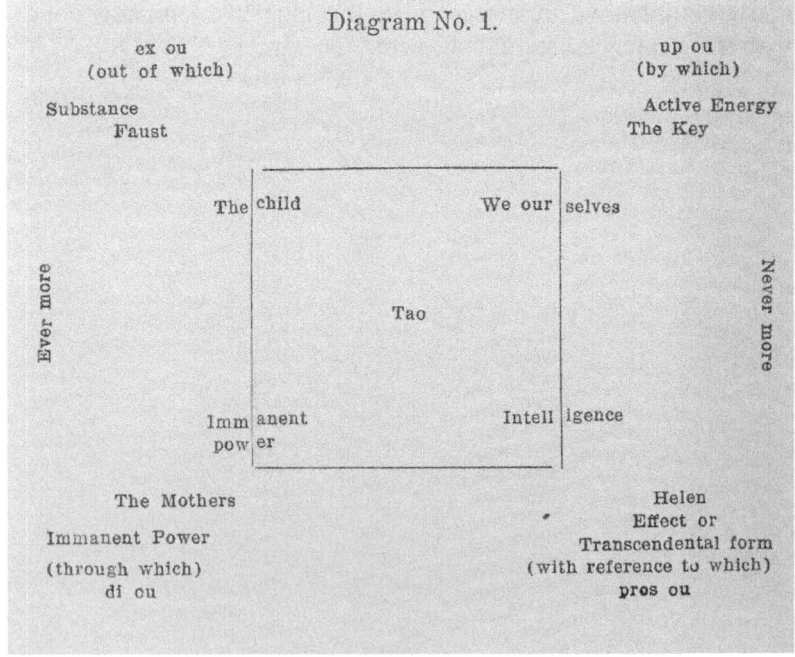

Diagram No. 1.

THE INNER LIFE AND THE TAO TEH KING

(I) Observe the child. It knows what it is to be in the condition of having the thumb in the month, but it does not know what thumb means nor what mouth means. It has not the ability to substitute the technical terms thumb and mouth for the condition which I call "thumb-in-mouth" condition. The child knows quality, but not the name for quality.

(II) Again; we all as children know something shining brightly, now, as in daytime all around us, then in the darkness as coming from certain objects; how we do not know. We may be taught to call it light and we may call it so, and most of us continue so throughout our whole life, never even suspecting that we talk merely like parrots, not knowing what we say. How many know why brightness is called light and how that conception arose? This condition is sense-consciousness; it is not intelligence. Intelligence does not arise till we in our inner man have found for ourselves a solution and a term for that brightness we have been taught to call light. As an adjunct to this, the second point, I will have you realize how much injury we receive by being educated, as we call it. We learn certain results attained by others and that, of course, is useful, but it kills all originality; it kills the initiative in most people. In the schools we are not even warned of our danger.

(III) Again; cotton cannot weave itself into cloth. Neither can sensations transform themselves into thoughts. Machinery weaves cotton into cloth. The thought-form system transforms sensations into intelligence.

(IV) Again; our value as human beings depends first of all upon intelligence. Where there is no intelligence there is no humanity, properly speaking.

These four points are really a chapter in themselves, and stand independent of the sequence of this chapter, but they are nevertheless the fundamental ideas that lie at the bottom of it and are four sides of Tao, and that will appear by and by. Without exaggerating much, I can say that this diagram (No. 1) is a diagram of the motions of your life and mine, not only in the four large divisions of life from birth to death, but it also represents the stages and the driving forces of our thinking and acting. Our life swings around the four points, whether we will or not, and, the diagram may be compared to a clock; a clock that has a voice. If you listen closely you hear in the "tick-tack" a song of "evermore", "nevermore." With the triad added, this tetrad becomes our templum.

You know what that word means; I explained it in two forgone chapters. Yes! this diagram is the ground plan of our templum and with the triad added it reaches into the heavens. Being of so much signification, I may well urge you to pay much attention to it. The Innermost Squre is characterized by four terms: the child, we ourselves, inherent power, intelligence. These terms express the four stages of our spiritual evolution. I need not describe them. It happens that Aristotle has already done it. The small Greek words on the corners corresponding to the terms I already have mentioned, explain them. The *ex ou* is the "out of which" the evolution starts. The *up ou* is the "by which" it starts. The *di ou* is the "through which" it is accomplished, and the pros owl is the final end "with reference to which" the whole evolution has taken place.

The diagram will be of great practical value to those who wish to see the workings of their own psychological movements. All ought to wish to see that, because intelligence wishes to see itself and you can never be sure of your motives or your fate on the Path unless you follow yourself step by step through these four. This is the first exposition. Now for the second. Since the beginning of our present cycle, there is in human consciousness, in most people, an unconscious and in the few a conscious demand to understand, or let me say to absorb understandingly the object. After we have grasped it with the feelings, we crave to draw it into ourselves; we crave to possess the object. To grasp the object by the feelings is true action, but the craving is a perversion of an inherent and otherwise correct longing for an identification with the object. So long we do not in understanding grasp an object, so long it remains outside of us and is of no use to us, nor do we possess it, which we wish to and have a right to. In the preceding chapter I have already stated that if we do not attain such a grasp of the object, we miss the opportunity of the present cycle and live for nothing. It is in the understanding that I possess an object; in no other way do I possess it. A flower in my buttonhole, or, a house, even if my legal title is perfect, is not in my possession. They are no part of me and remain no part of me, no matter what I do. But if I understand them in their principles, they and I become one, and, in that oneness, I become a ruler. This identification and blending is a law of Nature. Nature is a system of nuptials. Not only the poet (Shelley) knows that, but science and common observation shows it.

> "The fountains mingle with the river
> And the rivers with the ocean,
> The winds of heaven mix forever
> With a sweet emotion;
> Nothing in the world is single;
> All things, by a law divine
> In one spirit meet and mingle"

Why not Thou with the Beloved?

> "See, the mountains kiss high heaven,
> And the waves clasp one another;
> No sister-flower would be forgiven
> If it disdained its brother;
> And the sunlight clasps the earth
> And the moonbeams kiss the sea;
> What are all these kissings worth-
> If Thou kiss not the Beloved!"

163

THE INNER LIFE AND THE TAO TEH KING

This is Shelley's rendering of the law, and also his statement why this mingling takes place- it is for a sign and symbol, that we kiss the Divine, or come to the great mystic object: union with God. In the Vedanta it is said that Nature is like a dancer, who comes upon the scene to charm the spectator and to be carried home. The meaning is of course this, that we shall learn the higher lesson of love, which is that between the soul and the Deity. "All things work together for good to them that love God," is the old gospel truth. I shall not stop further and show you the details in Nature's life. They are easy enough to see if you will but look. Everywhere there is Beauty, and the word Beauty correctly translated means "coming together" and nothing else. But it is not merely in nature that this happens. In your own life you have had experiences that are of the same kind. You know how often you have heard the same wisdom taught, for instance, set forth by lecturers or friends, and you could never catch on to it, apprehend it or re-express it in your own terms, till some day, all of a sudden, a happy word or phrase or expression at once made everything clear and you burst out, Ah! now I see it! In such an experience the law of these psychological matters is to be seen. In the novels you read, if they are skillfully written, there are many psychological moments in which the hero or heroine argue for or against their love or other actions. Such argumentations also show the method according to which the thought-form system works. They always lead to a climax in which the hero or heroine "sees," "understands,"or "realizes," and, the trend of the whole story takes a new and decided turn.

Human consciousness, where it is awakened, is not satisfied with a mere view of an object, a view obtained by merely seeing the object. If we were satisfied, our consciousness would be worth no more than the stare of a cow upon a red-painted door. To know about a thing is not the same as to know it. You may know a great deal about Europe, without knowing it. You may know about Theosophy without being a theosophist. No bliss is bliss unless realized intelligently; no thought is thought to us unless translated into mental substance. In Nature, no sweets will be absorbed as health, unless the system needs them, otherwise they are poison. Nor is human consciousness satisfied by the mere excited feelings or emotions that may pass over it. What are emotions worth if they are not translated into intelligible words? Surely no more than opium dreams, or more than the gusts of wind that have struck us and which we have forgotten and perhaps not even noticed. Human consciousness to be worth its name, demands an understanding, an intellectual possession, or a mental transmutation of that which the senses experience.

I have much against the way life is lived in our own day and in the present cycle, and, have several times in the foregone chapters expressed myself very strongly in condemnation of the authorities who are responsible for the degradation of the age. I shall not add anything at present, but say, that the only point which saves this age is that it still contains those who profess that all philosophical, moral and aesthetic schools, ought to be keyed in the note of the thought-form system, or set in the principles of order, form, rule, number, method, and so forth. Those few balance that other mass, or those who let the sympathetic system run wild, allowing it to destroy them in their fury and burn them in its unquenchable fire. I referred to the senses. The senses are the windows of the soul, not its governors. The soul looks out through these windows and the sun looks in with the whole company of objective figures, movements and impulses. When all these forms enter through the window, our image-making power, one aspect of the thought-form system, gives them body or turns them into shapes, or, as Shakespeare in a fine line has it, "gives to airy nothing a local habitation and a name." They enter as "airy nothings", but by us they receive "a local habitation and a name," or, in other words, they become something substantial in our minds, and that is all the reality they have or ever will get, as far as we are concerned. But this substantiality they thus receive is our salvation or redemption or understanding of them, and, if they did not receive that substantial form they would be of no use, nor become a part of us, and would affect us no more than a wind that sweeps over our heads. We would know through our feelings or our sense consciousness that something had happened, but no more; and knowing no more, we should derive no mental, moral, or spiritual benefit from them.

Dryden speaks of his work when it was only a confused mass of thoughts, tumbling over one another in the dark, when the fancy (he meant image-making power) was yet in its first work, moving the sleeping images of things towards the light, there to be distinguished (that is, separated), and then either to be chosen or rejected by the judgment, namely, reason. This, which Dryden here calls the "sleeping images of things," are those first or original shapes which our image-making power gives all our sense perceptions, and they are the ones we have to deal with and out of which comes complete consciousness. You must notice this point, that they get their sustenance from our minds or personality and have no other. The process is that of the seed laid in the soil. It grows and develops by means of the substance it derives from the soil, but is and remains itself. The growth or the shape acquired is the middle link, the child, if I may so call it, born of the potentiality of the seed and the soil. Without it, no union, no at-one-ment. This child, as I call it, is the thought-form manifesting itself. You see not only how the thought-form manifests itself, but also its tremendous importance in what we call life. The personality in which this has taken place is worthy to be called intelligent; and it is on the Path. Some people say that now the christ-child has been born in them. Meister Eckardt said so, too. I will now attempt to illustrate this process and I shall vary the nature of illustrations. In the foregone chapters, I have drawn my illustrations from our moral consciousness and sometimes from our sense consciousness. Now I will take them from our aesthetic consciousness and lead into it by one illustration from our intellectual consciousness.

It is the inherent demand to bear "the child," a demand for

transmutation, for reconciliation, for personal appropriation, that in the philosopher demands a "notion" or an idea or a word which will contain the object in a mental form, and thus give him a mental equivalent for the outside object. When he finds or conceives this notion, or idea, then he is free of the object, and the object is subject to him, and he controls it in such a way that it practically is taken out of the universe as an independent power and becomes his and his only. You have heard of magicians possessing words which enabled them to perform wonders. Such words are acquired by the process I mentioned. They are not gotten by mere transmission from a master to a pupil. They can only be acquired by the magian himself, by the magian himself passing through the alchemical process. Of course, I cannot here, even if I were able to do it, explain the alchemical process, but, as I at present am dealing with our aesthetic consciousness, I can picture it to some extent, and thereby perhaps cause you to "work," as it is called alchemically, or to enter the Path, as they say in the Orient and among mystics. I will take a scene from Goethe's Faust. It is found in the second part, first act. Faust demands that Mephistopheles shall produce Helen, the most beautiful, but also the most baneful Greek woman. Mephistopheles objects, but Faust persists. Mephistopheles says:

"The Heathen-folk I am glad to let alone;
In their own hell is cast their lot,..."

...but admits there are ways and, forced by Faust, he declares:

"Loth am I higher secrets to unfold.
In solitude, where reigns nor space nor time,
Are goddesses enthroned from early ages
'Tis hard to speak of beings so sublime-
The Mothers are they..."

At this word, the "mothers," Faust shrinks back terrified,

but recovers under Mephistopheles' sarcasm and admits he is in fear and trembling. Mephistopheles explains that these goddesses are unknown to men, and unwillingly named by him. He also tells Faust, who demands to know the way to them, that there is...

> "No way; to the untrodden none,
> No locks nor bolts-
> Only solitudes."

Do you know what the void is? Faust, as usual, stops Mephisto's dilatory talk and persists in his demands. Finally Mephisto hands Faust a little key which, he tells him: "Follow! thee to the Mothers it will lead!"

Again upon hearing the word "the Mothers" Faust shudders, but soon springs up in ecstasy, because now he has found the word, the liberating power, the key. "Good! Firmly I grasp it. New strength is mine; My breast expands! Now on to accomplish my great purpose."

And Mephistopheles approvingly cries out:

"So, that is right!
The key cleaves to thee; it follows like a slave!"

I need not continue Goethe's drama any further. Faust has the key and Helen is brought forth. Now, what is it that takes place f It is this, that Faust immediately grasps the situation in that moment he discovers what the key can do. The key to him is the same as the "notion" to the philosopher. At that moment he rises as master; all confusion is blown away, and no longer overwhelmed with fears or tremblings or the power of the situation, he exclaims: "Good! Firmly I grasp it. New strength is mine My breast expands! Now on to accomplish my great purpose;" and Mephisto also knows that Faust has "seen," has "understood," has "realized," or in other words, has undergone that psychological transmutation I have explained in details. Let Faust represent the philosopher, and my illustration will point to one of the methods of the thought-form system by which the reflective mind attains control over itself, or awakens to the value of life and its means of salvation.

At present I shall say nothing further about Faust and Helen. The two other powers are far more interesting. "The key" is of course "the active energy" in existence, and in these chapters called the thought-form system. I have chosen that term, I have said before, because it best expresses the Tao of the Tao-Teh-King, such as it slowly is coming to the front in these chapters and as you shall see it fully when we come to the end of them. I can give you several equivalents for it in Occidental philosophy, but I shall not use them myself because they are to me no more than suggestions and not full expressions. It was the Greek mind that first began to search for an abstract and technical term and found it in Anaxagoras. He named it Nous and meant thereby the ordering principle, that principle which as active energy gave unity, system and movement to the universe. Pythagoras later called it Number, a wonderful term, for law and order. Nous with Plato became an attribute of deity, and psychologically also the highest form of mental insight, or reason, as we are wont to call it. All knowledge and insight depends upon nous. This is sufficient for the present. It may help you somewhat. The later senses given to nous will appear in due time. At present I call it the thought-form, and I speak of the thought-form system when I say "the key" that Faust got, and which brought him to the mothers and unlocked the power that could lift Helen into the world. Next come the mothers before us and crave our attention.

The mothers are modern names for nature-goddesses among the Pelasgians, the prehistoric races of large parts of southern Europe. The Greek and Roman goddesses Persephone and Demeter were survivals of these nature-goddesses. The mothers as conceived by the Pelasgians were identical with the tripod upon which and inside of which they lived. They were the types of all conceptions, causes and energies; hence Faust must go to them. All of which, of course, means that he must descend to the core of the universe, to the "Immanent Power," through which alone things happen in our sphere of existence. He attained his object by "the key," or the "active energy." All of this is, of course, symbolism and life-truth, and can be studied in various ways. At present, I present it all as the thought-form system and have represented it in the diagram. If you follow the inscriptions and this Faustic scene, you will see how they explain each other. I shall not dwell much upon the diagram now. It will receive many more inscriptions as I refer to it in the future, when we shall see Tao under all four forms.

In this scene of Goethe's we have the four elements, the quaternary represented by Faust, the Key, the Mothers, Helen. Mephisto is the *deus ex machina* and does not belong to either quaternary or ternary. For the present study of Taoism, the Tetrad, the 4, is the most important, and among its many names, I will mention the most interesting in the connection with the subject in hand. Four is called "the fountain of nature," and many peoples of antiquity had a name for Deity consisting of four letters; hence I surmise, for that reason, four was called "the keybearer." Four also is the constituent of a virtuous life, the four virtues being Prudence, Temperance, Fortitude and Justice. But the most interesting at present is this, that Taoism distinguishes Tao under four aspects, four aspects which coincide with the four causes of Aristotle and the four forms already presented. What is Tao? The answer, I shall give, I take from an eminent Taoist, Huai-Nan-Tzu. "What is Tao?" he asked; and answers:

(I) "It is that which supports heaven and covers the earth; it has no boundaries, no limits; its heights cannot be measured, nor its depths fathomed; it enfolds the entire universe in its embrace, and confers visibility upon that which of itself is formless.

(II) It is so tenuous and subtle that it pervades everything just as water pervades mire. It is by Tao that mountains are high and abysses deep; that beasts walk and birds fly; that the sun and moon are bright, and the stars revolve in their courses.

(III) When the Spring winds blow, the sweet rain falls; and all things live and grow. The feathered ones brood and hatch, the furry ones breed and bear; plants and trees put forth all their glorious exuberance of foliage; birds lay eggs, and animals produce their young.

(IV) No action is visible outwardly, and yet the work is completed. Shadowy and indistinct, it has no form. Indistinct and shadowy, its resources have no end. Hidden and obscure, it reinforces all things out of formlessness. Penetrating and permeating everything, it never acts in vain."

Now what is this in our language of the Occident but Nature, the creating and forming principle of existence and also the substance of all we know. It is the *natura naturans* of the philosophers as well as the *natura naturata*, the cause of all phenomena as well as the phenomena themselves. Tao, then, is Nature. That is the first translation of the word; others will follow. If we analyze the description given, we see how the author begins by (1) the ideas of substance; (2) then he defines Tao as immanent power; (3) then as active energy; and finally he sums up by (4) transcendental terms and definitions. In other words, he begins in the tangible and ends in the intangible, and, that is so beautiful, because that is the order of regeneration both intellectually and volitionally. It is Nature 's way of training us.

(I) Laotzse, the master, like the disciple, speaks of Tao under four forms, and speaks of it as being from before the beginning, immaterial, and a primordial mystery. It is everywhere, and can be on the right side at the same time as it is on the left. In other words it is substance.

THE INNER LIFE AND THE TAO TEH KING

(II) Laotzse also speaks of Tao as manifested or individualized: in man, for instance, as reason or immediate knowledge. This is Tao as immanent power.

(III) Laotzse finally says: "These two are one and the same and differ only in name" and this "sameness" leads to a new signification of Tao, namely, as "the abyss of abysses."

(IV) But Laotzse also emphasizes again and again that Tao cannot be comprehended, or, in other words, that Tao is transcendental. Here, then, are four important aspects of Tao and I must try to elucidate them, but not at present.

Thus far I have been dealing with the thought-form system mainly as it manifests itself in the philosophical mind or in the form of our mind which reasons. I said before I would do that, introductory to some forms of our aesthetic consciousness under the influence of the thought-form system. I now come to these aesthetic forms, and will first speak of the musical mind. A musician builds a tune-architecture, which is a visible, rather than an audible form, and this form overcomes the corporeal. That form scintillates with light; light which never was on sea nor land. I said visible, not audible form, because music, of all arts, is the most powerful image-maker. True enough, we hear it in its first appearance, but it stays with us as a visible image, because it is an image. And ever afterwards its appearance is before the inner eye as a light, a form without extension; or to put it in another way, it is ever afterwards spirit appearing as spirit, or spirit focusing itself. It is therefore that I call it a visual image rather than an audible image. Of course, I am speaking of music in its real or occult sense. I mean by Music; the inner Word, or Logos. I mean sounds which, when they enter us, transform themselves to intelligence, to mind. Music is mind speaking to mind, or cosmic emotions vibrating in unison with subjective emotions, and as such, reflecting themselves in the musician. Music is not the same as harmonious sounds, however charming. Music is the speaking voice of the Divine. It is a message to the world coming through the musician. All this is of course of transcendental nature, something that takes place in the sublime solitude of genius and in that stillness spoken of before. The world outside of solitude and stillness hears a manifoldness of sounds, perhaps in geometric or mathematical order, and it trembles at times into ecstasy and feels the transcendental has come very near. But the outside cannot retain the musical images; it cannot translate them into rational terms. And music is not music unless such translations take place. Only genius in stillness can do it. One prophet understands another; one mystic perceives immediately the inspiration of another. As I already have said, all this takes place in the sublime solitude of genius, in stillness. And when it does take place, Tao has taken the spirit in its arms. If we wish to hear the fabled music of the spheres, and wish to rise to the goddess of beauty that keeps the immortally tuned harp, we must retire to the solitude or quiet places of our own souls, there, and, there only, do we find the universe reflected and see those tune-architectures which stand in that sea, whence sprang the Anadyomene. The wave-born Venus Anadyomene is not wantonness, she is Music, a celestial love-song.

In the first chapter I stated that "solitude means that the ego is alone with itself." That solitude is the plane of "the twice-born", all of which means that the noisy and clamorous sense-consciousness has been subdued and that the thought-form system rules. Such are the conditions necessary for the birth of music and for the birth of the musician, or, as applied to ourselves, for the opening and energizing of the musical consciousness of ours. The sculptor reduces his perceptions to a form, let me say a human one, and this form or image he builds up by lines, in such a way that his image represents to him the true or real man, and, moreover, in such a way that this image fills him with the power of the ideal world. And he is both the conception and the birth. His image becomes himself, and, unless he becomes that image, the eternal form is not found.

THE INNER LIFE AND THE TAO TEH KING

This image, or the finished statue, is to him his reconciliation or at-one-ing of an outer objective world and his own consciousness. In it, the dualism is at-one-ed and he calls his art higher than the nature which it represents. This image or finished statue makes him feel that he is a master-creator, and it lifts him beyond himself. In his own work he sees the immortal power that worked in him and by him and for him. And if he has reverence, he does not call the work his own in any special sense. I do not think that Michael Angelo for a moment thought of "the Aurora" on the tomb of Lorenzo de Medici, as his in a special sense. I do not think that the artist who caused the daemonic expression on the Venus of Milo, dreamed of it as his. The sculptor's work is the seal of his election, and that is his pay. He lies in the arms of Tao. He has tasted the waters of Pythagoras' well at Crotona, and is no longer at war with himself and his surroundings. He is one of the immortals. And that is enough. This is done in solitude, in stillness. In solitude he and the objective were married, and the child of that marriage is himself. Here again I quote what I said in the first chapter about solitude, that it strips us naked of all the incidental and trivial and burns these up. In solitude none of the five senses work, they are merely doors by which the soul passes in and out, in to itself and out to Nature. How is the poet born and how does he lie in the arms of Tao? As for the poet: "He must come to us, another Numa, radiant and inspired from the kisses of Egeria." Egeria was a nymph, and nymphs do not live in market places; they are only found on solitary woodpaths and secluded places in Nature's secret haunts, in stillness. There the poet retires, when he seeks the word that shall overcome and slay the hydra of confusion and discord. The word, namely, which for him is the thought-form that can supplant the passion, which thrilled him. The word, in which he and the eternal become one. Whether the storm rushes into the woods like Boreas, or breathes like gentle Zephyrs, he perceives and lays hold of the rhythmic swing which vibrates solutions and conceptions to his genius. And in that moment he is free, and master over those very vibrations. The poet is like the musician.

THE INNER LIFE AND THE TAO TEH KING

They both formulate sentient life, and thereby attain their freedom, but the poet is not satisfied by merely rousing sentiment, he wants to portray it, too. Hence he endeavors to translate his passion into thought, and to awaken the image-making power that he may fasten his images in that power. He does this by language. His language is best or only learned in Nature's solitudes, in the stillness of Tao. In fact, the poet is the only one who speaks an original language; all others are his imitators. The poet is the one who translates Mother-Nature's sentiments into set terms for the rest of us, and thereby he becomes an interpreter for us and gives us that insight, that understanding we longed for but were not able to give ourselves. He can do so because Egeria, the nymph, kisses him, and Hybla, another nymph, bathes him in the ethereal dews. Of Nature's original stillness, the poet was the first prophet, the first revealer, the one who set man free by giving him the word.

You are all familiar with the story of the New Testament, I suppose, and have all probably read the life of Jesus, told in it. You will agree with me, that it is a most marvelous and beautiful tale. Indeed, that story will as Renan prophetically saw it, be told throughout all ages and never grow stale or lose its charm. You have perhaps also discovered that unwritten poem of the Christ, which vibrates between the lines and trembles in the accords of the life of Jesus, as it is played upon New Testament strings. It is the mystic life, the life of immaculate conception. It is a form of the Inner Life told in the terms of a living man, and thereby giving us that understanding I spoke of, which we long for in order to get a tangible symbol, like the idea, which the philosopher conceived, or the accord that composes itself in the heart of the musician, or the word that placed itself upon the poet's tongue. It is the divine life, the Inner Life, as it was conceived in the soul of Mary. It is that life which is born in solitude, through Mary, not by Mary. It is the life that eternally was with the Father and which comes into the world, but the world sees it not. This mystic story interwoven with the gospel story is the "eternal gospel" of which older mystics-such as, for instance, Joachim of Flores- speak much. It is the life

of "the indwelling Christ" in "the twice born." It is the life that
makes Jesus a master mystic. It is the life of which Jesus testified,
that it would be lived, when men no longer worshiped in
Jerusalem; it is that life which Jesus refers to when he says "I
am the truth, the way and the life," and, when he declared that no
one comes to the Father except by him. Need I say that that life is
the life of re-conciliation and that it is learned in solitude? It is a
life in the arms of Tao. Jesus, the poets, the musicians, the
sculptors and the other artists take us into the white light of life's
flame; but the religionist, the professional, the priest, plunges into
the abyss of the red and terrible fire that burns in the core of every
flame. In intense passion and fanatic self-destructiveness, he seeks
destruction as a solution of life's dualism. Sacrifice to him is
reconciliation. Sacrifice is his cry! Immolation is the means; he
teaches, not of redemption here- it is too patent that it does not
come here- but yonder, in another world- he does not know where
located, and does not care. In frenzy he has relished and in
fierceness he has reveled in the blood of his sacrifice and thought
he bought his peace. But no! That understanding we long for, that
verbal key we seek to Nature's mystery, is not found in the cry of
the sacrificial victim. The sacrificial method is not the method of
our cycle; our thought-form system cannot use it. If the cries of his
victims could be steered into one stream, that stream would be
powerful enough to unhinge the universe, I think, but could never
give freedom and the peace of Tao's arms.

Nay, my friends, Empedokles did not find the solution he
sought by plunging into the Etna volcano. It is only at a distance
that the volcano is beautiful; it is only on the stage that violence
becomes dramatic; it is only in fancy that lust can be made
luminous, and, it is only when the lightening behind the thunder
cloud illumines its edges, that it becomes sublime. The actuality is
terrible and carries no redemption from burdens; offers no
reconciliation of opposites and blood cries for revenge.
Reconciliation is not attained by sacrifice or by blood! It comes
only in stillness. Over all this religiousness lies a solitude which is

dismay, isolation, and the death, that is death. Tao's arm is not underneath. And now I come back to Shelley's poem quoted in the beginning of this chapter: "What are all these kissings worth" and the final line "If Thou kiss not thy Beloved"? What are they worth? Are they worth-ships? (weorth-scip.)

You remember what I said in a foregone chapter on worship and its value, its character as an expression of our union with the Divine. "All these kissings"- that of the philosopher and the notion- that of the musician and his visual image- that of the sculptor and the line- that of the poet and the passionate language- "all these kissings" are conquests of elemental powers and, to be real blessings, we lay them upon the alter of an humble heart. They are conquests, I said. The musician can, after the method of Faust, use the fire-power to create, recreate and to dissolve worlds. The simple experiment of breaking a glass by a violin bow is enough to prove it. The poet, by the same method, becomes an embodiment of the Over-Soul, and, the sculptor touches that which ordinary man can neither see nor touch and he draws that ethereal line which constitutes the heavenly mathematics. The philosopher forges a tool for all of these souls whereby they literally build their astral and spiritual bodies. Each and all bring these powers to the worship (Weorth-scip) of the Supreme.

All that which I have expressed by forms drawn from our aesthetic consciousness has also practical value and can by you be applied to will and moral consciousness. That which I have said is not merely entertaining thought (if it is that), it is occult philosophy and Inner Life. No matter on what plane you break through- on the aesthetic or the moral- break through you must. The breaking through is the second birth and none shall live but those who are born again. It is not necessary that you or I should become philosophers, musicians, sculptors or poets, but it is necessary that the principles which these genial souls embody should be awakened in us and set in activity.

CHAPTER X

TEH

I shall now speak about Teh, which, as already said in past chapters, is the realization of Tao, or Tao as manifested in life at large and especially by the sage. The Chinese sign, which spells Teh, is a double sign and made up of two others, which respectively mean "to go," "to walk," or "to pass," and "an upright heart"; in other words, the sign means "the walk of an upright heart," or, as we would say, virtue. Chinese dictionaries connect the word Teh with the word Tek, which means "to attain" or "to be able to."

If this word Tek be the older word- that is, the word which expresses physical ability, which it probably does, then Teh could be construed to mean "that which we are able to do or which we must do." In either case the word will carry the sense of virtue, in the former it will mean moral virtue, in the latter something physical. In both cases something to strive for. So much for the technical meaning of the sign and the word Teh. Inasmuch as Teh is the realization of Tao, it is necessary that I re-state the main quality of Tao in order to show how Teh is a realization. I will re-state what Tao is by a re-reading of Huan-Nan-Tzu's explanation, and you will recollect the fourfold aspect of Tao as I pointed it out before. Huan-Nan-Tzu explains what Tao is by saying:

(1) "It is that which supports heaven and covers the earth; it has no boundaries, no limits; its heights cannot be measured, nor its depths fathomed; it enfolds the entire universe in its embrace, and confers visibility upon that which of itself is formless."

(2) "It is so tenuous and subtle that it pervades everything, just as water pervades mire. It is by Tao that mountains are high and abysses deep; that beasts walk and birds fly; that the sun and

moon are bright, and the stars revolve in their courses."

(3) "When the Spring winds blow, the sweet rain falls, and all things live and grow. The feathered ones brood and hatch, the furry ones breed and bear; plants and trees put forth all their glorious exuberance of foliage; birds lay eggs and animals produce their young; no action is visible outwardly, and yet the work is completed."

(4) "Shadowy and indistinct, it has no form. Indistinct and shadowy, its resources have no end. Hidden and obscure, it reinforces all things out of formlessness. Penetrating and permeating everything, it never acts in vain." (*Religious Systems of the World*, F. H. Balfour: Taoism.)

On diagram No. 1 I have already indicated by four terms these four aspects of Tao. I called them (1) Substance, (2) Energetic Power, (3) Immanent Power, (4) The Transcendental. The fourfoldness of manifestation is easily seen and is, moreover, indicated in diagram No. 1, given with last chapter and illustrated by me in various ways. The same fourfoldness is seen in Teh, but instead of giving you numerous quotations gathered here and there from the Tao-Teh-King, I have summarized them in the terms: Life, Love, Light, "Will, inscribed on the square, (Diagram No. 2.) These four terms I shall use to describe the fourfold manifestation of Teh. I have also written on this diagram (No. 2) a German sentence from Goethe: "Im Ganzen, Guten, Schonen resolut zu leben," and split the sentence into four parts, which correspond to the other four terms already inscribed. I have also written four words in English, which represent the sense of the German words. If you place Diagram No. 2, Teh, over Diagram No. 1, Tao, the respective fours all correspond, and No. 2 will be seen to be the psychological counterpart to No. 1 just as it ought to be if Teh is the realization of Tao.

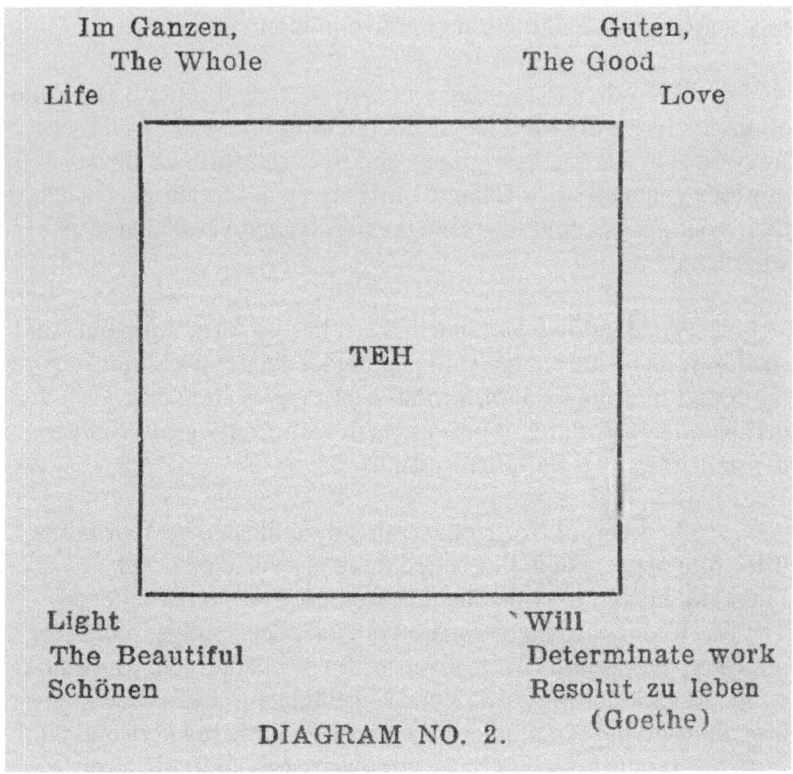

Im Ganzen,   Guten,
    The Whole   The Good
Life   Love

TEH

Light   `Will
The Beautiful   Determinate work
Schönen   Resolut zu leben
            DIAGRAM NO. 2.   (Goethe)

So much for the diagrams for the present. I have said that I shall not now give a number of quotations to prove what Teh is. I will instead give a totality view of Teh and yet never for a moment swerve from my diagram (No. 2.) To give this totality view I shall use a phrase from Goethe: "Im Ganzen, Guten, Schonen resolut zu leben" or in English, "to live with determination in the whole, the good and the beautiful." I have chosen the phrase because it is so apt and because you may hear it elsewhere. It is often quoted in philosophical discussions in this country and in England. To live in the whole, the good and the beautiful implies an attention to self, which needs explanation to forestall misunderstanding. I shall speak a great deal about self-realization in this and the next chapter. When I speak of self-realization I must not be understood to mean self in separateness, self as imagining itself as better or higher than its origin, nor the self that individually can set itself up against the not-self. Self-realization in that sense cannot be condemned too severely. The East acts in harmony with the West in raising the condemning hand against it. Both East and West consider self-realization in that sense a sin, a rebellion against the Higher Self and the order of the universe. Self-realization is the distinctive crime of our own age and perhaps no more marked in any country than in the United States. Without being a pessimist or a professional reformer, I predict great trouble coming upon this age because of its fall from the ideal, the true self.

When I speak of self in a good sense I mean the self which is a manifestation, or which approximately manifests the Higher Self, the Divinity. In one sense Auguste Comie spoke the eternal truth when he asserted that the old saying, "The heavens declare the glory of God" had lost its meaning and that the names of Hipparchus, Kepler and Newton meant much more than the starry heavens. It will be true, and will be true to us all, when our soul shall have become identified with the Absolute, that the heavens no more declare the glory of God, because we then shall have become the souls of the starry heavens, but now for the present "ourselves" dare not claim so much as Comte claimed. To do so now would be to persist in a grievous error and sin and totally to misconceive what self-realization means.

Self-realization is Teh as defined by Laotzse, or that which we can do and must do in this present moment in order to be representations of Tao. Self-realization means that man becomes the true manifestation of the Universal, whether we name this Universal impersonally or personally. Self-realization means a perfect substitution of all that which I in the past have called "Inner Life," and all that which this term implies; a substitution of that for all and everything that can be called external, separate and individual. Such self-realization does not imply the destruction of anything human of eternal value; on the contrary, it means the full blossom of humanity. Ourselves at present, our personality, as we call it, is no more than an ever changing plurality. "When our personality shall have been cut down on all its sharp edges, hammered into its inherent plan and purpose, and re-invigorated with eternal life, then, and first then, can we talk about "realized selves," about self-realization accomplished. Then we are eternal units. Until then we can only dream about the accomplishment of that high and ultimate ideal. Such dreams will pass before your vision in my present discourse; no more. I propose to claim that Goethe's phrase, "To live determinedly in the whole, in the good and in the beautiful," is a very good transcription of the meaning of Teh. Goethe did not know either Tao or Teh of the Tao-Teh-King, hence did not use the phrase in the sense I do. But that does not matter. The sentence is full of meaning just in the line of my discourse, and I shall use it with entire freedom. I will use the four parts of it in their natural succession and as arranged on the diagram. They stand grouped around Teh because they in the square represent the outer, while Teh represents the inner, whence they have sprung.

By "Im Ganzen" "in the whole," in general, I shall understand To Pan "the All" as a unit, both as known scientifically and as known intuitively; both objectively, subjectively and transcendentally; "the All," both personally as God and impersonally as the universe; both as life and as death, and "the All" in all forms and moods indefinable. By living "Im Ganzen," "in the whole," I shall understand to live "in consciousness of the whole"; the very opposite of living in "separateness" or isolation from it. How can we live determinedly "with a will" in "the All" such as I have attempted to suggest what "the All" may be; I will use an illustration. This candle may suggest the ideal! (See Diagram 3.) I shall, of course, be able only to show "the All" in one aspect. I will show it as light or truth; light or truth as quality; light or truth as form and judge; as the ordering principle in existence; or as I also shall call it, the Apollo, and the Christ

182

principle. While I thus only show one aspect, that aspect will suggest the Whole.

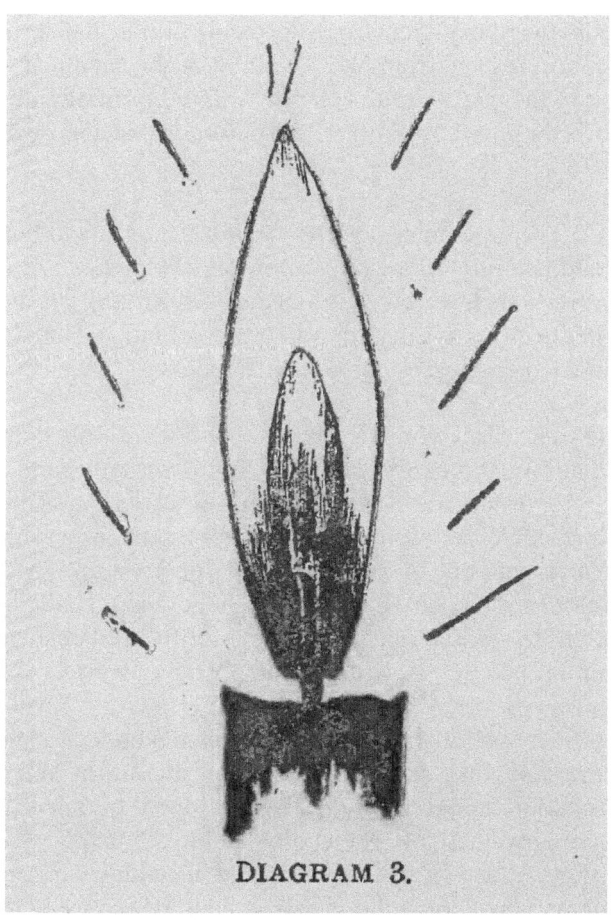

DIAGRAM 3.

My text is this candle. How does it illustrate? I will show you and show it in the psychological process of development, leaving out all other views.

(1) The wax (tallow) represents the sub-conscious

183

existence of the soul and corresponds to soil for the plant. The sub-conscious existence is the sum total of all the soul's foregone life, good, bad and indifferent. It is made up of natural qualities, of the soul's magical experiences, of its recollections, its karma, its struggles, failures and triumphs. The light of the candle is according to the quality of the tallow. And the form of embodied Teh is according to the quality of the natural basis upon which it rests.

(2) The taper makes it possible for the tallow to burn steadily and usefully. In the psychological life the taper represents consciousness, such as it is developed by education. The Teh appears in the consciousness of a Laotzse, a Plato, a Buddha, as well as in a Congo negro- but how differently!

(3) The black core is heat, and the not yet fully consumed taper and tallow. It therefore represents sub-consciousness and also the more or less developed consciousness; let me call it self-consciousness. Self-consciousness in a good sense is a step beyond consciousness and one toward spirituality or freedom. The black core is Teh in a glow, or what Frederik Hegel would call "diremption," a state of interior struggle for full self-realization and dominion over the Not-Me, or the objective world.

(4) The yellow light represents what is understood by the phrase "the soul is the candle of the Lord"; that is, the Teh is fully born in the soul, though not yet fully developed. In this degree the night or the Law, the Path, is receding and the "Sun of righteousness is arising with salvation on his wings." In human psychological development it is that stage in which we begin truly to say "I"- that marvelous word!

(5) The white light represents the full illumination. Individuality or separateness has vanished and the pure soul spreads its beneficent light and warmth round about. The Teh has not only taken the place of all law or the path or objectivity, but

law or path has been completed by being dissolved and transmuted into it.

(6) The diffused light is Tao and Teh, or Divinity in All, and All lifted into heavenly blessedness.

Here then are revealed six psychological stages, or six stages of Teh's inner nature. No amount of quotations or definitions could illustrate it as fully and as easily as a lighted candle. Light a candle at home and sit down quietly to meditate, and you shall find the candle a master guru, a sage. The candle burns in simplicity and stillness such as you have heard these two words explained in the past chapters. All this is not only psychologically true, but also historically.

(1) The wax or tallow is the Orient, say China, or mankind's unconscious will, the soil in which grows all the coming civilization.

(2) The taper is the dawning life. For instance, in India and Assyria and Egypt.

(3) The black core is Greek consciousness.

(4) The yellow light is the Hebrew awakening in the Messiah.

(5) The white light is primitive Christianity, and:

(6) The diffused light is that realization of the union of God and Man, "perfected humanity," Teh, which is yet to come.

Again I call your attention to the former chapter, in which I drew a parallelogram enclosing a geographical sphere, within which was shown the life of our cycle and the people who represented it. By comparison you will see further confirmation of the assertions I made at the time. Though this last, the "perfect humanity," Teh is yet to come, history fully proves that Teh is the fulfillment of the law of evolution, both the natural and the moral law. And that it is the fulfillment means that where Teh is dominant, there the law or path, the isolating principle in the evolution, has vanished because it has been transmuted into a higher reality! In this candle you have an illustration of one mode of existence of "the All," the mode of light, Teh as light. The comparison of soul to a light or candle is a common figure of speech in all occult lore. There are many reasons for it; too many, however, to enumerate here. Your own intuitions can easily supply them.

Realize the different stages of the light ; the tallow or wax, the taper, the black core, the yellow light, the white light, the diffused light in your own existence; live them all freely and fully at the same time, and you realize self- that is, that you are a universal self, not an isolated one, not one standing apart and dying. This is the ideal! How to do it in particulars in actual life?

By "Im Ganzen," "in the whole," specially, I shall understand to holon (totum), the idea of experience as a collection, a special kind of whole. In contradistinction to "the All" in general, this conception implies something that is changeable. Nature, (natura, physis, prakriti) for instance, is such a conception; the word "Nature" implies all sense perceptions of objects in the outer world and the variability of these objects. We ourselves, as we actually are, are such a changeable form of the All. We grow! Realizing this changeable nature, many of us have fallen into the grievous error of running about asking for salvation, as if salvation had anything to do with self-realization. Salvation is given to all! We never were anything else than saved! What we want is to assert our God-likeness and God-call, to realize "I am that I am." Let us assert:

(1) "A cosmos I am," both nature and spirit, therefore I

claim the perfect body and perfect spirit.

(2) Let man realize the woman in him- let women realize the man in themselves.

(3) Trust in thine own untried capacity
As thou wouldst trust in God himself.
Thou dost not dream what forces lie in thee,
Vast and unfathomed as the grandest sea.
No man shall place a limit to thy strength;
Such triumphs as no mortal ever gained
May yet be thine if thou wilt but believe
In... thyself.
(E. W. Wilcox.)

Such ideas are the power of "the All," and they lead life to sovereign power! They are of the form of the new consciousness! By "Im Guten," "in the good," in a general sense, I shall understand (agathon-bonum), that which is the final aim and end of all ethical action, both externally and spiritually. The good in this sense is synonymous with deity, the ultimate ground, not only of moral activity, but of all reality. It is the cosmic and ethic principle, and this more closely denned as love. By living "Im Guten," "in the good," I shall understand living in consciousness of the soul's essential identity with the good or God (the very opposite of "evil," such as for instance Shakespeare's Richard III. declares it to be his principle.) How do we live determinately, with a will, in this condition!

Here again I shall fall back upon an illustration, and the suggestion that comes from the illustration. (See Diagram No. 4.) This flower shall be the suggester. It shall represent love, the good. Under the form of those terms it is full of suggestions. As I did before, when I recommended the candle as a master guru, so now I recommend a living flower. The facts here are the pot and the plant, but these facts are not the flower or Teh. (A) The flower or

Teh, (1), is that passion which gripped the seed and forced it out of itself, and (2) that passion in the sub-conscious which drew it into its womb, the soil, and (3) that passion which here blossoms before you, and (4) that passion or "cosmic emotion" which reaches from this plant in phenomenal appearance to your image-building power; that passion which connects the two, and (5) that passion or "cosmic consciousness" which turns away from the sun's light (which is conditioned by earth atmosphere) and hastens inward towards a sphere, which is its infinite antecedents, and it is (6) a passion that seeks its own, its own family marks in intensity, not in immensity; it is eternal being.

(B) The flower or Teh in symbol is also the trembling stem. If you could have seen concentrated into a few moments the growth that took time, you would have seen and heard harmonies built upon harmonies, visible melody, an outward rushing, an uplift, and an inward "coming to be." That is Teh.

(C) And finally the flower or Teh in symbol are the blossoms. What is a blossom? Nature baring her bosom, showing her beauty! Did you ever see blossoms? Plants are passions, torrents of "Teh," sometimes in minor key, mournful and melancholy; sometimes fast and animated; sometimes a murmur, and sometimes a roar; always wild children, though they look so quiet. Do not misunderstand! Do not think of human passions, those self-destructive tires! Teh as passion is not a destructive fire. The central idea of the word passion in its origin is suffering. Teh is Tao incarnated in the world, and therefore "suffering," therefore full of pain, but always animated. The root of the plant is the eternal "being" of Teh; the stem is "the coming to be"; the blossom is revelation in all fullness, in all fulfillment.

But this is hard of comprehension. Let me therefore for Teh substitute a living idea, such as that of Jesus, for instance, and you shall see Teh before your eyes. Jesus is not a man, but type of a passionate movement. His life resembles a passionate movement like that of a flower. The story of Jesus is like this: (1) He strikes roots in oriental earth. He is Oriental, not European or American. (2) He is from Abraham; that is, Abrahm (out-of-Brahm.) So is a flower out-of-Brahm, substance. (3) The story of Jesus breaks fully through in the Law by Moses, in the Song by David, in the shadow pictures by Isaiah. (4) The story rises to consciousness in classical culture. What is culture but the breaking through the soil, that the flower and blossom may appear? It was Jesus breaking with the existing bondage that awakened his consciousness of a call, and his call became the flower of his life. (5) Finally the story blossoms in the New Testament, and the blossom is an at-one-ing, a redeeming note of love, passion and despair in harmony; fullness, fulfilling the whole past course. And that blossom was the revelation of the purpose of the whole movement. The history of Teh. (6) The flower is bewildering in its majesty and seductive in its calm; and so is the story of Jesus, overwhelming in his declaration of the oneness of the Almighty, the All-good, the All-wise and the Soul. ("The father and I are one.") And a flower plant is just such oneness. The plant is neither the root, the stem, the leaves, the blossom, but all these in one. Teh is not any special act. The life story of the soul is Teh. No wonder that Jesus of the legend so often dealt with plants and referred to nature's harmonies. He felt himself to be "God with us," or the present nature. He is Teh or enthusiasm, a plant that grows everywhere in the universe.

Jesus is not a scientific fact, nor a man, nor a thought. He is great passion- enthusiasm. Enthusiasm translated from Greek thought to Hebrew thought gives us the Greek word Jesus as Jehovah-Hosea, and that contracted is Jehosuah, and that translated into English is "God with us." Jesus thus is an expression for Teh in you and me. Without passion or enthusiasm we shall never understand the mystery of Jesus. No belief or Bible study will reveal the mystery. Teh seen as Jesus is the voice of Tao calling in "the cool of the evening" upon the sinner, and is also the bell to morning prayer and adoration.

DIAGRAM 4.

Jesus is no mere man, he is love; he is Teh, a present God. I see him wherever there is life and love, light and law; in the landscape, in the boisterous and wild ocean, in the calm starlit night, in the amorous lines of the human body, in the monotonous beat of an Indian's drum, in an axiom of Euclid; in the bended back that carries the hoe, yes, I hear his cry in the factory and the prison. The Jesus idea was familiar to the ancient world. It meant passion, color, enthusiasm, and resembles the Dionysios idea, if we look for pictures in Greek life; not Bacchus, the drunkard, but

THE INNER LIFE AND THE TAO TEH KING

Dionysios of the Orphic Mysteries. It is worth your while to study this aspect of the Jesus idea. It reveals Teh as an evolutionary force, and Teh will be seen to be the root idea of religion, science, poetry and philosophy. It will also give the true understanding of the desperately misunderstood idea of incarnation. If we look for parallels to the Christ idea we find an excellent one in the Greek Apollo. That, too, would be for all a most useful study. It will reveal the inter-relationship of the idea Jesus and Christ, Teh and Tao.

The Jewish-Christian converts thought of Christ very much as the Dorian Greeks thought of Apollo. Apollo to the Greek was the god of law, order or righteousness, the chief of the polls, or city government, and the revenger of all infractions. Apollonism in Doric aspects is much like Paulinism of the New Testament. The Attic Greeks, on the other hand, understood Apollo very nearly like the Christ of St. John's Gospel. Apollo to them was the aesthetic and plastic element in existence. He was god of music or rhythm, and the ideal of beauty, the god of reason, Logos- the same names are given the Christ. Apollonism in Attic aspect is very much like Johanism of the New Testament. In both aspects there is a strong parallelism between the Apollo idea and the Christ idea.

By "Im Guten" "in the good," in a special sense, I shall understand to mean a thing possessing worth. The various races and the changing times have varying ideas about "the highest good." The new consciousness, that of the New Ages, realizes its idea of the good by fulfilling its own law. Our own law tells us that our everlasting, joyous and undeniable duty is to impress our stamp upon others. Our self-sacrifice is therefore not negative, as the old law was, but it is positive. In passionate activity we and the New Age fulfill the ideal of the flower, of Teh. Passionate activity is a magic phrase, but easily understood in the light of what I have said. It was said of Jesus: "He went about and did good!" For us it does not merely mean laboring to do good, but also to show the example, to inspire by presence. Thus far I have shown Teh in the process of "self-realization," "Im Ganzen" (the All), under aspect of the Christ or light, by means of a candle; and "Im Guten" under aspect of Jesus or love, and by means of a flower. It remains to show Teh "Im Schonen." I shall try to do it by still another illustration, the ocean. I will show the ocean under the aspect of beauty, the sublime. The ocean is the most uncertain and unstable of all things in the world, and so is beauty, in spite of appearance. And so is Teh. Yet both ocean, beauty and Teh impress us constantly with the idea of "eternity, immensity and power." I will try to show it. My description of the traits of the ocean are taken from Richard Henry Stoddard's "Hymn to the Sea."

> "Thou wert before the continents, before
> The hollow heavens, which, like another sea,
> Encircles them and Thee; but whence Thou wert
> And when Thou wast created, is not known."

"The self" or soul that has been in the trance of beauty or Teh and identified itself with it, knows beauty or Teh as being eternal like love, and beauty is love's form. The three, love and beauty and Teh, are inseparable and encircling the earth and sky-yea, reaching beyond! The soul perceives this and is itself such a far-reaching power. Beauty's or Teh's origin is not known outside of the soul. Nor is the origin of soul known.

> "Antiquity was young when Thou wast old.
> There is no limit to Thy strength, no end
> To Thy magnificence."

Antiquity is of time; beauty or Teh has no limit to its strength. Already Plato had discovered that when "justice" and wisdom, and all other things that are held in honor, find no avenue to the soul, beauty has still some passage and entrance. The soul and Teh have entrance where no law can penetrate. What grand personality the ocean manifests! It is the soul or Teh in form unknown to science and philosophy!

> "Thou goest forth
> On thy long journeys to remotest lands,
> And comest back unwearied."

How could beauty or Teh ever weary? Beauty's smile never yawns. Beauty's virginal lines never jade and beauty's untiring colors are never exhausted. Neither is Teh weary or getting old; is ever young blood. There is Teh or beauty of soul that never dies; there is Teh or beauty on tropic isles and Arctic icebergs; in "the sullen sorrow of the sky," and the "laughter of the Sun." Teh or beauty is the constitutive element. Try to separate them if you can.

> "Thou art terrible
> In thy tempestuous moods, when the loud winds
> Precipitate their strength against the waves."

Ah, who thought beauty was only "the long, slow rolling summer days on beaches far away?" Surely they have never seen "a soul on fire," nor heard of Apollo's arrows or cowered under Athena's stern face, nor ever experienced Teh's demands upon the soul. They have never understood life's set purpose with us.

> "The heavens look down and see themselves in Thee.
> And splendors seen not elsewhere."

Yea, so it is! Teh is magnificent! The angels are desirous of knowing the mystery of a soul. They are themselves only naked spirits desiring body. The heavens see their own color in the ocean. The angels see splendors not seen elsewhere. But men experience Teh! Should we not rejoice in Teh, in Beauty; our Teh, our Beauty! Beauty or Teh of body, Beauty or Teh of soul!

THE INNER LIFE AND THE TAO TEH KING

"Thine the silent, happy, awful night,
When over Thee and Thy charmed waves the moon
Rides high."

When the poet here speaks of the silent, happy, awful
night, we think only of conditions that are without sound, but not
without voice. The night, the self, the ocean, Teh are never without
voice, though sometimes silent. Teh or Beauty is the voice that
calls all creation to come forth. The voice, the word, is the
incarnated love. Beauty! Teh! The poet finally starts in to talk
about death, but corrects himself at once and exclaims:

"No!
There is no death. The thing that we call death
Is but another, sadder name for life,
Which is itself an insufficient name,
Faint recognition of that unknown life-
That power whose shadow is the universe."

Yes, "shadow" is the word! Shadow paints Teh, beauty,
by contrast. Teh is not death! Teh is life and always was! I think I
have said sufficient to suggest what self-realization, "Im
Schonen," is. Where are there such worshipers of beauty? Where
can they be found? A religion of beauty is as much a necessity for
us as a religion of goodness, or forms that embrace the whole.
How much there is still to be done before our humanity can reflect
Tao as Teh! How much before my diagrams can be said to be line
drawings of our ways of life!

By "Im Schonen" in a special sense, I shall understand any
one of the innumerable terms of love, which we may be attracted
to individually, or which may be our form or plan of life. I need
not detail the thought. Pictures of beauty hover before your
imagination. Realize one of them!

By "resolut zu leben," I shall in general understand to live determinately, or according to the whole trend or plan of our life as we know it, both in consciousness and conscience. We need resolutely to assert our God-likeness! Finally I must, at least, indicate the special mode of "living determinedly."

Again I will substitute a picture for the abstract term Teh. You can see the picture in the book that contains the Christ poem. The Christ idea is the determined realization of the whole, the good, the beautiful, thus:

(1) The Christ "is the principle in whom all things stand together," as it was said in Paul's letter to the Collossians.

(2) Jesus said: "I and the Father are one."

(3) All the parables are in the Beautiful.

(4) Finally "the determinate living" is expressed by "faithful unto death."

You are familiar with these expressions. They all contain the conception Teh.

CHAPTER XI

LIFE, LOVE, LIGHT AND WILL

In the last chapter I described how to live the life which is of Teh by using a phrase of Goethe's: "Im Ganzen, Guten, Schonen resolut zu leben." I will now show how this fourfold life connects with corresponding powers within our own constitution, and, that this corresponding fourfoldness makes it not only possible, but easy to live with determination in the Whole, the Good and the Beautiful.

On Diagram II. I designate the four inherent powers as Life, Love, Light and determined Will. The terms are entirely my own, and not used by anybody else, as far as I know. I have used them for many years in my studies of the subject, but I would not lay any special weight upon them. Other terms may be as suitable and perhaps convey the same ideas. What I do mean by them I shall explain, and, I shall hope that you for yourself will substitute other terms if you have such and if they convey to you the ideas I intend to express. The main point is the idea or the psychological fact, not the name we give the fact. These four terms inscribed in the respective four corners of Diagram II. represent ideas connected with the ancient classification of temperaments into four groups, usually attributed to Hippocrates: the sanguine, choleric, melancholic and phlegmatic.

I say ideas distinctly connected with this classification, because I do not bind myself to it nor do I think that classification exhaustive. However, defective as it is, it serves admirably for a broad classification of our congenital constitution, and it has the advantage of being biological. We get the best psychology where we begin biologically, on sure foundations in nature. Moreover, back of these four temperaments lie the elements fire, air, earth, water, such as the ancients named them, and, also the four forms of the spiritual world: supreme goodness, nous, psyche, hyle, and, also the influences from the four corners of the universe. Our bodily constitution gives a bias to our disposition, and that bias is usually called temperament and distinguished in a four fold way as sanguinic, choleric, melancholic and phlegmatic. Temperament is nothing else than a predominant characteristic of our natural inclinations and tendencies, and the four names I have put on the diagram are simply my transcriptions of the four terms; sanguinic, choleric, melancholic and phlegmatic, which I have not put down on the diagram, because I wanted to avoid the confusion that was apt to arise if I wrote too much on. it. I only mention this about the temperaments to give you a clue to my terms; life, love, light and will, and to indicate that I begin in biology, the true psychological basis. Besides the four terms I have used, there are others which I might have written on the diagram, but which I also have left out in order to avoid confusion. You can readily add them yourself if you wish.

Among such terms are those of a four-foldness described in Paul's letter to the Ephesians (Eph. 4.11-15). Paul speaks of the appointment of apostles, prophets, evangelists and pastoral teachers, who were set in the church in order to perfect the saints, to build up the church, that all might attain to the unity of faith and grow to be full grown men and no more be children driven by any and every wind of doctrine. That which Paul here describes as the order of the ministry of the early church is admirable psychology. If we understand what apostles, prophets, evangelists and pastoral teachers mean, the whole psychological system of the Path and of Teh, as understood by Paul, is marvelous in its simplicity. I will try to elucidate. The apostolic power is the spirit in rational preeminence. It is the power that has the eye upon the Whole, both in its outer features and in its inner. It is the embodiment of Logos-Reason or the fundamental human power which is the spring of all mental, moral and spiritual manifestations. In the apostolic power there is something dominant like that silent but weighty force which the earth exhibits everywhere. In the catacombs, the apostle's symbol is a lion and his robe is yellow, like the earth under the burning sun in the Orient. The apostolic character lies in the first Kabbalistic world of Aziah, the world of activity or earth. The prophetic power spoken of is the Wisdom-power or, as the classical people called it, the Hermes. Hermes was messenger from the Highest and his nature was represented as being that of the Wind, a term which to the ancients was synonymous with Spirit. The prophet was not a soothsayer but a divine messenger or witness. In the ancient church he was the preacher or which was the same the witness, the witness or proclaimer of the divine truth. The prophet was a sort of executive officer of the Spirit. The ancient symbol used as an expression for his office was an eagle and usually shown on blue felt, clearly indicative of his soaring spirit. The prophetic character lies in the second Kabbalistic world of Yetzirah, the world of formation.

The evangelist is also a messenger, but one sent by an authority, not directly from heaven like the prophet. The evangelist is the man with the large warm heart who goes out into the world with the "glad tidings" and who brings milk and honey, to the hungry. His symbol is double. He is represented by the "human face divine" back of him, and with the figure of an ass at his side. The idea being that he has human feeling as motive power and also the steadiness, ye, obstinacy of the ass, that will not be driven away by stripes, and, which moreover is satisfied to eat that on the fields which the ox or other animals will not eat. The evangelistic character lies in the third Kabbalistic world, the world of Briah, the world of creation. The pastoral teacher is symbolically represented as the patient ox on the threshing floor in the East, which treads out the corn by steady and patient walking round and round. This symbol explains him as the more or less phlegmatic or patient teacher who by persistent labor brings out the fruit in the pupil, who is being trained in spiritual life. He is not original like the prophet, nor authoritative like the apostle, nor fiery like the evangelist, but he is really the cornerstone in the spiritual edifice, for what does all the work of the other offices amount to, if the teaching pastor did not teach the initiate how to masticate and assimilate? The pastor and teachers' character lies in the fourth Kabbalistic world, the world of Atziloth, the archetypal world. Reviewing the four offices as now described, you can readily see the truth of Paul's statement, that they are necessary for full growth, for unity and perfection, not only in an outer organization made up of people of the four temperaments, but also in each one of us. Though we have only one temperament predominant, we have the other three in less degree and they need training and guidance as much as the one which is dominant. I shall come back to this fourfoldness at the end of this chapter and make a personal application of it.

The square represents man as a temple. The square is ethically an emblem of sincerity; it means wholeness, health and harmony on a plane of life different from that of nature. The circle, the line that runs into itself, stands for similar perfections in nature. The square in the sense I use it was discovered, or at any rate is credited, to operative Masonry and Freemasonry. The circle could not be used as a symbol for temple, and has not been used, because a temple is not a nature-product; a temple is a human symbol for a human creative act. The word square has gone into human language as a term for integrity and beauty. We are square physically when we form an equilateral quadrature by standing upright, feet joined and arms outstretched. We are square spiritually when the events of our lives follow the principle of fourfoldness expressed by the law of "the limbs." The metaphysical and physical supplement one another. We are square cosmologically and theologically by other figures and measurements unnecessary to detail at present. The idea of the square I have derived from the Apocalypse of St. John. I use it because of its psychological character. I will explain what that means. St. John saw the New Jerusalem descend in the form of a man and that form was described as being a square. That mystery only becomes intelligible when you place the human figure with outstretched arms inscribed in a square, making the length of the body from head to sole equal to the length of the arms and hands from finger tip to finger tip. A square drawn around such a figure may well represent the human temple and the psychological fourfoldness of man in his temperamental actions. Such a figure in a square is to be recommended to all who study man's constitution and their own. For microcosmic man. it answers to the macrocosmic man's figure in that temple I gave in a former chapter, and located geographically from China to the Mediterranean sea and a few degrees north of the tropic of Cancer. Laotzse knew the fourfoldness. The cosmogony of the Tao-Teh-King is this:

> Tao gave birth to 1 (Tao-sen-yit).
> 1 gave birth to 2 (Yit-sen-ri).
> 2 gave birth to 3 (Ei-sen-sam).
> 3 gave birth to 4 (Sam-sen-wan-wut or the 10,000 things),

and the 10,000 things carry (1) Yin on the back and hold, (2) Yang in the arms, and these two produce, (3) Harmony, or the living principle, and, these three together constitute (4) the world; in other words Yin, Yang, Harmony and the world also constitute a fourfoldness. Rather interesting; is it not? Yin and Yang mean Mother and Father.

So much for Diagram II. and its construction. The word Teh, stands in the center of the Diagram and I shall now try to make you see these four as emanations from Teh. Those who have given serious attention to the life that seems to rush by them; anybody who has observed phenomena and thought about their causes, must have become aware that existence, either in cosmic or human form, is something dynamic, something living, is much like a stream. To be sure, none of us know either the stream's spring nor its outlet to an ocean, if there be any ocean. We see only that something under space and time conditions. It is even possible that there is no stream and that we read our own changeable nature into that which we call the universe. However, we see change. Even fire, if it be not stirred, will go to sleep and die. Like ships swinging around on the anchor chain, we do not really get away, but nevertheless we are always in motion, because life itself moves by ebb and flood. Water without circulation becomes stagnant and pollutes itself. Moral bugles are always calling us; we are never allowed rest except we wed ourselves to death. Streams, physical, mental and moral, winds, spiritual or otherwise, keep up a circulation everywhere. Some of us in pessimistic moods see these currents only as destructive and point to all the flotsam and jetsam they carry along. Others more optimistic see only how great majestic ships of human dignity and worth sail down in the deep waters and safely pass all dangers.

Wherever mankind has had an eye for such a movement it has usually also seen that movement under a twofold aspect and named these aspects variously. In China the twofold aspect was seen long ago, and by Laotzse the two were named Tao and Teh; and he, like the other ancient sages, by these two terms described what he perceived, and he did it in the Tao-Teh-King. I have already set forth what Laotzse meant by Tao and there is but little more to say. I began to speak about Teh in the last chapter and shall now give some more information. I will claim that the word Teh represents such movements, changes, emanations, streams and dynamic forces, as those I have hinted at as descriptions of That which takes place around us. I have frequently used the word Teh and given suggestions about it; yet much is still left to be said. Something of that still unsaid I shall try to bring out by placing the Teh in relationship to the conceptions evolution and karma, and thereby gain some means by which to explain it. I shall not define evolution nor karma. By evolution I shall in general understand the movement in the universe so aptly defined by Herbert Spencer and Science in general, and I shall take the word largely in a physical sense. By Karma I shall understand practically the same as I understand by evolution, but I shall take the word mainly in a moral and spiritual sense. At any rate I shall give the word a very wide and universal meaning. These two words, evolution and karma, have many equivalents, varying according to views taken, and it will have its interest that I give you some of these equivalents and explain them to some extent, because the equivalents will help to explain Tao and Teh, the two old Chinese terms for thoughts similar to some aspects of evolution, karma and the other terms, as I shall now mention them in the following and elucidate them.

The classical people, Greeks and Romans, used the term destiny or fate, and the fullest explanation of this word is that given by Seneca in his epistles. I will therefore reproduce this Stoic's words. I will quote Seneca in full because his definition is probably least known.

"They (our ancestors) did not by any means believe this, that Jupiter, as we worship him at the Capitol and in other shrines, sent down thunderbolts from his hand; but they recognized the same Jupiter as we do, the same director and guardian of the universe, the mind and soul of the world, the lord and maker of this work, to whom each name belongs. You wish to say that he is Providence, you will speak correctly; for he is the one by whose wisdom the world is cared for, so that it may proceed safely and perform its tasks. You wish to call him Nature; you will not sin. He is the One from whom all come; by whose spirit we live. You wish to call him the World, you will not be deceived, for he is all this which is visible, set in his own members, sustaining himself and his." (Seneca Naturalium Quest. Lib. 11. Cap. 45.1, 2, 3.)

If you speak of Nature, Fate, Fortune, all are names of the same God, who is manifesting himself in these various ways." (Seneca. De Beneficiis Lib. lv.8.)

I need not say much in explanation of Seneca. As you noticed, he advises not to care for names but to get at the fact behind names. And speaking in the language of the Tao-Teh-King, the fact he cares for is named Teh. And Teh as a fact is presented by Laotzse as a "power that makes for righteousness," a power that has its being in all our modes of existence. A power and purpose, a will and a way, name it as we may, exists as a fact and cannot be denied. Look upon it as evolution, as karma or under any of the aspects mentioned by Seneca- there it is, and, as Seneca (Ep, 107.11) also says, "it leads the willing and drags the unwilling."

An ancient Greek poet describing the mother of the gods, said she was "One shape of many names." That description fits Teh admirably. Not only is Teh of motherly nature (though the Tao-Teh-King knows no gods) but Teh is multiform and many named, as I have said, and that because Teh enters into all human actions as the organizing reason, the forming and plastic principle, and gets its many names from these incarnations. Such a principle as Teh is peculiar to humanity. Throughout the organic world, action is regulated mainly by hereditary structure; and secondarily by reflex action or instinct derived from hereditary structure. But action with man is modified by intelligent use of experience, by the reflex action of the accumulated results of mankind's past experiences. That action and those accumulated results of mankind's past experiences is in Chinese called Teh; with us, scientifically, Morals, principles of morals or principles for the conduct of our spiritual life. The Calvinist among christian theologians chose the term election and understood one small action of that which other christians call Providence, a term so personal that they are constantly in trouble when asked to explain it. Among scientists you meet with the biologist who has a term of his own, by which he accounts for both cause and effect and motion, too. "Selection" is his magic word. I need not spend any time on it; you are familiar with it if you have followed the literature of the last thirty years. The same is the case with the phrase "cosmic process" so handy to the evolutionist as an explanation of facts he does not understand and which his narrow science has no room for. Pantheistic poets of modern days speak of "cosmic emotion" and quote Sidgwick and Romanes as their authorities; other poets of the same color have varied the phrase and speak of "tides of eternal emotions." The mystics of all ages have called the same phenomena and their causes "love." The future will probably see other terms and hear other expressions. And it is well that new terms and expressions should come forth. They prove that some parts of mankind are neither dead nor asleep. Whatever terms be applied, they all signify that the power they name is one that works for uplift, for evolution, for progress, for spiritual life, for the Inner Life. The terms employed always signify quality in contradistinction to quantity, and they all have a tendency to be personal in character and all stand somewhat in opposition to something impersonal. It seems that no teacher can avoid personification. Whatever terms be employed and whether they be considered personally or impersonally they can all be translated, by Teh, as the Tao-Teh-King uses that word.

I, myself, shall not offer new terms. I am engaged in restoring Teh to its right place and I mean to use with perfectly liberty and whenever I want any of the terms I have just now enumerated, because they express various aspects of the Chinese conception of Teh. But this I will say right here, that with the exception of Seneca's explication of all that which lies in the word fate, all the other terms apply principally to Tao and only secondarily to Teh. With the exception of Stoicism, the West knows next to nothing of such a conception as that of Teh as the mother of the universe; or as we can say, since Goethe, the "eternally feminine." Western thought is so exclusively masculine in cast and formal in its philosophy, that it has become terribly one-sided and barren. If it were not for the mystic leaven of love, that, here and there, now and then, has softened its rudeness and added a little affection and color to its mentality, the Western mind would be a dreary desert and look like barren rocks. And the pity is, the West believes itself superior.

The names given to Deity by the ancients were always descriptions of the character of their deity, such as they perceived it. In conformity to that practice, I shall give Teh the sense of "the eternally feminine," the sense of "a power that makes for righteousness," the sense of "providence" the sense of "cosmic process," the sense of "moral force" the sense of "mother," besides all the other senses already given the word. The reason for these many names of Teh or senses given to Teh is this, that Teh is as an old saw says a soul and a light that reveals all things, but hides itself from sight. All the world sees by Teh, but never saw Teh.

> "I find thee, Most High, where'er my glance I send,
> At the beginning Thee; Thee also at the end.
> If towards the source I fly, in Thee 't is lost to me.
> The outlet would I spy- that, too, breaks forth from Thee.
> Thou the beginning art, that doth its end enclose.
> Thou art the end that back to the beginning flows.
> And in the midst art Thou, and all things are in Thee,
> And I am I, because Thou art the midst in me."
> (Friedrich Rückert: *The Wisdom of the Brahmin*, lv.50.
Translated by C. T. Brooks, Boston, 1882.)

According to the Tao-Teh-King, the relationship of Tao and Teh is something like this: "If Tao perishes," it is said, "then Teh will also perish." Teh is called the manifestation of Tao, and, Tao cannot be reached except by means of Teh. Teh is multiform, but Tao is a unit. These two ideas, that Teh is the manifestation of Tao and is multiform, explain the syncretism of the Teh. All virtue is necessarily manifold and ever varying. In one moment it is heavenward and a worth-ship; in the next it is earthward or love to the neighbor. These two ideas of "manifestation" and "multiformity" explain the great variety of names and descriptions of Teh already given. In one place it is said that Tao is the Lord of Teh, but nowhere does any commentary explain in what that lordship consists. Whatever it does mean, it does not mean that Tao is superior to Teh, because Tao does not and cannot exist without Teh. It will not do to call Tao the masculine and Teh the feminine principle of existence, because the Tao-Teh-King not only does not do it, but knows both Yang and Yin and calls them the masculine and feminine principles. If Tao and Teh are related to Yang and Yin, then it must be as superior spiritual principles behind them and it is in this sense that I take Teh, when I call it "the eternally feminine."

It is exceedingly difficult to define Tao and Teh fully and satisfactory to a Western critical and intellectual mind. Both terms are too elastic for logic and both represent something universal, that cannot be put into a philosophical form. Truly the Tao-Teh-King declares that their nature "baffles investigation" but the same book also declares that if we "use" Tao and Teh, we shall know them. Thus an examination of the nature of Tao and Teh ends like all examinations of mystic principles; they are beyond comprehension, but ready for our use at any time and anywhere. The mystic principles desire incorporation; they wish to be placed in the human heart and to be allowed to lead man to his eternal good. They never mislead, however exacting they may be. They never teach us, as we understand teaching, but they are ready to lead us, and, they are always near us, yea, they dwell in our hearts. I have just said that I should give Teh the sense of "the eternally feminine" and the sense of "mother." These two senses have been given Teh by explicit language. All the other senses are implied in various teachings. But before I draw out the colors and the life that lies in the terms of the sixth chapter of the Tao-Teh-King on the mother-power Teh, I will give you a translation of it. And I will say a few words about the direct meaning before I apply this conception mother-power to Teh, for Teh is the mother-power, considered morally, out of which springs our whole mental, moral and spiritual life. Teh as the mother of all things is described in the sixth chapter as follows:

"The Valley-God never dies. I call it the Mother of the Abyss and she is the Root of Heaven-Earth (or the All-things.) She endures forever, and forever she produces."

THE INNER LIFE AND THE TAO TEH KING

     I might have disposed of this short chapter by saying that this Valley-God is the same as sakti, as deva matri, but I should then have been reading Brahminical ideas and modern methods into Chinese Theosophy and that would have been a false commentary. It has been done by others, I am sorry to say. I will admit, that the root idea of the Tao-Teh-King's description is probably physical and sexual. So much in the East begins that way. So much in the East is cast mainly in prehistoric forms, and only too many of modern students of Eastern lore stick in these forms. While the signs and forms of the Tao-Teh-King are often physical and sexual, simply because the writer had no other means at hand for his use, these signs and forms of the Tao-Teh-King always bear a high and noble, a spiritual and transcendental signification, and are so understood by genuine Taoists. In this case, "the Valley-God" cannot mean anything else than Teh or Virtue. The sign for Valley-Spirit is a double one. It is composed of ku and sen.

     The sign for ku is a mouth out of which flows water, hence it is a sign for valley, but simply for a valley without a stream. To indicate that the valley gives out water, the sign sen is added, which indicates that the valley is living. That is the way the Chinese commentator understands it. For short, the signs is a name for the activity of Teh in all the realms of its operation. But the realistic conception connected with the term must not be ignored. There is such an one in it, which is evident from the fact that Laotzse also calls it "nourishing mother" (ss'i-mu). A prominent Taoist and philosopher, Liet-tsi (400 B.C), declares Laotzse's teaching and words to be cited from the books of the fabled King Hoang-ti (about 27 Cent. B.C). If so, then the meaning of the sign and term would be physical and sexual. Be this declaration of Liet-tsi so or not, we cannot prove or deny the allegation. The word ku-sen means now the "emanating spirit" or "the out flowing spirit," indicating the invisible power behind all objective appearances, or, in other words, the spiritual or invisible mother of all things already mentioned in the opening chapter of the book.

THE INNER LIFE AND THE TAO TEH KING

The chapter on the valley-god already given in translation divides itself naturally into three thoughts. The first relates to the valley-god as the original power through which as the mysterious mother all things come forth; the second thought relates to the valley-god as the root of heaven and earth specially; and the third thought is this that these two already mentioned do not exist separately but are really one, and, it has been suggested by the German commentator, Strausz, that these two in union correspond to Chokma of the Old Testament, to the Idea of Plato, to Sophia of the Gnostics and the Magic of Jacob Bohme. I think the suggestion an admirable one. I would add that the two in union also correspond to Sephira, mother of the Sephiroth, of the Kabbalah. It would be very interesting to work out the details of these correspondences, but space and time forbid it, at present. I wish to bring Teh down to the level of our own daily life and individual existence. That will be more practical and useful, at present. Let me now apply this fourfoldness of Teh to you and myself and try to find out our exact place in the temple, and thereby necessarily the work we can and must do in that universal ministry of Teh to which we all without exception are called. If we find ourselves individually of a warm and pure red blood condition; if our blood is not loaded with foreign substances, but readily heals a wound; if our nerves are in a corresponding healthy condition and neither "cracked" nor weak; if we enjoy to live and to be active in great and good work and do a work for the benefit of mankind, not merely because we are paid for it or profit by it in some way, but do such a work because we find our call in it and an innermost satisfaction in doing it, then, I say, we are Life people, people of the apostolic temper, workers in the universal ministry. Our genius is activity and it will be a sin for us to be unfaithful. Our place on the Diagram and in the temple is readily seen. We know what Teh wants of us.

If we are introspective of disposition, if we always are inclined to look behind a phenomenon to see its spirit, if possible; if the blue sky draws us out of ourselves and robs us of the solid ground under our feet; if things and persons do not appear to our souls like the seeming solid things our senses declare them to be; if we are disinclined for all kinds of "small talk," "gossip," or the like, but from time to time are moved by a mighty impulse to "speak out," to "witness," to give testimony in the name of the Highest; then, we are of the prophetic temper, or at least poets or philosophers. Our genius is clearly spirit and our work in the universal ministry so clearly marked off for us that we never can mistake it. We know our place on the Diagram and in the temple. We know what Teh wants of us. If our hearts bleed at the sight of human misery, both physical and spiritual, if we burn to go out into the world to preach the glad tidings that there is hope for all, even the deepest fallen, if we proclaim that hope in love to mankind and without any condemnation, not even with reproach; if we cheerfully stand abuse, even stripes and never lose courage in our work; if we persist in working for others as if they were our own relatives, though separated from us by race or color or enmity, then, I say, we are of the evangelistic temper. Our genius is clearly Love and nobody can do the work laid out for us in our ministry as well as we can. We know our place in the temple and what Teh wants of us.

If we are disposed to teach and take care, to lead and to guide, and be a daily and hourly sacrifice of which others take freely and eat, never even realizing that they torture us, if we have a patience that never wearies over repetitions and monotony; if compensation is never thought of; if we run after the lost sheep, comfort the obstinate ones, and bear over with the unreasonable, then, our work in the temple of humanity is pastoral teaching and we are indeed pillars in the sanctuary of Teh. It is evident that this last group of sanctified tempers and human beings are those who live with determination (see Diagram II.). That the first group described (the apostolic) is living in the Whole is self-evident. I hardly need to say that the prophetic temper as described is the light bearer of beauty, and that the evangelistic temper is a real incarnation of goodness. Let none try to stifle their own conscience and say that they have not felt any motion in the direction of the four forms mentioned. They do not speak the truth, ignorantly or willfully. All feel the motions of Teh! The Tao-Teh-King (LI) declares "To produce and not possess- to act and not expect- to enlarge and not control- that is Teh." If such people have not felt the drawings of Teh under such forms as those I have described, they have felt them under other forms. Perhaps the four to them should be named, God, Reason, Nature, Highest Life; perhaps they should be named Eight, Justice, Love, Reciprocity of life; perhaps they should be named as on Diagram I. No matter how they are named. Each age has named them differently, but each age has known the fact that Teh manifests itself in a temple square or human individuality. Not only each age knows the fact, but the fact presents itself to each individual, even to those who cannot express the fact or translate the moving power into words. No man is sufficient for himself. Life is so constituted that we need reservoirs of every kind of excellence, of intelligence, of knowledge, of power. The four forms are such reservoirs in which Teh is present and they are for us to draw from, both to live by and to work by.

Now in which ever of these four groups our work may lie, it is the spirit of Teh, the Great Mother, that works that temper in us. And to be in Truth, we must obey, yea we wish to obey and we do obey as surely as the water runs out of the valley. You remember the sign of ku-sen, the great symbol of Teh! I say it is Teh that both works in us and wishes to work in us, and, if we amount to anything at all in the universal ministry to which we all are called by Teh, even while we still struggle on the Path, then we show eagerness to do that work as we say "with a will"; we do it determinedly and that eagerness proves what we amount to. This is Teh and teaching about Teh. And Teh now witnesses within each one of us for or against us, according to the truth in which we stand in this matter. There is a spurious Biblical phrase which reads, "It is a terrible thing to fall into the hands of the living God." It may be spurious as regards the Bible, but this I say, "It is a terrible thing to fall into the hands of Teh" for those who are unfaithful. It can only mean destruction. I said in the beginning of this chapter that the fourfold life of Teh corresponded to similar powers within our constitution and that this corresponding fourfoldness made it not only possible but easy to live with determination in the Whole, the Good, the True and the Beautiful. I have shown you the corresponding forms, both the inner in yourself and the outer in Teh's universal life, and, I have said that Teh works spontaneously in us all, because Teh is a river of active goodness or virtue that flows into the world from out a valley, which is called the Abyss of Abysses. It is now for you and me to live up to this light and make ourselves living realizations of that stupendous fact. Terstegen was a Dutch mystic. As a mystic, he is especially remarkable on account of his intuitive perceptions of the motions of the Spirit, of Teh such as I have defined Teh. Here are a few lines from his poetry describing these motions of Teh:

> "Hath not each heart a passion and a dream-
> Each, some companionship forever sweet-
> And each, in saddest skies some silver gleam
> And each, some passing joy too faint and fleet
> And each, a staff and stay, though frail it prove-
> And each, a face he fain would ever see?"

These are some of the beckonings of Teh, that come to all. He finally asks:

> "And what have I?- a glory and a calm,
> A life that is an everlasting psalm,
> A heaven of endless joy in Thee."

That is Teh. Terstegen thus declares that Teh is an "everlasting presence" and an endless joy. May that be your lot! You shall then know that all this about Teh is of the Inner Life.

CHAPTER XII

A SHAWNEE TALE

In the last chapter, I introduced and discussed several new subjects, necessarily leaving a great deal for this and the following chapters. The subjects were Teh, the human temple, our temperaments, and the work we are called to do both on the Path and in the Universal Ministry for the benefit of our fellowmen.

I shall now continue the same subjects and endeavor to explain certain important aspects of them by means of a folklore tale from our American plains. Strange as it may appear, the story I shall read contains the most valuable material for a study of Teh and a life on the Path, the life of regeneration. The story I shall read is a Shawnee tale, and I give it as told in Schoolcraft's "Algic researches" under the title of "The Celestial Sisters." The book is now scarce. Inner evidences and the undisputed veracity of Schoolcraft is sufficient evidence against any charge or suspicion of a manipulation of the story, in the interest of romance or continuity or spiritual symbolism. This is the story.

The Celestial Sisters:

Waupee, or the White Hawk, lived in a remote part of the forest, where animals abounded. Every day he returned from the chase with a large spoil, for he was one of the most skillful and lucky of hunters of his tribe. His form was like the cedar; the fire of youth beamed from his eye; there was no forest too gloomy for him to penetrate, and no track made by bird or beast of any kind which he could not readily follow. One day he had gone beyond any point which he had ever before visited. He traveled through an open wood, which enabled him to see a great distance. At length he beheld a light breaking through the foliage of the distant trees, which made him sure that he was on the borders of a prairie. It was a wide plain, covered with long blue grass, and enameled with flowers of a thousand lovely tints. After walking for some time without a path, musing upon the open country, and enjoying the fragrant breeze, he suddenly came to a ring worn among the grass and the flowers, as if it had been made by footsteps moving lightly round and round. But it was strange, so strange as to cause the White Hawk to pause and gaze long and fixedly upon the ground, there was no path which led to this flowery circle. There was not even a crushed leaf nor a broken twig, nor the least trace of a footstep, approaching or retiring, to be found. He thought he would hide himself and lie in wait to discover, if he could, what this strange circle meant.

Presently he heard the faint sounds of music in the air. He looked up in the direction they came from, and as the magic notes died away he saw a small object, like a little summer cloud that approaches the earth, floating down from above. At first it was very small, and seemed as if it could have been blown away by the first breeze that came along; but it rapidly grew as he gazed upon it, and the music every moment came clearer and more sweetly to his ear. As it neared the earth it appeared as a basket, and it was filled with twelve sisters, of the most lovely forms and enchanting beauty. As soon as the basket touched the ground they leaped out, and began straightway to dance, in the most joyous manner, around the magic ring, striking, as they did so, a shining ball, which uttered the most ravishing melodies, and kept time as they danced. The White Hawk, from his concealment, entranced, gazed upon their graceful forms and movements. He admired them all, but he was most pleased with the youngest. He longed to be at her side, to embrace her, to call her his own; and unable to remain longer a silent admirer, he rushed out and endeavored to seize this twelfth beauty who so enchanted him. But the sisters, with the quickness of birds, the moment they descried the form of a man, leaped back into the basket, and were drawn up into the sky.

Lamenting his ill-luck, Waupee gazed longingly upon the

fairy basket as it ascended and bore the lovely sisters from his view. "They are gone," he said, "and I shall see them no more."

He returned to his solitary lodge, but he found no relief to his mind. He walked abroad, but to look at the sky, which had withdrawn from his sight the only being he had ever loved, was painful to him now. The next day, selecting the same hour, the White Hawk went back to the prairie, and took his station near the ring; in order to deceive the sisters, he assumed the form of an opossum, and sat among the grass as if he were there engaged in chewing the cud. He had not waited long when he saw the cloudy basket descend, and heard the same sweet music falling as before. He crept slowly toward the ring; but the instant the sisters caught sight of him they were startled, and sprang into their car. It rose a short distance when one of the older sisters spoke: "Perhaps" she said, "it is come to show us how the game is played by mortals."

"Oh no," the youngest replied; "quick, let us ascend." And all joining in a chant, they rose out of sight. Waupee, casting off his disguise, walked sorrowfully back to his lodge, but ah, the night seemed very long to lonely White Hawk! His whole soul was filled with the thought of the beautiful sister.

Betimes, the next day, he returned to the haunted spot, hoping and fearing, and sighing as though his very soul would leave his body in its anguish. He reflected upon the plan he should follow to secure success. He had already failed twice; to fail a third time would be fatal. Near by he found an old stump, much covered with moss, and just then in use as the residence of a number of mice, who had stopped there on a pilgrimage to some relatives on the other side of the prairie. The White Hawk was so pleased with their tidy little forms that he thought he, too, would be a mouse, especially as they were by no means formidable to look at, and would not be at all likely to create alarm. He accordingly, having first brought the stump and set it near the ring, without further notice became a mouse, and peeped and sported about, and kept his sharp little eyes busy with the others; but he did not forget to keep one eye up toward the sky, and one ear wide open in the same direction. It was not long before the sisters, at their customary hour, came down and resumed their sport. "But see," cried the young sister, "that stump was not there before."

She ran off, frightened, toward the basket. Her sisters only smiled, and gathering round the old tree-stump, they struck it, in jest, when out ran the mice, and among them Waupee. They killed them all but one, which was pursued by the young sister. Just as she had raised a silver stick which she held in her hand to put an end to it, too, the form of the White Hawk arose, and he clasped his prize in his arms. The other eleven sprang to their basket, and were drawn up to the skies. Waupee exerted all his skill to please his bride and win her affections. He wiped the tears from her eyes; he related his adventures in the chase; he dwelt upon the charms of life on the earth. He was constant in his attentions, keeping fondly by her side, and picking out the way, for her to walk as he led her gently toward his lodge. He felt his heart glow with joy as he entered it, and from that moment he was one of the happiest of men. Winter and summer passed rapidly away, and as the spring drew near with its balmy gales and its many-colored flowers, their happiness was increased by the presence of a beautiful boy in their lodge. What more of earthly blessing was there for them to enjoy?

Waupee's wife was a daughter of one of the stars; and as the scenes of earth began to pall upon her sight, she sighed to revisit her father. But she was obliged to hide these feelings from her husband. She remembered the charm that would carry her up, and while White Hawk was engaged in the chase, she took occasion to construct a wicker basket, which she kept concealed. In the meantime, she collected such rarities from the earth as she thought would please her father, as well as the most dainty kinds of food. One day when Waupee was absent and all was in readiness, she went out to the charmed ring, taking with her her little son. As they entered the car she commenced her magical song, and the basket rose. The song was sad, and lowly and mournful, and as it was wafted far away by the wind, it caught her husband's ear. It was a voice which he well knew and he instantly ran to the prairie. Though he made breathless speed, he could not reach the ring before his wife and child had ascended beyond his reach. He lifted up his voice in loud appeals, but they were unavailing. The basket still went up. He watched it till it became a small speck, and finally it vanished in the sky. He then bent his head down to the ground, and was miserable. Through a long winter and a long summer Waupee bewailed his loss, but he found no relief. The beautiful spirit had come and gone, and he should see it no more! He mourned his wife's loss sorely, but his son's still more; for the boy had both the mother's beauty and the father's strength.

His wife had reached her home in the stars, and in the blissful employments of her father's house she had almost forgotten that she had left a husband upon the earth. But her son, as he grew up, resembled more and more his father, and every day he was restless and anxious to visit the scene of his birth. His grandfather said to his daughter, one day: "Go, my child, and take your son down to his father, and ask him to come up and live with us. But tell him to bring along a specimen of each kind of bird and animal he kills in the chase."

She accordingly took the boy and descended. The White Hawk, who was ever near the enchanted spot, heard her voice as she came down from the sky. His heart beat with impatience as he saw her form and that of his son, and they were soon clasped in his arms. He heard the message of the Star, and he began to hunt with the greatest activity, that he might collect the present with all dispatch. He spent whole nights, as well as days, in searching for every curious and beautiful animal and bird. He only preserved a foot, a wing, or a tail of each. When all was ready, Waupee visited once more each favorite spot- the hill-top when he had been used to see the rising sun; the stream where he had sported as a boy; the old lodge, now looking sad and solemn, which he was to sit in no more; and last of all, coming to the magic circle, he gazed widely around him with tearful eyes, and, taking his wife and child by the hand, they entered the car and were drawn up- into a country far beyond the flight of birds, or the power of mortal eye to pierce.

This is the story.

I would indeed like to dwell minutely upon all the details of the rich symbolism of the story, but that would lead beyond the limits of my present discourses on the Inner Life and the Tao-Teh-King. I must therefore take only the salient features of the story and they happen to be just the very details, that I need to explain how Teh comes to us; what Wu-Wei is and how our temperaments are to be ruled and turned into use for the spiritual life. Now then, to the application.

First about Waupee. He is plainly what we ordinarily call "the natural man"; a fine specimen of human possibilities, but he is not on the Path as yet. He is truly a man of temperaments, both as these are potentially in themselves and also as hindrances to spiritual life. The natural man is seen in the hunter and his skill. The un-free man is also seen in this same skillful man, who at first is only killing such passions and dispositions as he meets with in the forest of his own spiritual wilderness. It is not till he, as the story has it, on the third day comes upon the Open that he enters upon the larger life. He passes through three degrees of development before he is ready to concentrate upon the one object in his life. On the first day he discovers that there is an "opening" and on the next he, like the natural man, who knows nothing about "Wu Wei" or "non-action," fails because his very temperamental strength and natural excellence is in his way. His faults are these, he hides and lies in wait; he rushes out to seize the youngest sister; he plays possum; these are temperamental faults, but perfectly natural on his part. He, an Indian, could not be expected to act otherwise. His whole character is determined by his natural will and by his training. His actions are simply forms of his habits. The only hope we can see for him in the story, and, before we learn of the trick of the mice, is his boldness, his frankness and courage. He is not a weakling, either in soul or body. He is full of determination, and in those traits appear the first rudiments of the future spiritual man. Though the conflicts that arise within him at the sight of the sister threaten to destroy him, the very conflict is the sign of coming freedom. And how does he finally succeed? After having tried several kinds of direct methods for the attainment of his object and failed, he becomes a mouse and is about to be destroyed, and then he succeeds, that is, he becomes humble, so humble that he is no more than a mouse. Could an Indian well conceive of an animal more insignificant, even more contemptible than a mouse! And when he is about to be destroyed he has reached the very point of "non-action," or Wu Wei, which he, and all of us must reach before we embrace the heavenly maiden, Teh. Teh comes out of Wu Wei, "non-action"; Teh is taken possession of in Wu Wei "non-action"; and Teh really is Wu Wei, "non-action," and thus the very soul of the story, the motive force of all that takes place.

And here for the present, I must drop Waupee as a subject and talk about Wu Wei. Waupee and his history is not my main subject. He is only an illustration. The main subject is Wu Wei and the ideas connected with that conception. In my last chapter, I have treated Teh from the universal point of view. Now I came to Teh as the sum total of practical virtue or Wu Wei, as it is called in the Tao-Teh-King. It is of greatest importance that we should get a clear understanding of that term, not only because an understanding of the moral tendency of the whole book depends upon it, but also because Wu Wei represents the wisdom of all ages on how to begin to travel on the Path, and how to continue on the Path, and on how to be identified with the Path. The word in literal translation is this: "Wu" means "not having" "to be destitute of"; "Wei" means "small," "fading away," "bodiless," "secret," or, put together in Wu Wei we get the conception, "not doing," "non-action," "non-assertion."

That is the literal signification of the two words. Based upon this literal translation of the two Chinese signs, we may establish the doctrine which we in the West call Quietism, and which also exists under the name of Wu Wei in China, though not elaborated so definitely as it was in Southern Europe by John of the Cross, Molinos, Teresa, Madam Guyon, Fenelon, and among the Germans by Angelus Silecious, and many others. Quietism means first of all, resignation and absolute subjection under the Universal Will; but this is not its main characteristics; in resignation and absolute subjection it resembles all other mysticism. It is also a passive and receptive mode of receiving a divine influx and making little or nothing of activity in religious matters, whether ceremonial or moral. In this respect it is known to the Tao-Teh-King and implied in the word Wu Wei! Next, Quietism has been practiced as a disinterested love for a personal god. In this last form it is not known in China, simply because the Tao-Teh-King knows no personal God. It is the form especially practiced by Madam Guyon, Molinos and Fenelon. Practical forms of Quietism, such as the form among the Quakers, is also implied in Wu Wei. Forms of Quietism which have run into extremes of Pietism are unknown to Wu Wei and Tao-Teh-King. This is enough about Quietism and Wu Wei in general.

If you wish a literary and poetic interpretation, but no translation of Wu Wei, I can recommend no better than that little charming book by Henri Borel called "Wu Wei, a fantasy based on the philosophy of Laotzse." It is indeed the cream of the Tao-Teh-King, and if you read that you can get no better practical insight into the mind of the Tao-Teh-King and Laotzse. If you can absorb the sense of BorePs book, you may forget all these twelve chapters of mine and you shall find that you have lost nothing but the husks that covered the nut. As I said, this is enough about Wu Wei in general. I will now go into details. Wu Wei defined as a principle for the "conduct of life" means "non-interference," "non-exertion," "not-doing," "masterly inactivity"; that is, we must discard all thoughts of helping nature in her work. It is laid down as a sine qua non (LXIII.) "Act non-action. Be occupied with non-occupation. Taste the tasteless. Find your great in what is little, and your many in the few." This is metaphysical. But the same chapter says also, "Recompense injury with kindness." That savors of the New Testament and is intensely practical and useful in real life. It is said in Chapter LXXIX, "to let matters rest will be found to be the best way. Therefore, the wise man takes care of his own part of the compact and exacts nothing of others"; and "he who undertakes to do the work for the Great Architect rarely fails to cut his own hands." It is so hard for people to learn that to be passionless and motionless does not mean stupidity and mental or spiritual ruin, but the contrary. Rigid inactivity frees a man from entanglements and bad karma. All efforts defeat themselves, because they are efforts and not spontaneous actions. Wu Wei means "non-interference" in politics as well as in people's personal affairs. The Taoist demands that the people be left to develop their own resources. Conformity to nature will bring best results. In my next chapter I shall speak of Wu Wei in Chinese politics and ancient history. The metaphysics of Wu Wei or "non-action" is this, that "emptiness" or "vacancy" or "space," words which also correctly translate Wu Wei, is not a negative force, but a most positive one; one, of which it is said (V) that "though empty, it never collapses, and the more it is exercised the more it brings forth." Emptiness is even called "the abyss-mother," which is "the root of heaven and earth"; because the sage, the holy man, the mystic, employs "emptiness" as a working principle (VII.), and as he "puts himself last, he is first; abandoning himself, he is preserved."

To get at the full meanings of "emptiness" or "vacancy" or "space" as a translation of Wu Wei I must come back to the term Ku-sen as I explained it in the last chapter. Ku means literally a valley, that is, the space or empty room enclosed by hills; not the valley as it appears to the eye or as civilization uses it for railroads or cities. It is the cosmic emptiness symbolized, but not marked off by mountain ridges. It is taught (XL): "thirty spokes unite in one nave, and by that part which is non-existent (that is, the hole in the center of the nave) it is useful for a carriage wheel. Clay is molded into vessels and by their hollowness they are useful as vessels. Roofs and floors, doors and windows, are arranged in such a way that they make a house by the hollowness they produce."

You understand then that it is the hole in the nave that represents but does not constitute the essential of the wheel, that the space inside of the clay walls represents but does not constitute the essential of the vessels, and that the hollow space of the room stands for the real part of the house. Of course it is so, because the number of spokes, or their length, is certainly immaterial to the main office which the wheel is to serve as a wheel; and it is immaterial whether the vessel is made of clay or silver; whether it is round or square or oblong. The main thing is that it can contain something, and the same is the case as regards the house. In the Tao-Teh-King much is made of this vacuum, this emptiness, this hollow space and that tendency is thoroughly oriental and mystic.

That which Laotzse here illustrates by realistic terms, Buddha also illustrated and in his own characteristic way. In the Milinda Panha there is reported a conversation between the Buddhist sage Nagasena and King Milinda, which runs as follows. The sage tells the king: "My fellow-priests address me as Nagasena, but that is merely a name, for I am no independent ego-entity, no atman." The king replies: "If you are no ego-entity, pray tell me who it is that acts, that eats, that drinks, that thinks?"And the king continues to ask if Nagasena is hair, nails, lungs, sensation, perception or consciousness, and receives a denial to all his questions. Finally the king comes to the natural conclusion that he fails to discover any Nagasena; that Nagasena is an empty sound and at last declares: "Venerable Sir, you speak a falsehood, a lie. There is no Nagasena."

Then comes the turning of the tables. The sage asks the king if he came in a chariot or on foot, and the king answers: "I came in a chariot." Nagasena then asks: "What is a chariot? Is it the axle, the wheels, the box, the yoke or the reins?" The king answers no! to all the questions and Nagasena then declares: "I fail to see any chariot. The word chariot is an empty sound. Your majesty speaks a falsehood, a lie. There is no chariot." The king defends himself and says: "Venerable Sir; I speak no lie; the word 'chariot' is only a way of speaking, a term, a name for that which is made up of pole, axle, box, wheels." Nagasena now draws the conclusion he has been waiting to make, which is, that in an absolute sense there is really no more person or chariot than the unity that is made by the combination of the various phenomenal parts that go to make a person or a chariot. In other words a person, a chariot, is no reality, but only a name for a combination. In Plato the same problem was discussed under the form of "the One and the Many." In the Middle Ages, it was again discussed in Scholasticism and the problem was called "Nominalism and Realism." Both with Plato and in Scholasticism the result was the same as in Buddhism, that is, the thing is not real, and the name we give it is a name merely and not an equivalent expression for reality. All mystics and Inner Life people hold that the real is not known and that which we call real is only a name for a mystery. The mystery cannot be known, but may be communed with in the Inner Life. When Laotzse uses the illustration of the valley, the hole in the nave, he means to lead the thoughts from the phenomenal to the real; from the name of the thing to that which in earlier chapters I denned as Simplicity and Stillness. In our own conception we approach this idea of emptiness, vacuity, when we say for instance "beauty unadorned is most adorned." A human body can never be truly represented in its native beauty except by its nakedness.

The older mystics preferred nakedness to dress while

meditating, because nakedness gave them a freedom, that never can be attained with garments on. This, of course, may not appear intelligent to those who do not know what meditation and contemplation are. We have the same idea symbolized in the hermit, the yogi, who sacrifices everything in withdrawing to the desert. He wishes to liberate himself, that freedom from cares may help him to escape all trammels; he literally "empties" himself. But perhaps the idea of emptiness may be clear when I tell you that innermost in all Egyptian temples there was an adytum, a most holy chamber, and that that chamber was dark and empty- why? It was the residence of the god! the god resided in space and space was symbolized by emptiness! Can you see the mystery!

Here is another illustration taken from a totally different sphere of life. The Japanese have tea-rooms, which they call the "Abodes of Vacancy." The tea-room is an empty room. It is absolutely empty, except for what may be placed there for the time being to satisfy some aesthetic mood. In its emptiness, the tea-room answers to the adytum or the innermost of the Egyptian temples, which was dark and empty. The tea-room gets its significance from its temporary use by visitors and their presence. It is nothing but emptiness in itself. The visitors give it its character; they are the main thing; the room itself is nothing.

A room or its name means nothing to the Japanese mystic, it is its use he inquires about; its consecration. Its name means nothing; its character is the all to him. Yet a room is of course a room and of architectural signification whether consecrated or not. In the tea-room the wall decorations are landscapes, birds, flowers, rather than the human figure, the latter being present in the person of the beholder himself. How subtle that, too! How ingenious is not the teaching that the tea-room is for silence or solitude, for Man; for Presence; for the real! In short the idea of emptiness, nakedness, is expressed. Nakedness, that individual truth may be revealed. Again the idea of isolation is expressed by the very emptiness of the room. Man is to learn emptiness, which in China and Japan means vastness or the Great Mother, Teh, the universal womb in which and out of which the actual comes forth. Space ig the divinity thought of as female. In India it is Aditi, the "boundless one" and sometimes Sakti. In China it is Ku-sen, the "valley spirit" You see how different the Oriental and mystic sanctuaries are from the Western and the church peoples! Look into a real blue sky and you shall see how full and rich it is in its emptiness! You will see how much more rational and sublime the Orientals are! How overwhelmingly so. No cathedral can rival them in their simplicity and forceful teachings. Truly said Jesus, that the lilies in their simplicity or nakedness or emptiness surpassed Solomon in all his glory; lilies and the lotus are sanctuaries on account of their very simplicity, emptiness in their purity, which is a sublime Nakedness. We do not obtain the Real by simply "having our will." Obtaining the thing is not obtaining it at all. The object of our desire does not fascinate; it is the life which passes through it that fascinates. The flower I put in my buttonhole is a victim of my greed and cannot be expected to give me any real pleasure. It is the moonlight that bewitches, not the moon. It is beauty that elevates, not the art object. It is the dignity in a man that a woman submits to, not to the mere man. And vice versa it is the "eternally feminine" a real man worships, not flesh and blood.

We are such "spaces," or "emptiness," or we ought to empty ourselves that we may be such a room filled with the mysterious presence, symbolized by the Japanese Tea-room and. the adytum of Egyptian temples. Any and all endeavor to realize such a condition is called Wu Wei, "non-action," and you must have understood that it is not a negativity, that on the contrary it is Reality. Now apply these later teachings to the definitions of Wu Wei, given before, and you observe how the terms already used have expanded enormously. Literally translated they were merely negative terms on our ordinary plan of life, but they have now grown to positive statements of occult truths. Wu Wei is now no more "not having" nor merely Quietism and resignation; it is now an eternal quality, a Presence. And that presence is Teh. Follow the word further and see how it keeps on growing as we get nearer and nearer to it, by what I now shall state. You shall now hear why non-action, Wu Wei, is so highly praised in the Tao-Teh-King. It is because "The non-existent enters into all things without any crevice, (XLIII), and by non-action there is nothing that may not be done" (XLVIII), and "there is no sin greater than giving rein to desire. There is no misery greater than discontent." (XLVI). It is, therefore, also advised, "Shut the lips and close the portals of eyes and ears and as long as you live you will have no trouble; but open your lips and meddle with things and as long as you live you will not get out of trouble." (LII).

All these statements would have no meaning if Wu Wei, or "non-action," had not become something positive. The West is active in its excellence: It strives for the first place by doing. The East is passive in its excellence; it does not strive, it yields, and it attains the first place spiritually, by yielding. It is this latter method which the Tao-Teh-King recommends on every page, and calls Wu Wei, and understands to be the essence of Teh. It is difficult for the West to understand this method. The method of "not-doing" is unfortunately always understood as doing nothing, and that is not at all the sense of "not doing." And it can be truly asserted that "not doing" is the under-current of all spiritual life in the world. Buddhism and Christian Mysticism meet Taoism in teaching the same method. They have their own way with it, but they aim exactly at the same point. Buddhism in world-weariness tells disciples to leave the world and have nothing to do with it. Taoism does that, too, but at the same time exhorts its followers to rule the world by nonresistance, by subjection, by not desiring it, and, not even acknowledge to self that they rule it by that method. You shall now hear some singular teachings on that subject. Such as that the real world comes from something not real (that "existence comes from non-existence") and that "the sage manages affairs without doing anything, and conveys his instructions without the use of speech."

THE INNER LIFE AND THE TAO TEH KING

The Buddha looks upon the world through the large glass end of the telescope and rejects all its things as insignificant, because he sees everything diminutively as you do when you look in at the large end of a telescope. Taoism looks in from the small glass end of the telescope and sees the "infinitely great," and identifies itself with it, calls it Tao and Teh and means thereby the Primal Force, the Absolute, Brahm (neuter), Buddhism comes in from one end of the bridge and Taoism from the other. They meet in the Middle, in the recognition that the bridge is not "it," but that the Middle is the Path, the way of "not doing."

As it is, Buddhism produces intermediaries between God and man, real saints. Taoism by Wu Wei or non action is suitable for a practical world and makes wise men, who can be in the world and rule it and yet not be of it, nor lost in it. A Taoist knows as much as a Buddhist about sin and sorrow and the illusory nature of the phenomenal world, but he does not run away from any of these. A Taoist knows no "Sorrows of Werther" and "Weltschmertz." He practices Wu Wei because he has no use for fraudulent phenomena; he does not shun them because of any pathological condition. The Taoist by Wu Wei becomes the sage among the unwise; the physician among the sick and a teacher to those who are blind. A Buddhist cannot fight, a Taoist can! And, about "not doing" it should here be stated, that the Christian Mystics of the Middle Ages, had a sensible understanding of it in spite of all their insane ascetic practices. They were intensely practical people, which they proved by their actions during the Black Death horrors, and the papal interdict, details of which I must pass over for the present. This terribly active world of ours places a man's value on what a man does, not on what he is. And in overlooking quality and preferring quantity, we of the West have lost the best parts of life. Go into public institutions and, in many cases, you there find moral outcasts in important positions, because they can labor much.

If you ask why the institution keeps such people, you will

be told that the institution is soulless and therefore does not care about morals, but only about the amount of labor they can perform. Not so in the Greater Life as lived by mystics and true people. To them the eternal personal value of the worker is the most important. They place a man's value not in what he does, but in what he is, upon quality, not upon quantity. It is that which a man is, which makes his acts good; the deeds do not make the man. There is nothing to hinder a mystic from being active in the world. No; nothing! He will, however, not follow the world's methods. He may sell his services to the world, but he never sells his person or his soul or his convictions. Again, there is nothing the modern man will object to more vigorously than to be told to be quiet, to lie low, to become reconciled to things, even if they are bad. We cannot blame him. He has seen how church and state have frightfully misused the principle of quietness, and that is his reason for fears and noncompliance.

Rebellion against restraint is the keynote to all that is going on in modern progressive society, politics, social affairs, yet I must maintain against all contradiction that the principle of Wu Wei is fundamentally right and that we shall never come to a true reorganization of society unless we re-adopt it; not as it is preached by the hirelings of the various crafts, but as Nature enforces it and as the Tao-Teh-King teaches it. Nature everywhere calls for submission. On this subject of submitting we must persuade our fellowmen and ourselves that Wu Wei does not mean the ruin of ourselves and our eternal purposes and aims. It means that we must still the noise of the senses and the clamorous desires, which constantly are in our way for the attainment of truth, and we must also eliminate all intellectual notions. All sages, and none of them have been hypocrites or time-servants, have realized for themselves and have taught their disciples that life is only found by losing it; that "a man is rich in proportion to the number of things he can afford to let alone" (Thoreau); that desires are limitless and cause all our troubles; that they only create more thirst, as does salt water when we drink it; that our senses, our tempers, are to be used but are not to rule us, and that death follows if they rule; that our desires sing like the Sirens of old and prevent our hearing "the voice of the silence," and, that they color the images that arise in our minds and consequently blur them and their truth; that silence, solitude and lowliness are the soil, the sun, the air, in which spiritual life grows. All these facts of the spiritual life we must persuade ourselves and our fellowmen to learn and to submit to. They are wisdom! They are power! They are Wu Wei. On none of these points are we expected to destroy ourselves, whether by submitting to the will of another or to an abstract principle. We are simply to bow down to wisdom, to place the individual under the universal and no more. It ought to be easy, for as one master said: "the yoke is easy and the burden light."

But let it at once be understood that Wu Wei, Quietism, is not merely submission, not merely a negative virtue. It is in itself very positive. A Quietist radiates happiness, and good cheer flows from him. A Quietist is never discouraged, and is therefore able to be a rallying point for others. A Quietist is resolute and never turns back from his purpose, and his purpose is always sublime. A Quietist is brave, and others have confidence in him. His presence inspires confidence. And all this because we feel his presence permeated with a deep power, and his nearness gives us the impression of something sublime. Ask anybody who has met a great soul, and they will tell you about the influence that comes from him. In the third chapter, I gave an illustration of a Quietist, in the beggar at the church door, who converted Tauler.

THE INNER LIFE AND THE TAO TEH KING

CHAPTER XIII

NON ACTION

You remember that "non-action" does not mean inactivity; doing nothing and expecting stewed chickens to come in through the windows, ready for the table. Wu Wei or "non-action," means having nothing to do with the incidental, the trivial, the "passing show," the phenomenal, and devoting oneself exclusively and with energy to the essential and the real. Wu Wei is simply the Chinese name from the Tao-Teh-King for the idea and teaching found among all kinds of mystics, namely, that the earthly, the temporal, is a prison, a chain, a hindrance and an obstruction on the Path, and must therefore be let alone and shunned. How shall a Taoist attain results or do his duty to the world in which he lives ? The doctrine of Wu Wei does not allow the use of means or efforts. Taoism teaches distinctly "avoid activity" "dispense with the use of means" and Tao, as you read in another chapter, is called "nameless simplicity"; it teaches:

"Simplicity without a name
Is free from all external aim.
With no desire, at rest and still,
All things go right, as of their own will."

And why should they not? The world is not ours! Who set us to manage the affairs of the universe? Surely nobody! We cannot manage our own affairs, how much less those of the world's! The sage "takes no action" (XXIX.) because all efforts with a personal purpose are sure to fail. It is said (XXIX.) that "things" are spirit-like and cannot be got by active doing. He who would so win them, destroys them. "He who would hold them in his grasp, loses them." That is the way a Taoist does his duty and avoids cutting his hands in the world's machinery. Things are "spirit-like," that is, they slip out of our hands like elastic rubber bands and spring back with pain. Things, so called, are not so real as many of us think. They are merely centers of force and that is the reason we cannot "get hold of them by active doings." Things, so called, are time and space combinations of activities beyond our reach. We may and we do use these combinations, but they are only, so to say, loaned us; they are not subject to us. We get things worth having without excessive efforts. Have you not observed sometimes that that which you got and which was of any real value to you came like a gift, not by an effort of yours? You called it luck, good luck, and let it pass. Was that quite right? You may have thought it was good karma. Was that enough? You may have said "God is good"; "this was providential." Was that a right attitude? Well, you may have said or thought thus, but you ought also to have withdrawn to solitude and silence and studied the law, which teaches that we get things worth having without efforts, by Wu Wei, and because things have their own way without regard to us; they crush us if we are in the way; they lift us if we are obedient.

We live in a house not ours. We are tenants merely. If we adapt ourselves to the laws of this cosmic house, we call the world, it will be well with us. If we disobey, the landlord dispossesses us. Retirement will reveal many mysteries of Wu Wei, of "non-action," and you cannot afford to ignore that law. By "non-action" or by Wu Wei, all good things are gotten and brought about. Strange as it seems to all of us, till we have experienced the fact, it is nevertheless the moral law of our lives. And it ought not be hard to learn to obey. This is the way we should live according to the Tao-Teh King, (LXIII.), "This is the way of Tao and Teh (or the true path) to act without thinking of acting; to conduct affairs without feeling the trouble of them; to taste without discerning any flavor; to consider the small as great and the few as many and to recompense injury with love and kindness." If we act that way, we are in Teh and follow Wu Wei. This for the present is enough about Wu Wei in the individual life. Now, about Wu Wei in the public life, in the state, in politics. I shall now quote Laotzse and

THE INNER LIFE AND THE TAO TEH KING

Kwangtzse on the paradisiacal state of early China, a state that was a result of Wu Wei, and, that you may be able to get some chronological idea of the time when that state existed, I will tell you what European scholars have found out regarding early Chinese chronology and history.

Chinese history, before 771 B. C. or up to about 150 years before Laotzse, is nothing but a record of internal feuds between many and various states or settlements, and, toward the end of that period, a record of striving for the establishment of an empire, which is finally established in 771 B. C. The next period of history, from 771 B. C. to 221 B. C, is a period of struggle for the total extinction of feudal power, which is finally extinguished totally in 221 B. C. by the first emperor of Tsin. Before all this lies a period of "paradise," if I may so call it, and most of that which Laotzse says about the "people of ancient days," relates to that period which, generally speaking, I should say was at least three to four thousand years ago, counting back from today.

We are told in the Tao-Teh-King that Tao, as Teh, ruled the world at first and at that time the world was in a paradisaical state. Taoists do not tell us how long it lasted, but Laotzse says (XVIII.), it lasted till "Tao ceased to be observed," and Kwang-tzse explains what this means. He calls that age "the age of Perfect Virtue" or "the age of Teh" and describes it as follows: "In that age, they attached no value to knowledge and did not employ men of action (soldiers or police). Superiors were no more than the higher branches of a tree; and the people lived freely in the Open. They were upright and correct, without knowing that to be so was to be righteous; they loved one another, without knowing that to be real goodness; they were honest, without knowing that to be loyalty; they fulfilled their engagements, without knowing that to do so, was to act in good faith; in their daily life they employed the services of one another without thinking that they were conferring or receiving gifts. Because they lived that way we cannot find any trace of their actions and no records of their affairs' and that is all in their favor and to their glory." These people lived in Wu Wei and were full of Teh. Let me call them simpleminded in the best sense of that phrase. Kwang-tzse gives several other descriptions of "the age of perfect virtue," but this will be sufficient for the present. I will only mention that he tells us that people in those days did not form themselves into castes and classes of social distinctions; they were all alike and lived according to nature; they were, as he said, "on terms of equality with all creatures, as forming one family." Surely we are far remote from any such state of nature today!

Let me warn you! you must not take this description to mean that the early Chinese were savages, as some scientists and sociologists will explain that state to be. These people were far from savagery, if ever their ancestors had been savages. They were tillers of the soil and knew the loom. Such people are not savages. The loom is sufficient evidence that they were not savages. Savages do not know the loom and cannot weave. They were simple. Theirs was the simple life; they did not talk it, they lived it. The reason why "the simple life" was lost, says Kwangtzse, as you heard, was that the people began to aim at "knowledge" rather than life, and at that which later was called "culture." (On this subject, of culture as a hindrance to spiritual life, I have already spoken in an earlier chapter.) Laotzse and Kwang-tzse again and again repeat that the sage (I.) constantly tries to keep the people without "knowledge" and without desire, and, where there are those who have "knowledge," to keep them from acting their own will, and where there are those who have will, to weaken it. In chapter VII. Laotzse points to Heaven and Earth as patterns for the sage. They have no personal or private ends; they do not seek "knowledge" or cultivate desires. Nature in all movements is placid and contented (like water) and not self-conscious. Of this I have also spoken in an earlier chapter.

Kwang-tzse tells a grim story of how men came to lose themselves in culture, so called: The ruler of the southern ocean was named "The Hasty" and he of the northern "Heedless." The ruler of the center was named "Chaos." "Heedless" and "Hasty" met often with "Chaos" and were treated well. They consulted together how they might repay his kindness and said: "Men have all seven orifices for purposes of the senses, such as seeing, hearing, but this poor ruler has none. Let us try and make them for him. Accordingly they cut one orifice in him every day and at the end of the seven days Chaos died. Fitting Chaos with senses and thereby with desires, they killed him.

About the government by the sage, the Tao-Teh-King (III.), says that it consists in "emptying the heart of the people," that is, of desires, and in "weakening the will of the people," that is, "the will to live," Tanha. By such "non-action nothing is ungoverned," and why? Because Tao and Teh then govern. It is the interference of the governor, be he imperial or democratic, in the affairs that hinders the actions of Tao and Teh. And this has been the general rule, for the better and the worse in the Chinese empire and elsewhere. And so it is to-day. And Laotzse's advice (XIX.) is a good one today. It was: "Abandon your saintliness (that is a hint to preachers); put away your cleverness (that is a hint to so-called statesmen), and the people would be benefited a hundredfold. Abandon your charity and put away your righteousness and people would become more brotherly and more kind; put away your riches and scheming and there will be no robbers or frauds (that is a hint to those who establish charities, like universities, hospitals, museums, after they have amassed enormous wealth by robbery of all kinds.)" Culture is insufficient for the highest purpose:

> "Hold fast to that which will endure,
> Show thyself simple; preserve thee pure;
> Thine own keep small; thy desires poor."

If any of you would object and say that no progress is possible under such conditions, I am ready to answer you; first by the question: How do you know? Has it ever been tried! And next

THE INNER LIFE AND THE TAO TEH KING

I will declare that that which we call "progress" is a sad caricature of that which your own ideas demand.

Thus far I have been speaking more or less abstractly. I must therefore bring this subject of Wu Wei or "non-action" down on a practical plane, down to our level. And I can do it by employing four forms of Tao, of which Laotzse speaks. The first form is called humility. How does the Tao-Teh-King itself explain humility? Here is the answer (LXL), "When a great kingdom takes a lowly position, it becomes the place of concourse for the world; it is the wife of the world. The wife by quietness invariably conquers the man. And since quietness is also lowliness, therefore a great kingdom by lowliness towards a small kingdom, may take that small kingdom. And a small kingdom, by lowliness towards a small kingdom, may take that small kingdom. And a small kingdom, by lowliness towards a great kingdom may take that great kingdom. So that either the one stoops to conquer, or the other is low and conquers. If the great kingdom only desires to attach to itself and nourish (that is, to benefit), others, then the small kingdom will only wish to enter its service. But, in order that both may have their wish the great should be lowly." In the same vein it is said (XXXIX.) "princes and kings speak of themselves as orphans, lonely men and wheel-less carts."

In the 67th chapter Laotzse associates with humility what he calls his three "precious things or jewels," which are: gentleness, economy, and shrinking from taking precedence of others. "With gentleness," he says, "I can he hold; with economy I can he liberal; shrinking from taking precedence of others, I become a vessel of the highest honor."

These three, gentleness, economy and shrinking from taking precedence of others, together with humility, are the four forms of Tao or rather of Teh, which make Wu Wei possible for us in daily life. We are only too apt to say that the bad succeed in this world and that the good go down. I question the truth of the assertion. Look closely and you shall find as I have found, that it is not so. There is justice everywhere; karma rules. To understand fully how Wu Wei or the principle of non-action can work as a principle in state government, it is necessary that I should explain the fundamentals of the Chinese state organism, which is so different from ours. The life of Nature-peoples, as I call them, or of people who "live according to Nature" as we say popularly, is like that of a child. I will take as an example a child four or five years old. How does it live? Does it know that it lives? Can it have any consciousness or reflective thought about its own existence? No! none! The moment it has reflective consciousness of itself it is no more a child.

Excepting the important fact, that the child lives outside its mother, and, that of course is most important, it is after all still so much dependent upon its mother that it can be said, that it is still in the womb, or in the mother's environment, and bound so closely that it depends upon her altogether. In the main it is merely a hereditary expression of the race, family or society, in which it lives. The child lives in generals, not in particulars, in Wu Wei, not in self-assertion. The child does not live its own life, strictly speaking. The mother lives for it, thinks for it, plans for it, feeds it, clothes it. The child lives according to nature, at least in normal cases. It is not concerned in any way with the problems which it meets later in life. It does not even know that they exist, and could not be made to understand them if they were presented. The child may say "I" about itself and it may more or less selfishly assert itself in cries and volitions and be naughty, but it does not know what it is to be naughty except by being told, nor has it any shame, gratitude or any so called moral sense, except by drill. The child has neither intellectual nor moral pains or joys. It has no aesthetic feelings for the beautiful either. But the child is imitative. Imitation is the most characteristic thing about it and has been so since the second half of its first year of existence, and, the workings of imitation show the presence of will and becomes the beginning of learning and of individual development.

THE INNER LIFE AND THE TAO TEH KING

But if the child does not possess these ideas, it normally has all the joy and pains that come from the play of impulse and from feeding, sleeping and growing, including the pains that come naturally from teething and the like of children's troubles. Its little imagination entertains itself when the child hears stories told. And the child is a complex thing of personal pride, habits and self-consciousness. Spontaneously and without duplicity, formality or reserve, its mental life comes out in action. It has no prejudice and conventionality till these two are implanted by social formalities or by the parent's vanity. In these, the positive sides of its life, the child is just as dependent as it is in the negative described before. Under both conditions it can be said that the child cares for nothing; it takes life as it comes. The child born among poor people is no worse off for the moment than that born among the rich. Neither of them know what riches or poverty are. The child has possibilities for growth, for intellect, for spiritual sense, but it is practically an animal in its life. The difference lies in the possibilities. The child is a possible human being, but no real one yet. This criticism is by no means unfavorable to the child. On the contrary. For good and for bad the child is a dependent creature as I have described. It lives in generals, not in particulars; in Wu Wei, not in self-assertions. As it is, we say correctly that the child lives according to nature. Hear how an old Tao-ist talks about a life according to nature. Huai-nan-tzu said:

"What is it that we mean when we talk about the natural or inherent? It is that which is homogeneous, pure, simple, filed, unvarnished, upright, luminous and immaculate, and which has never undergone any mixture or adulteration from the beginning. And what is the human or artificial? It is that which has been adulterated with shrewdness, crookedness, dexterity, hypocrisy and deceit; that which bends itself into compliance with the world, and defers to the customs of the age. For instance, the ox has horns and a divided hoof, while the horse has a disheveled mane and a complete foot; this is the heavenly or natural. But if you put a bit into the horse's mouth and pierce the nose of the ox, this is human or artificial."

The following is in the same vein: "If Nature has given you black hair, don't try to dye it yellow; if you have a sallow or pale complexion, don't daub it with pink paint; if your waist measures five and twenty inches around, don't try to squeeze it into eighteen. All such attempts are violations of Nature, and are sure to bring their own punishment along with them."

As you see, those old people knew perfectly well what it is to be natural. The principle of naturalness is the principle of the child's life and this principle may be attained by Wu Wei. Now, all this about the child applies to peoples. It is for that reason that I have entered upon so many details. It applies directly to the conditions of Chinese life in which the Tao-Teh-King plays such an important part. I must now describe the Chinese life and let me say to you that neither this description nor the one of the child is merely for your entertainment. The Chinese life of which you now shall hear, and, that of the child of which you just heard, are looking glasses that faithfully reflect conditions in which you and I now are, or, which you and I have just left, or are about leaving. Bear in mind that Tao and the early followers of Laotzse are not included among the Chinese I describe, nor is the village life as described in the Tao-Teh-King to be included.

The Chinese is an old man still in the cradle. When I say that, I have really given his characteristic in a nutshell. He is old; a very, very old race; he seems to be a remnant of prehistoric times; but he is still in the cradle, that is, he is still a child as far as historic life is concerned; just such a child as I have described. He is still living "according to nature." But as he has not passed through the evolution of mind and regeneration of spirit, he is still in the cradle, or nature 's womb. In this respect he is like a boy that never becomes a man. Go to China and you shall see that people of all ages play children's games, knowing nothing higher; that state officials are spanked, as are children where spanking is the custom. You shall find them so naive that you cannot understand them, even when you know their language; exactly as it is with the true child. Read their books and you shall see that their writings are merely aphorisms and totally lack rational connection of sentences, and, that is because the Chinese mind lacks perspective. How funny a child's letter is! How funny a Chinese painting without perspective! You shall also notice that Chinese writings are mostly collections of traditions and lack the incentives to actions now or in the future. They live in the past. That, too, is the child. In China you will see that agriculture is a religious and devotional cult. By toil, not by psalm singing or flattery they worship Mother Nature. Labor is to a Chinese a religious act. Nature is to him, as it is to other primitive people, the Mother. They kneel down and kiss the earth. Our farmers think only of crops, and they spread manures, plow and harrow for self-interest, not on account of any ideas of sacrifice, offerings, or like cults. The Chinaman's offering is work, hard labor.

The Chinese mind is natural history rather than psychology. It resembles the child described. Our education aims at new developments, but the Chinese object is preservation of results, reverence for tradition; quickening of memory rather than thinking. He imitates and does not care to create anything new. His art is craft, artifice, and his language is monosyllabic, totally without grammatical reflective forms. What we do by grammatical forms, such as tense, or case, he does by modulation of voice. You will remember the curious mistakes of missionaries, which I mentioned in a former chapter, all caused by false intonation. His music contains no inner note. It is merely sounds in succession, noise. His village life is merely an extension of a number of families living in one place and with a so-called governor appointed over them by the emperor. Somewhat like our territories; patriarchal government we call it in history. City life as we know it in theory is totally unknown. Where it has been attempted under foreign influence it even beats the outcast life of such places as London, New York, or Yokahama, in degradation and depravity, as might be expected. I need mention only Shanghai as an example. Religion as a transcendental longing and spiritual regeneration is as incomprehensible to the Chinese as it is to the child. He knows only this life and thinks his departed ancestors live in the astral spheres, and he fears them. You should remember that this does not apply to Tao-ists. We are able to make a tolerably clear picture of the state of things in the five centuries from 771 to 220 B. C. I shall speak of some of the points that relate to my subject. Religion in a Western sense did not exist; even the word did not exist. Neither did notions or words for church or temple or priestly caste exist. "Gods" were known and offenses against "gods" were defined, but people had not yet sunk down to too much belief in "gods," and extravagant belief was called superstition. You see then that some purity or originality still existed. "Sin" meant no offense against a god, but an infraction of nature's general laws, such as these laws were defined by imperial command or by vassal princes delegated to define them. When the emperor defined these laws he was called "son of heaven."

Prayer was common enough. Here is an illustration. When the Chou conqueror fell ill, his brother, later regent, prayed to Heaven for the recovery of his brother and offered himself as a substitute; the clerk was instructed to commit the offer to writing, and this solemn document was locked up. Other similar instances are on record. It is even recorded that the emperor of Tsin, who was steeped in Laotzse's philosophy, in 210 B. C. prayed and offered sacrifices because of a bad dream, and was thus advised by his soothsayers. But though the Chinese had to some extent sunk to sacrificial prayers, and the blood of the victim was constantly called for, they were yet ignorant of the occidental ideas connected with conscience, fear of God, mortal sins, repentance, absolution, alms-giving, self-mortification, charity, sackcloth and ashes, praise, glorification, all those notions which to Jews, Christians and Mohammedans mean so much. Morally he is a materialist in the extreme; his manners and customs do not rest upon spiritual values, but upon extreme realities and the expedient. His ethics is

Nature-life, both good and bad. That is childlike also. All this applies to the Chinese in general.

In China, there are, as elsewhere three classes of people: (1) The mass; (2) the learned and (3) the ruling class. The relationship of the people and prince may be seen from a quotation from Mentgzse's works. "The people are the most important and the prince the least important (because), the people can make the prince, but the prince cannot make the people." Further elucidation of this statement that the prince is of little importance you can find in the Tao-Teh-King. In all of this you recognize the child. Some of it is childishness and some of it is child-likeness and the child-likeness is the condition we come into by means of Wu Wei or "non action," as it is called. The childishness of it is the result of activity or interference with Tao and Teh. I have given you a faithful description of the psychological conditions of the child and of the Chinese people. In your opinion none of these conditions are desirable, because you naturally judge them from the modern point of view of history and from an advanced point of growth in evolution. I will not say that those conditions suit us today, that would be absurd and impossible to prove, but I will say that the principles back of the child's conditions and the principles back of the Chinaman's condition are most desirable, and moreover, I will say that they must be recovered. I will put some arguments before you to prove both of my assertions.

The principle that lies in Wu Wei and which is back of the child and of that condition I described the Chinaman in, is in occidental philosophical language called by various names, some of the most important of which I will mention. The first is immediacy. The term explains a condition which is original, or so direct and unconditioned that it comes without any efforts or means; and, which needs no proof. It means that which is natural to us; the heart's revelations; the truths implanted in man by nature and spirit and, in a broad way, that which is self-evident. Upon this fact of an inner direct and immediate knowledge is built the doctrine that such knowledge, with the exclusion of all immediateness, is the truth. Immediacy is also called (spiritual) instinct implanted, or innate ideas, "natural reason," common sense, "Faith." When the sage says "I know I am I" he needs not give any proof. His knowledge is an immediate knowledge, or a knowledge without proof. This phrase, "I know I am I" does not mean that he can make a reasonable statement of that fact if called upon to do it; it means simply that he has a sense of identity, a sense of being an individual in contradistinction to another individual. As a mere elementary fact, the same truth applies also to my dog who demonstrates his individuality on the street by rushing for the first dog he sees and getting into a fight. The dog's case is also one of immediacy, but one on a lower plane. The point of identity between the sage's immediacy and that of the dog's is this, that both realize themselves and truth directly and without proof or demonstration. The two states are opposite poles of intelligence, but within intelligence. In the middle lies our common everyday world with all its volitions, reasonings, desires and squabbles. People without realization of the value of the sage's immediacy stay in the dog's condition; they, like the dog, live their lives in desires, and take no thought for higher things. The thoughts they have are engaged in the affairs of the day, for self-satisfaction and all other selfish ends.

The sage at the other pole has abandoned all such desires and volitions and thinkings; yea, even more, he has become so settled in the direct vision of truth and is so completely in the company of the highest powers, that he even does not know the lower conditions any more ; they are not only forgotten, but no more make a part of his mental, moral and spiritual condition. Who and what the sage really is, I have described in earlier chapters, in phraseology drawn from the Tao-Teh-King. I will now add thereto some of my own ideas in order to throw further light upon immediacy, or the state we are in when we live in Wu Wei or "non-action" and beyond. The sage in the condition of immediacy seizes his point with an intuition almost feminine, no matter what the point may be, intellectual, volitional or perceptional. And when he has got his point, he realizes it with enthusiasm. These realizations are thoroughly individual, that is, when he presents a philosophical idea, he does not do it in cool rationality, nay, his presentation is thoroughly personal. It is himself. There is no abstraction about it; it is his idea, and, we see and feel his individuality. In the Occident we are disposed to throw contempt upon such a man and his teachings. We have become so accustomed to the worship of words, or literary idols, that we cannot perceive the life that comes to us through a sage, and our loss is consequently enormous. We get empty shells, and no more. The sage's immediacy contains a revelation, but we miss it. Immediacy as it works in the sage is the main characteristic of all Inner Life. Immediacy means feeling the truth, not reasoning it out. It lives in faculties of inner perceptions not cultivated in the Occident except among the mystics or Inner-Life-people. These people rest in their own subjectivity, and that subjectivity is molded according to the eternal pattern, and all they need to do is to look and describe what they perceive themselves. An inner illumination is always present and that loosens the fetters of the mind and allows the mind, according to the degrees of its culture, to set forth the perceptions in words or deeds. When we meet such immediacy we should not argue, but prefer insight to argument; subjectivity to objective forms. The insight allowed us will show the universe one glorious and eternally active whole. It will show us that mankind literally is divinity "in the making" that each one of us potentially is a living divine attribute. It will show us that we are not made by circumstances or by our environment, but from within. All this is gained by Wu Wei.

Immediacy discards or rather does not possess understanding as a degree of reason. It is like the child I have described; still a part of the whole and not claiming separate existence. It discards reasoning, but glories in its image-making power, a power which to it is everything and which does everything for it. In fact immediacy and the image-making faculty are twins, and between them they weave the real into individual forms. Immediacy is the loom and the image-making faculty is the weaver. Most of us cannot see, much less understand, the pattern that is woven, but when it is finished we see the sage. I have said that when we meet immediacy we should not argue, but prefer insight to argument. Now I add, when we meet the sage we should not ask for a system of wisdom or an intellectual structure, but we should learn of him and through him as an individual; and relationship should be one of life, not one of thought, one of personal intercourse, not of distance. I think the true relationship is expressed by Jesus' command to eat his flesh and drink his blood. In Tao and Teh all distinctions disappear and things are identical, universal, in unity. Common people who regard the objective or the tangible world as the only reality, will acknowledge existence is an unsolved riddle and a perpetual conflict. The sage understands the principle of identity of things. Kwang-tze tells an anecdote to show how little value one ought to place upon distinctions. A keeper of monkeys ordered that their rations of nuts should be three in the morning and four at night; at this the monkeys were very angry and complained, and so the keeper ruled that the monkeys should have four nuts in the morning and three at night. And with this the monkeys were very well satisfied. They got no more nuts, but their whims or subjective views were satisfied. Another lesson can be drawn from that anecdote and Kwang-tzse draws it. It is this, that the sage cares not for distinctions; contraries to him are identical and by following what he calls "two courses at once" he follows the laws of heaven; what "two courses at once" is I will explain.

The real Taoist is "both-and"; not "this" or "that"; he is the reconciliation of opposites. Says Tao-Teh-King (XXVIII):

"Who his manhood shows
And his womanhood knows
Becomes the empire's river-
All come to him, yea all beneath the sky,"

THE INNER LIFE AND THE TAO TEH KING

And he is...

"The simple child again, free from all stains..."

"Who his brightness knows
And his blackness shows
Becomes the empire's model-
He in the unchanging virtue arrayed,
Man's first estate, the absolute.
Who knows his fame
And guards disgrace
Becomes a specious valley-
And men come to him from all beneath the sky,"

And in him:

"They hail the simple infant."

Such a state is immediacy of the sage's kind and the very state we wish to attain and do attain by Wu Wei. It was so in olden time, when mankind was still young. Then the sage was the leader of men and in undisputed possession of the truth. Alas! The age of innocence is lost- for good and for bad! We cannot recover what Mother Nature has taken back. The wheel of existence can neither be stopped nor made to revolve in the opposite direction. What Time has devoured cannot be restored, nor do we ask for the age of innocence or for the return of anything past. We have no need of these things, because the ages are still rotating and a new age of innocence is always possible; the wheel of existence is still revolving and offering the same possibilities as of yore, and time is everlastingly renewing all things. The mechanism of the universe is as young as ever. What we can do; what we must do; what we want to do is to learn Wu Wei of these ancient people, for it was by Wu Wei that they obtained happiness and immortality, and that is what we want.

THE INNER LIFE AND THE TAO TEH KING

Thus far I have been concerned with immediacy, and thereby with intelligence and knowledge as one aspect of Wu Wei. But there is also another and a most important side of our nature to be considered and that side also represents principles back of the life of the child and the Chinese as above described. That side is the side of conduct.

To perfect wisdom corresponds perfect goodness or love or affection. They correspond like masculine and feminine and like intellect and will. It is good practice to consider goodness, love, affection and will as the interior, and wisdom and intellect as the exterior, and in that respect we shall be in agreement with all Inner-Life-people. They all consider Love a direct form of Divinity, and say that when one acts from love he acts divinely. Love is to them divinity immanently present in the world and as such the principle that binds the world and its parts together. Plato might well and truthfully say "that love is the mediator and interpreter between God and men." It is this principle that works at the root of the child's life and also back of the Chinaman's childishness and which is also in Wu Wei. They are both, the child and the Chinaman, wisdom and love, types of the power that binds things together. They both act intuitively and through the will. They are both flames of good, though unwittingly and often to the scorn of others.

These two principles of Wu Wei dominated in those ancient days of China, such as I have told you the Chinese Taoists reported them. Those ancient days they called "the age of perfect virtue" or Teh. They were, as I have said so often, a result of Wu Wei and worthy of our imitation.

THE INNER LIFE AND THE TAO TEH KING

CHAPTER XIV

NATURE

In this chapter I will give a few hints to the understanding of the Shawnee tale told before. A full interpretation I have given elsewhere. The present hints will help to an understanding of Teh and conclude the exposition of the subject. Waupee and his life may be looked upon from the standpoint of the three gunas and that view will show how great he is. The introductory description of him in the story shows the two gunas: Tamas, the fundamental quality of bigness in rest, both in activity and in passivity; it shows him in nature's primary state of preparation or "inertia," if this word be properly understood. The same description also shows him in the guna of Bajas or as a youth full of energy and motion. He is always in action, hunting, fishing, exploring and studying his surroundings. These two qualities, for good and bad dominate him until the time he weds the celestial sister. Her advent, the story tells us, makes him perfectly happy and that is an evidence of the sattwa quality, the force and power of harmony, of truth. The three taken together show him as no mere specimen of a man, but as a species of man.

You know that the three gunas are modified in seven kinds of ways or in a seven-fold way. All of these I also see in Waupee. Let me show them in the seven steps in his life. "We hear first a description of the simple minded Waupee who, to begin with, is without any special development in any direction. The first step is his first day's discovery and the rise of selfhood in him, caused by the marvels of the open plain and his first vision of the sisters. The second is his assertion of selfhood in deceit, when he "plays the possum." The third is renunciation of self, at the time he became a mouse. The fourth is his marriage to his own Higher Self, represented by wedding the celestial sister. The fifth is his "fall," "described as his being," "absent," and the loss of the sister as a result of these "absences." The sixth is his condition of suffering because of his loss and his resultant "penances," represented by his "returns" to the haunted spot or the condition in which the Celestial had come to him in the beginning. And finally his seventh degree is his restoration by the "celestial marriage," at the time he comes up on the heavenly plains. His return to earth has nothing to do with his development. That represents a new feature of what I will call a second series of development. The story of the return may also be looked upon as Indian folk lore to account for the origin and character of the White Hawk. It is curious, but it is a fact, people will rather walk that Path, which is Teh, positive, than the Path, which is Teh, negative. It appears that we will rather stand a strenuous life than a negative, and yet, the negative, Wu-Wei, would quickly give us the fulfillment of all legitimate desires. We will rather be killed by overwork than by non-action. That appears to be the condition of mankind in general.

Yet a closer examination will easily show that no one can live positively without being "hammered" from time to time. Death is a necessary element in the universe. Nobody likes a cross. Yet, Teh, positive, is not finished before we learn to love the cross and approve of afflictions. The reason is this, that only submission produces genuine simplicity. The eternal "No!" that follows some people, finally frees them. The closed doors are closed to prevent side-tracking. The ball that some drag after them fastened to the foot hinders hastiness. And all the endless chains that hold so many of us in conditions we call prison life are so many ropes that connect with bells that hang in the tower of conscience. And these bells are always sounding the alarm, when evil desires set us on fire- still we will not listen or obey! Crosses are set against all kinds of lawlessness and place us in conflict with ourselves; conflicts that always end in victory for the eternal Self. The last thing we discover is that it is always justice that cuts down the tree for our cross, and, that it is justice which nails it together and hangs us upon it.

THE INNER LIFE AND THE TAO TEH KING

No cross, no crown! But as little as you or I can manufacture the eternal crown with our hands, as little can we manufacture crosses of eternal value. Saints, so called, have done it. They have tortured themselves, and some have even calculated the value of the coming crown in proportion to the manufactured cross. Do not manufacture crosses. Those that come to us in the natural course of life are quite sufficient. It sounds paradoxical, but it is true. Suffering, or the negative in life, has no power to hurt us if we live in Wu-Wei, that is, in non-action. It is my own action that makes suffering what it is. Teh, negative, is of our own making and that is why we walk the road. Nobody compels us.

Who and what is this celestial sister? I claim she answers to Teh. You have read what I have said about Teh, and, rather abstractly at that. I must therefore add to my foregone statements a view of Teh, hitherto held back. I have purposely ignored the view which I now present, in order to avoid confusion, and, to connect the conception Teh with Tao, which I, in earlier chapters, explained to be Nature, without qualifying the term. The connection is now easily made and seen by you; when I recall to your mind that all goddesses in the various mythologies are no more than personifications of forces or nature-powers. I take for granted, that my readers know this. That, too, is the case in folklore, and my story is folklore. The heroines of folklore are no more than similar personifications. This celestial sister of the Indian tale, I have related and now endeavor to explain, is such a personification of the Higher Self, which reveals itself to Waupee. All heroines and supernatural personalities that appear in folklore, folk-songs and old religious legends, have no meaning for us unless understood that way. Psychology as studied now-a-days endorses this statement. It says that the human mind cannot express itself (whatever it may feel) or give form to its ideals except by images taken from its own subjectivity, nor can we human beings commune with another human being except through mind or the Higher Self. In no other way can we possibly blend. Mind or the Highest Self is the alembic for the smelting of human personalities and the extraction of the pure metal, called Entity. Many mystics, however, deny this and claim direct communion with the Highest.

I will offer a few thoughts on the subject of Teh or Mother Nature as a personality and then apply these thoughts to an understanding of this celestial sister. Mother Nature is not a person like you or I; yet we cannot liberate ourselves from a realization and the feeling that at times we are guided, checked, even pushed; that at times "the voice of the silence" has something in it akin to us; that at times we long so intensely for what we call "the heart of nature" that we intellectually cannot escape the conclusion that there must be an essential affinity between the spirit of man and the life of nature. Our feeling asserts a personality, something akin to ourselves. But we never can get an intellectual verity before us. We are never directly approached. The whole activity is going out from us. It is so with most of us. Mystics of all ages and all lands however tell us that they have been spoken to, have walked with and otherwise met such a personality. And they have a surety against deception in their "inner sense," so they say. Most of us must leave that assertion to them. We cannot follow, though we will not for that reason deny.

This is a fact; we have a sense of the infinite, the boundless, the eternal, and, though that sense will not tolerate any limitation of this conception, yet that infinite, that boundless, that eternal seems to be something like ourselves. In reason, we cannot account for the sense, but in feeling we are perfectly at rest. And if we are not spoiled by reflective logic, we even become eloquent or poetic, as Plato would say. That again is the case with most of us, yet mystics assure us of their union with that Infinite! It cannot be verified for us. Who has or is in the Truth! We have a sense of beauty which responds to the beauty of the universe. At times our response is so powerful that we are lifted out of our temporary self and perceive ourselves in a strange mingling with Nature's beauty, a mingling that bears witness to a close relationship. That, too, is for mystics far more than mere perception. They are translated beyond themselves and their visit yonder leaves them transfigured. Again, I say, ordinarily for the mind, it cannot be proved. But that is no reason for a denial of such high perception. Someone is deceived, mistaking appearance for reality! Is it the mystic or the common mind! Is Nature merely appearance? May Nature not be the same as that great Personality the mystics speak of? But it is not merely emotional people and poets who realize the relationship. Greek philosophers were overcome when they realized the ordered arrangement of the universe, and the classical people all agreed that that which they saw was not confusion, but an universe, that is, an existence of one idea, one aim, one kind, a One. Of moderns, we know of Kepler's outburst: "Oh, God, to think thy thoughts- that is my religion." It was the uniformity of what astronomy showed him, and its response within that created this perception of a personality! And the Greek realization of the same caused the famous line of Aratus and that of Cleanthes: "For God's offspring we are." Laotzse, if he had heard it, would have said: "Amen! Yes Nature, Teh, is the queen and goddess of mortals." But Laotzse would never have clothed his thought in anthropomorphic forms. He felt Her, Mother, Nature, Teh, both positively and negatively, but no terms of language or art would exhaust his idea and he refrained from use of personifications.

As is well known, Christianity asserts a family relationship to the Highest, and that doctrine involves a communion far deeper than one of thought merely. Yes! cried Goethe, "We are surrounded and encompassed by Nature; unable to step out and unable to enter deeper into her." It is, however, a fact, she has never lifted her veil and no man has ever seen her face to face, yet it seems to us, that ever and ever she creates new forms, and, ever and ever she rushes them out of life again, acting like a person. She is ever sacrificing her own product, and, death seems her method for getting more life. We see a system resembling thought. This fact, that Mother Nature leaves a red trail after her, is often enough, and only too often observed and criticized in such a way that the critics only hurt themselves. But those of us who have spent a life-time with nature and in close observation, study and meditation, think differently. To us Nature is no slaughterer or murderer; no slayer or assassin, no Moloch or Thug, as is only too often said by the ignorant. The truth is that she herself is blind and is the sacrifice; she is the one slaughtered and slain; she is the one who is offered to Moloch and the Thug. She herself wonders why, and has never answered her own riddle, and could not lift the veil if she wanted to. She herself would like to know the answer to the everlasting flux: and transmutation which is her life and being. Well has William Harbutt Dawson (N. Y. Sun, Aug. 24, 1901) sung about this mystery.

> Giant of old am I,
> The rock-ribbed earth is my body;
> The mountains that rise on high,
> These are my hands, my fingers;
> The snow is my hair, and the clouds
> Gather around at my breathing-
> I whisper in wandering winds,
> But the avalanche crash is my calling.
> When I raise myself anon
> And shake my limbs in the sunlight
> The sweat flows forth in rivers.
> Sons and daughters of man
> Roam at will upon me-
> Climb to my utmost hand-tips,
> Hide in the hair on my shoulders,
> Glide in the blue of my eyes,
> In cor'acles made of the corn husks-
> But I heed not their coming and going.
>
> Mystery am I to myself.
> Knowing not why, whence, whither,
> Knowing not purpose or end,
> Or the things that were or shall be;

THE INNER LIFE AND THE TAO TEH KING

Only faintly surmising
That I was by another fashioned;
A being vaster than I,
Stronger in thew and sinew
Mightier in body and arm-girth:
"Giant of eld, thy child,
I greet thee Unknown, Great Maker!"

But a wonder stranger is mine,
From age to age enduring:
As I lie in the night's deep silence,
(When the light-giver rests in his chamber),
And gaze in the firmament o 'er me
Far from my utmost arm's reach,
Far from the sound of my calling,
And watch in the solemn distance
Of infinite space overshadowing
Those pale fires burning yonder,
Never farther or nearer,
Never brighter or dimmer,
Burning forever and ever:
This is the wonder unceasing
This is the light that appalls me!

It is the light, the counterpart that seems so far off, that becomes "the wonder unceasing."

You hear the melancholy all through this confession of self conscious earth-nature: "Giant I am- yet I am as naught!" And why? Because the light is so far off! The cry of the poem is the cry of life for light, a cry that can be heard everywhere, not only where the moose calls across the lake, but in the roll of the thunder, when lightning leaps from cloud to cloud; not only where human souls sigh in pain, but also when and where the angels, who have no body, look into the mysterious garment of men and wonder. And why this wonder!

THE INNER LIFE AND THE TAO TEH KING

Why "this wonder unceasing"? Because, Nature, ever in pain, ever bearing and reproducing is also self-sacrificing, and it is the cry of the victim and the smoke of the offering that throws the melancholy veil over her, preventing her from understanding the mystery of which she herself is the wonder. She is a sublime Nothing. Nature is like Teh. Teh is life and Tao is structure. They cannot exist apart. In the poem just read, Nature is life, and light is the counterpart; and, the two are inseparable and mutually call for each other, and are in pain when separated. Look into the eye of a dog or a bird and the melancholic question stands there is large letters! There is life seeking light. Look over the landscape, be it ever so smiling, you think, look long enough and the mystery shall be seen. Wherever she is, she is incarnate and manifested in a form of sacrifice. She does not live for her own sake, she is part of another. As you heard it in the poem, she wonders! she suffers! Now, see how this Mother Nature, is a savior, an ever present deliverer: Whenever things have come to an extreme and balance is lost- there is an explosion and things readjust themselves. That is deliverance, salvation.

When the day has been excessively hot and we are about to succumb for lack of air fit to breathe, Nature in the evening either provides a thunderstorm in which all the miasma of the air eats itself up and we are set free under a clear sky and to new hope and life, or she sends a cool night to redeem us. Is she not thus a deliverer, a savior! If she robs the shore on one side of the ocean, she gives freely on the other and the whole does not lose, but is set free from stagnant conditions. Is she not saving from death? Real death! She has no speech or language, but she takes care of me and saves me from fall by the tongue and the voice she creates in another for that purpose! Is that not redemption? Men do not see Salvation nor understand their own redemption, because the mother never betrays the mystery. She never betrays it openly, but she whispers it to her darlings. Another way of putting it would be to say that it is the essential character of Nature to sacrifice self, to consume self and to rise again from the ashes like the fabled bird

THE INNER LIFE AND THE TAO TEH KING

Phoenix. This is something we see daily, hourly, always and everywhere in organic life and in a little slower process, but none less certain, in inorganic existences. Change and transmutation everywhere!

Nature in us is that wonderful, strong and sharply drawn pattern according to which your separate individuality is built top in a personality. It is the throb of the blood and the excitability of the nerves that do the work of building, repairing and improving. It is that master-power Will which holds the rudder firmly and prevents your ship from wreck and ruin. It is the navigator, Intelligence, studying the charts and keeping the course straight. It is that quick and living perception which intuitively finds the way in darkness, distress and in all growth. It is that urge and those longings which restlessly call you, and invite you to search the depths and to scan the latitudes. It is those images of Eternal Beauty which stand as beacon lights in your life, and it is that intense wish to be good which from time to time enthuses you; it is also the dawn and the full daylight of understanding that leads you on and on. Everywhere it is motion, birth, rebirth and it never tires nor comes to an end; it is immortal; dreadfully immortal. All these phenomena we imagine to be the glories of existence- yes! they are that!, but they are also subtle falsities, shadow plays and impermanencies!

They are positive while on the early stages of the Path; they are negative later on. Two sides of Nature! some of the wise men declare they have seen this power beyond the universe and themselves, but have left no records of the vision! I will now gather together these various thoughts, opposites and contradictory as some of them are. When gathered and seen at one point, they represent to some extent that stupendous power and moving force called Teh in Laotzse's book, and also those personifications which we in mythology call goddesses, and in folklore hear of as celestial visitors, like the young sisters in the American Indian story about Waupee and the other visitors I referred to in a former chapter,

254

which came to Boethius and to that poor copyist who died saying, "I lost what I never possessed." In a summary the characteristics are somewhat like this:

There is about us a power, infinite and mighty; we feel it to be personal like ourselves, and, fail to express our feelings unless we choose anthropomorphic terms. Mystics assure us this power is personal, but common mortals have no experience by which to prove it. Ancient philosophers also expressed themselves and declared there is a close relationship between ourselves and that power. Laotzse felt the same, but used no personal terms for his feeling. Keen intelligence and pure emotional souls look upon this power as sacrificing its own product in order to create more life, and, they also see this power, which they call Mother-Nature as self-sacrificing, though it appears to them that she does not herself know the aim and end of her self sacrifice.

But they see her self-sacrificing to have the same aim and end as her sacrificing her own product, namely, the production of more life. These deeper seeing minds and more sensitive souls see in all this sacrificing both of her Self and her products the salvation or deliverance of man from thralldom and the earth from death. They see her as the fabled bird, Phoenix, as change and transmutation; they feel her as nervous force; as master will; as intelligence and quick perception; as unceasing longings and as an image of Eternal Beauty; as the wish to be good and the enthusiasm to be it; as birth, rebirth and immortality. The principle of all this is embodied in this mysterious Celestial Sister that comes to Waupee. She is to him both heavenly and earthly. She comes like a sacrifice to him, that he may be lifted into the higher plane and she sacrifices him in order to be his salvation.

Teh acts in the same way with us all.

AN APPENDIX ON JEAN JACQUES ROUSSEAU'S IDEAS OF "A RETURN TO NATURE"

I have made so many references to "A Return to Nature" that, to avoid misunderstandings, I now append a few words on Jean Jacques Rousseau's famous sentence, "The Return to Nature," a sentence my reader may easily suppose that I have had in mind and refer to.

In my use of the phrase "return to Nature" there is no other reference to Rousseau than the one that naturally arises when great men like Laotzse and Rousseau both draw from the great wells of the Inner Life, which as a Finnish proverb well says, "*Diupa brunnar torka icke*: Deep wells never dry up." The well they both drew from was Nature, and it is to Nature that both, in their own peculiar way, recommend a return. Both Laotzse and Rousseau understood by Nature: immediacy, simplicity, freedom and goodness, and they set Nature in those senses against culture by which they understood that which makes life complicated, constrained, evil and too reflective. By culture they meant the formalism, social and ecclesiastic, of their day. Their general tendencies were therefore the same and very much like those of the reformers of various times. It is in such senses that Rousseau and Laotze agree. Their methods and expressions naturally differed widely. Laotzse lived many centuries before our era and in a country of so much ceremonialism and formalism that we hardly can imagine its condition. Everything was overdone, in religion, ethics and societary order, though these were not evil or corrupt as we understand such terms. Order had become a tyrant and was no more a help to live rationally. Regulations or customs crushed expansion and competition. Men did not think for themselves, but observed rules laid down by others as ignorant and narrow as themselves, but in power of government.

This state of affairs was a result of the former age's

struggles for mental, moral and spiritual life and freedom. In that age, it was a living state of things, and it was a high form of civilization and culture and useful for progress, hut it was not taken over by the next age in its original vitality and progressive power, but as mere matter and form, and for that reason it became a curse. It was this curse and burden, that Laotzse labored against.

Rousseau lived many centuries after the beginning of our era and in an age which he declared, in his Dijon-Prize essay on the effect of the progress of civilization on morals (1750), had lost its soul and substituted corruption in the same measure as it had progressed in the sciences and arts. His age had denied a state of happy ignorance with its original spontaneous way of living and immediate relations to nature. It had allowed itself to be suppressed by externalities; it had tolerated restlessness to supplant the inner peace, that comes from a contented life. Rousseau's charges were set forth with much warmth and enthusiasm and it was felt that he was a new power. He became famous but, like Laotzse and all men of his stamp, in his old age a lonesome and deserted man. His enemies and the enemies of naturalness did not like originality, natural energy and the fresh and healthy aroma that comes from a life in the Open. Such people shun the cool and clear waters fresh from the springs. They prefer the compound drinks of intoxicating liquors and the rich sources of flattery offered at societies' testimonial dinners. As they were in Rousseau's day, so they are today, and right here among us. We have to fight them if we wish to help our age to truth and liberty. They are the real hindrances to all Inner Life and true social order. They are the associates of Kali, the dark and dreadful goddess, who has given the name to this age.

I shall not need to review Laotzse's principles and system, if any "system" can be attributed to him. Enough has been said in the foregone chapters. But I will give a resume of Rousseau's ideas and teachings and invite the reader to make comparisons. One special difference between Laotzse and the Inner Life on one side, and Rousseau on the other, must be noted at the outset. It colors all Rousseau's utterances and it places him apart when we speak of the Inner Life. He is a literary man, and neither religious nor philosophical. The fundamental type of Rousseau's thinking is the opposition he sees between the immediate, the original, the self-centered, the totality of the soul on the one side and the relative, the partial, the dependent and the mixed, on the other side. In the first he sees life as its own cause and effect, born of its own energy and endeavor, and in the second he sees limitations, compulsions and inner diremption. The first is the Absolute; the second is the relative. The first is Nature, the second is what he calls Culture.

Rousseau uses the word Nature in three senses. The first sense, the theological, appears when he speaks of the world as God's creation and the "heavenly and majestic simplicity with which its creator adorned it." That divine condition he calls Nature and contrasts it with the distortions, twists and obliquity introduced by man, which he calls Culture. Rousseau also says that all things proceed pure and good from their natural origin. The second sense, the "natural-history" sense, appears when he describes "the primitive condition" and explains how inequalities arose. In man's original "zoological" nature-condition there was perhaps no marked "majestic simplicity." It was an instinctive life. Man had no reflection nor imagination. He had but few necessities; they were physical and easily satisfied.

While Rousseau is not blind to the "primitive man's" low and brutal state, and seems to have seen its contradiction to "the majestic simplicity" elsewhere described, he laments its loss. The loss of the life of instinct is to him a sort of "fall" from a paradisaical state. The third sense of the word Nature appears in Rousseau's psychology. When he speaks in this sense he ignores the two others and plunges into introspection, that he may find man's original (natural) and fundamental powers and being. The result of his examination is that he declares that the original Man, or, Man according to his nature, is good and sound, though men may be bad. He wants men to return to this, the original good and sound nature, to heart-life, and shun all external relations which blur the vision and contaminate morals. He thinks that silence and solitude make it possible for mankind to find the original nature. By "being good" Rousseau meant that "we express our nature" and he himself in moments- *sans diversion, sans obstacle*- thought himself to have been so good such as Nature intended him to be. And he declares emphatically that all men have fundamentally a desire to be as they should and ought to be. There is in everybody a natural tendency to maintain his selfhood, an *amour de soi* as he calls it.

But this amour de soi, the healthy self maintenance, has to meet and fight an *amour propre*, self-love, something our surroundings develop, something not ourselves. The amour propre does not exist in a society where man has to do with himself alone. Such a society does not create a desire for distinction, preferment. In the amour de soi there is an abundance of energy, and it is all spent in natural self-development, while the amour propre paralyses man's energy by shattering his self-centredness. To be directed by Nature and to live according to Nature means a life according to amour de soi, and, moreover, such a life creates sympathy with other beings, the very opposite of amour propre which sets distinctions of separateness against other beings. In the amour de soi only are we free beings and may feel ourselves as gods: *on se suffit a soi-meme comme Dieu!* In the amour de soi we have few needs and make no comparisons. In the amour propre we multiply desires and defer to other people's opinions. Like Laotzse, Rousseau also thinks that much learning is a hindrance to a natural life. By self-rest, on the other hand, we open ourselves to all the natural influxes which correspond to our own nature.

Our best and true teacher in the natural life is feeling, and Rousseau has the merit of having placed the feelings in their right position in psychology, and, he has that merit in spite of previous work done by such men as Spinoza, Shaftesbury, Hutcheson and

Hume. We have (all of us) an inherent liking or disliking; and these are Nature's monitors; they act instinctively and speak clearly, where they are not corrupted. Feeling and reason are really two sides of the same nature. If we follow feeling we live in unity. By feeling is of course not meant our sensations, or what psychology generally calls the feelings. By feeling is understood broadly, the Inner Man. By feeling or which is the same, by inner perception or immediate knowledge, we get religion. City people who have no feeling except when they run against stone walls, who have no perceptions except when tired out by the length of their streets; who have no immediate knowledge, but are full of reports of crimes and the like from their newspapers- city people have no religion. How could any ecstasy strike them! Their hearts are not sensitive; their eyes do not know the wide views; their ears hear only noises, but never the rhythm of the winds sighing at sunrise. Let them withdraw from that unnatural existence. It never generated religion or mystic longings for the greatest, the Infinite. Rousseau never tires of calling to us to close our books and ecclesiastic conventions and retire to open-air-nature, there to find our own soul, who is our true god. In the first stages of education, says Rousseau, it is of prime importance that the original nature of the child has full and free play of its feelings for and against that which it wants or does not want. Only by so doing does it become possible to regulate the child's growth according to its own inherent character or nature and not according to somebody else's notions. This idea is the prevailing one in Rousseau's handling of the problem of education.

In the history of the development of human thought and life, Rousseau represents a revival of the ancient naturalism which placed instinct above reflection. A little before him there had already been an awakening of the Hellenic sense of Nature, with all its acceptances of objective joy in natural facts and natural simplicity and impulses. But Rousseau is the man whom history names as the father of the movement in Europe in a general way, and, in France in a special way, and as the opponent to abstract ideological notions. With Rousseau, feeling comes into the history of philosophy as an independent and absolute principle and in no way subject to the intellect. From feeling is henceforth derived religion, poetry and romanticism, represented by such famous names as those of Schleiermacher and Novalis, for instance. Everywhere humanity seems to "find its own" by turning against the dry intellect, and alas! humanity also finds itself tied by the new errors and sins! Ever since Rousseau's time genius has spread its wings as never before; common man, who before was not even supposed to be able to think, broke out from his social and mental prison, borne by the new overflowing life and images and thought, and combinations of these now made possible have enriched the human mind most marvelously. Never before had men directly from the soil come forth as leaders in life and thought. The New Age culture, such as it is known in the United States, could never have seen the day except for Rousseau.

A sensible study and intelligent application of the ideas and methods of Laotzse and Rousseau will go far to refresh individual souls and develop true self-reliance. It will create true will power and work, and, wealth both of mind and pocket. It will do away with our boastful self-complacency and the intolerable strain of trust associations, and also place these in their position as public servants rather than as tyrants. In my opinion the new ideas for our age and the coming age, ideas, we all long for in the name of religion, philosophy and social organization, lie slumbering in the teachings and methods left us by Laotzse and Jean Jacques Rousseau. In the confidence that I have done something to draw these teachings out of their unmerited obscurity, and in the hope that they sooner or later may be made useful, I conclude these chapters on The Inner Life and the Tao-Teh-King.

THE END

Made in the USA
Monee, IL
05 July 2023